the offer you can't refuse

the offer you can't refuse

What if customers want more than just excellent service?

Steven Van Belleghem

LANNOO
CAMPUS

Also published in Dutch: *The offer you can't refuse*, LannooCampus, 2020.

D/2020/45/327 – ISBN 978 94 014 7035 3 – NUR 802

Cover and interior design: Karl Demoen
Translation: Ian Connerty

LannooCampus Publishers is a subsidiary of Lannoo Publishers,
the book and multimedia division of Lannoo Publishers nv.

LannooCampus Publishers
Vaartkom 41 box 01.02
3000 Leuven
Belgium
www.lannoocampus.com

P.O. Box 23202
1100 DS Amsterdam
Netherlands

Contents

CHAPTER 2.
THE OFFER YOU CAN'T REFUSE MODEL

PART 2. GENERAL PURPOSE TECHNOLOGIES

CHAPTER 3.
FOUR TECHNOLOGIES THAT GO FURTHER THAN ULTIMATE EASE OF USE

PART 3. STRATEGIES FOR THE OFFER YOU CAN'T REFUSE

CHAPTER 4.
ULTIMATE CONVENIENCE

CHAPTER 5.
PARTNER IN LIFE

CHAPTER 6.
SAVE THE WORLD

PART 4. SUCCESSFUL IMPLEMENTATION

CHAPTER 7.
THE OFFER YOU CAN'T REFUSE FOR EMPLOYEES

CHAPTER 8.
THE HOURGLASS MODEL –
A PRACTICAL INNOVATION MODEL

CHAPTER 9.
DO IT BETTER

introduction

Social challenges

At the age of just sixteen, Greta Thunberg was chosen as TIME's Person of the Year for 2019. This made the Swedish climate activist the youngest ever winner of that prestigious distinction. Thunberg has both her haters and lovers. Some people were hugely in favour of the series of climate protests in 2019; others were appalled that children were allowed to miss school to take part in demonstrations. Her famous 'How dare you!' quote at the meeting of world leaders at the United Nations was received by both applause and a chorus of boos. Reaction to her has always been ambiguous.

Leaving aside the polarisation, no-one can deny that the climate discussion is now higher on the political agenda than it has ever been, thanks largely to the activism of Greta Thunberg and her followers. During recent months, initiatives have been launched all over the world to turn back the tide of climate change. More and more companies are also taking action to reduce their ecological footprint.

In fact, society is looking increasingly towards companies to help tackle society's problems. People's trust in the companies is greater than their trust in the government, as revealed by an annual study by the American PR and marketing advice bureau Edelman.[1] Companies like Unilever, Danone, Salesforce, Nestlé and many others now have very clear climate objectives, which are in keeping with the societal ambition to limit the effects of global warming.[2] Jeff Bezos, the CEO of Amazon, decided in February 2020 to invest 10 billion dollars in a fund to combat climate change. This money will be used to support scientists and activists in their efforts to protect our environment.

It is evident that both awareness of and actions to deal with climate change are moving into overdrive. But in spite of all this hopeful news, as few as 25 per cent of companies have a climate plan that is worth the name.[3] The opportunities for society to grow further in this direction are still enormous.

More than ever before, people are starting to worry almost daily about the challenges facing society. The climate problem is just one of the major concerns of the average citizen. Health care is, of course, another issue that is fairly close to the top of the list.

As a result of the unexpected outbreak of the coronavirus, we have all been forced to face up to our weakness. Humanity is vulnerable and it will only be thanks to a previously unseen degree of co-operation between the public, the business community, scientists and politicians that we will eventually be able to defeat this terrible contagion. From now on, every company will need to be active in some way in health care. That is a matter of concern to us all.

In the years ahead, the expectations of customers will also be increasingly coloured by such societal concerns. More and more consumers will be looking for companies that take their social responsibilities seriously.

The biggest digital transformation ever

At the same time, it needs to be recognised that customer expectations are not focused exclusively on societal problems. For most consumers, their personal challenges, dreams, fears and desires are still at the forefront of their minds. Benefiting society alone without meeting the basic expectations of customers (in terms of price, product and service) is a non-starter. Companies therefore face the task of making sure that they can also satisfy the personal challenges of their customers – if they want to keep them.

In 2020, we all took part in the largest digital training course ever. Everyone – young, old, rich, poor, pro or contra – had no other choice during the great lockdown than to embrace the use of digital tools. Not only to work, communicate and relax, but also to buy products. There was simply no other option than the digital option.

Consumers threw themselves wholeheartedly into the digital process, resulting in a rapid learning curve and a previously unexperienced peak of use. The chief technology officer of Shopify, the largest e-commerce platform for traders and companies, said at the end of April 2020: 'The number of daily purchases via the web is now comparable with the total number of purchases on Black Friday.'[4] Black Friday and Cyber Monday are the busiest online shopping days of the year in the United States. Those annual top-spots have now suddenly become the daily average.

For many companies, this need to switch rapidly to digital represented the largest transformation exercise they had ever faced. Many of them were simply not ready with the measures and procedures that would allow their employees to work from home, forcing them to improvise solutions at very short notice. Likewise, many of them had no readily available e-commerce option, so that they needed to develop something almost overnight. Satya Nadella, the CEO of Microsoft, has commented: 'The digital transformation in March and April was on a larger scale than the digital transformation we have witnessed during the past two years.'[5]

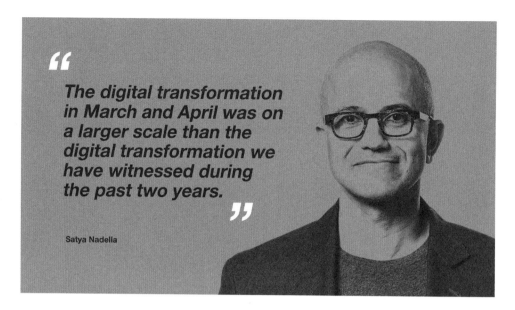

> **The digital transformation in March and April was on a larger scale than the digital transformation we have witnessed during the past two years.**
>
> Satya Nadella

This digital sprint has resulted in the disappearance of many digital barriers, both for customers and for companies. And those barriers will never be coming back. From now on, digital will more than ever be part of every aspect of our daily lives. If, as a company leader, you look out of your office window, you can only see a very small piece of the world. But the invisible digital segment of that world is getting bigger and more important all the time. When formulating the customer strategies of the future, it is crucial to ensure first and foremost that the digital components are 100 per cent in order. Customers now know which digital interfaces work well and which ones do not. The quality level of digital services has improved dramatically in recent years, so that this standard of excellence is now regarded as a minimum requirement. It is fast becoming the newest commodity.

The start of new customer expectations

Between 2010 and 2020 a new type of customer relationship came into being, based on the increasing ease of use of digital applications. Companies like Uber, Amazon, Zalando, WeChat, DiDi, Booking.com and many other digital enterprises responded perfectly to these changing expectations, allowing some of them to develop into the largest companies in the world. The underlying technologies that made this possible were 4G, mobile devices and social media. In the meantime, the curve of customer expectations based on these technologies has reached its ceiling. However, in the years ahead we will see the development of a new curve with yet another set of new customer expectations. In this book I will describe how you, as a company, can deal with and make best use of these new customer expectations, which are gradually becoming more and more visible. Today, we are only at the very bottom of the curve, but it is my hypothesis that by 2025 many of the elements explained in the following pages will have become the most normal thing in the world.

The new customer expectations are influenced by three elements:

- **General purpose technology:** the coming decade will see the growth of technologies such as 5G, artificial intelligence, quantum computing and robotics. Each of these technologies has the potential to change whole industries. But the combination of the four technologies together is set to revolutionise the way we live and work. The technologies will also offer new possibilities to take customer relations to a higher level.
- **Personal challenges:** everyone has their own personal dreams, fears, wishes and ambitions. As digital ease of use becomes the new norm, the question for companies will be how they can make the difference by responding successfully to the more emotional aspects of their customers' lives. Digital ease of use will guarantee transactional convenience. The next step is to provide greater ease and convenience for customers' emotional expectations.
- **Societal challenges:** more and more people are asking questions about the future of society. Challenges relating to technology, health and the climate are now at the top of many people's agendas. As a company, you can make use of your strengths to create a positive added value for the community.

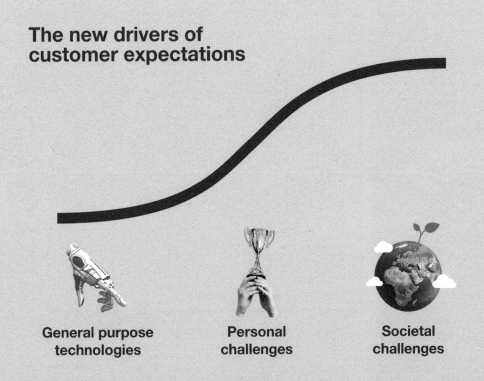

The new drivers of customer expectations

General purpose technologies

Personal challenges

Societal challenges

The Offer You Can't Refuse

If your company knows how to respond cleverly to the emergence of these three drivers, you will have the opportunity to develop a stronger relationship with your customers. In this book, I would like to take you on a journey; a journey that will help you to create that new kind of customer relationship. Based on a clear strategic vision, numerous practical examples and plenty of useful tips, I want to make it possible for your customers to receive an Offer They Can't Refuse in the very near future.

You can develop The Offer You Can't Refuse by investing in the following three axes, which will allow you to react in an appropriate manner to the new generation of customer expectations:

- **Ultimate Convenience:** this is the use of new technology in a smart way to make interfaces ever more automated, so that the customer needs to make no effort to do business with your company. This leads to the perfect transactional relationship.
- **Partner in Life:** this is not about your customer journey, but about the life journey of your customer. Which aspects in the lives of your customers create negative or positive energy? What things cost them too much effort? If you can provide answers to these questions, you can optimise your emotional relationship with your customers.
- **Save the World:** this is about companies taking their responsibility to do good for society as a whole. Every company has strengths that it can use to create a societal added value. Search for concrete solutions and contributions that will allow your company to make a truly tangible impact.

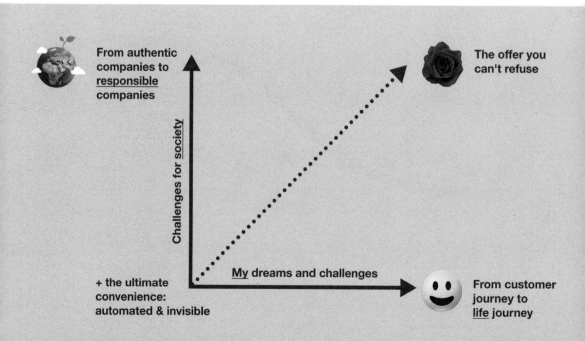

The research for The Offer You Can't Refuse

I wrote this book during the 'great lockdown' of 2020. Even so, this is not a COVID-19 book. All the concepts and all the research for *The Offer You Can't Refuse* were already completed by February 2020. During the nine months before the start of the crisis I worked hard to develop my new ideas and give them concrete shape and form.

Originally, I intended to write the book between May and August 2020. However, the unexpected imposition of the lockdown meant that I was able to start writing two months earlier, so that the book can also be published earlier than planned. Of course, in some places I still make reference to COVID-19, given the impact of the pandemic on the totality of society and therefore also on the customer experience.

I am also convinced that the ideas and models from this book (which were ready before we had ever even heard of COVID-19) will become indispensible for companies at a faster pace than even I initially anticipated. The rapid changes in the use of digital during the

> *I am convinced that the ideas and models from this book (which were ready before we had ever even heard of COVID-19) will become indispensible for companies.*

lockdown, coupled with changing attitudes in the public's thinking, give added urgency to the need for developing a new kind of customer relationship. The unparalleled crisis of spring 2020 was therefore an added motivation for me to finish this book as quickly as possible. With the

completion of each new chapter, I had the same recurring feeling: more than ever, this is the new reality.

The research for the book was primarily field research, supplemented by desk research. The large majority of the examples in the following pages are based on things that I either heard or experienced at first hand.

In recent years, I have spoken at hundreds of events, where I met many different business leaders, who came to share their stories. In addition, our company nexxworks organises fifty or so inspiration tours each year, taking managers and entrepreneurs to the four corners of the world, where they can discover the very latest innovations in real life situations. In this way, during the past three years I have been able to visit dozens of trendsetting organisations in the East, West, North and South. Finally, I also had the pleasure of being able to interview various people with interesting things to say about the world of business and customer relations. You can listen to many of these interviews on my podcast. You can even watch some of them on my YouTube channel. It was the combination of all these insights that led to the philosophy behind this book.

Feedback

As always, please feel free to send me all your questions and comments. My e-mail address is *Steven@VanBelleghem.biz*. I am always happy to read your feedback. I hope you enjoy my book: *The Offer You Can't Refuse*. Steven Van Belleghem
www.stevenvanbelleghem.com | www.youtube.com/stevenvanbelleghem

The soundtrack of The Offer You Can't Refuse

A book is more than a collection of letters on paper or on a screen. A book describes an idea, a story, a vision. With the writing of my books, I hope to generate enthusiasm, reveal new insights, encourage optimism and, above all, inspire a greater desire to help customers better. For this reason, I always like to add a little something extra. My previous book, *Customers The Day After Tomorrow*, had an added element of augmented reality. Readers were able to call up videos in which I talked with business leaders about some of the book's practical examples. But this time I want to take things even further, by adding a musical element.

During the past few years, I have had the pleasure of working together with Piet Goddaer. Piet has been writing, composing and producing music for more than a quarter of a century. He is best known under his artist name: Ozark Henry. During his career, he has been awarded various gold and platinum discs, won the Zamu Music Award in the 'best writer-composer-arranger' category and has travelled the world to make people happy with his music. I asked Piet if he would be willing to compose a soundtrack for my new book. Film music has been with us for decades, but the idea of book music is something new. Piet is a great believer that a musical component can and should be added to every aspect of life. With this in mind, he is working increasingly with companies to help them to develop their own unique sound. Museums, airlines, universities and many other organisations are discovering that it is important to have their own distinctive aural identity. In this respect, music adds an extra dimension to our lives. Music creates a certain type of atmosphere and puts us in a particular state of mind. As a result, I am happy and proud that I am now able to present to you the first ever management book with a soundtrack!

Before, during and after your reading, you can enjoy the music, which will hopefully help you to engage even more closely with the ethos and ambience of the book. You can access the soundtrack of *The Offer You Can't Refuse* via this QR code.

PART 1

the ☺ffer y🌍u can't refuse

customer
expectations
go further than
ease of use

The new minimum

The three dancing balls in Facebook Messenger or the 'typing' message at the top of the chat function in WhatsApp are a nightmare for our pattern of expectation. Go on, admit it! If you send a message to someone, you hope to see the balls start their dancing within a handful of seconds. Those balls are one of the biggest expectation-heightening symbols in the contemporary world. And the longer the balls dance, the greater your expectations become. Each extra dance, each additional time the balls jiggle up and down, your curiosity increases about the fantastic message that someone is typing for you in real time. But if all you get as an answer is a simple 'thumbs up', it can be a real disappointment.

In recent years, we have all witnessed how mobile technology, 4G and social media have influenced not only our behaviour, but also our pattern of expectations. My first book, *The Conversation Manager,* was published in 2010. In it, I argued for the use of tools like Facebook and Twitter to start conversations with customers. 'Provide relevant and pleasing messages, share them, and let the customers respond' was one of my main recommendations.

In this way, it was possible for companies – for the very first time – to engage in one-to-one conversations with thousands of customers each day. If you did this in the right manner, you could benefit from a word-of-mouth effect on a massive scale. Suddenly, conversations about companies were no longer conducted in the local coffee bar or over at half-time beer in the football stadium. No, from that moment on, the whole world was listening, with all the advantages and disadvantages this implies. Nowadays, of course, this way of thinking has become the most normal thing in the world. Companies in today's market who still fail to make use of social media must have been asleep for the past ten years.

If, a decade later, I now look at the impact of social media on customer experience, this impact has been far greater than anything I could have imagined back in 2010. But the most important aspect of this impact is not the mass of additional commercial content, the use of social media as a service tool or the countless individual conversations between customers and companies. No, as far as I am concerned, the most important change brought about by social media has been the way in which it has created huge transparency in the world of customer experience. Today's companies interact with their customers in a manner that is highly visual and abundantly clear, both for the entire market and for the classic media. The consistently poor treatment of customers now leads to greater negative PR than ever before. In contrast, companies that excel in customer friendliness reap huge rewards, with their story being spread (and praised) across the length and breadth of social media.

This transparency has turned customer focus into a matter of urgency, making it a theme of current concern in many board rooms. The result has been that companies now battle to outdo each other in terms of their range of customer-friendly measures.

How Big Tech moulded the digital norm

The period between 2010 and 2019 was coloured by social media, mobile technology and 4G. The combination of these three technologies created new business models, which had a powerful influence on our daily lives and on customer experience. Today, Netflix is available everywhere and in all circumstances. It makes no difference whether we are sitting on a plane, in a train or on the settee in our own front room. With the simple press of a button we have access to all our favourite series and films. Amazon has evolved from an online bookseller to become one of the largest stores on Earth. In addition, Amazon is also the world leader in cloud services, has an amazingly wide-ranging online content offer, makes smart hardware products, is the owner of offline retail shops, and so much more. In the hotel sector, we can now make our bookings with a few clicks of a mouse and thanks to the services of Booking.com we are able to outsource the risk completely to the hotel, since no-one is expected to pay in advance and free cancellation up to 24 hours before the date of arrival has become almost standard throughout the market.

It is the large tech-giants in Silicon Valley and China that have taken biggest advantage of the possibilities offered by 4G, mobile and social. The manner in which they gave new shape and form to digital interfaces has now become the norm. In whatever sector your company is active, the benchmark in respect of the user-friendliness of your technology is not your direct competitor, but the interface of Amazon, WeChat, Grab, DiDi or Uber. Their digital high-performance is the new minimum for digital service provision.

The largest digital training session ever

In March 2020, Europe and the United States embarked on the largest digital training session the world has ever seen. As a result of the corona crisis, 2.8 billion people were locked down in compulsory quarantine. To put this figure in perspective: 2.8 billion people in quarantine means that more people were confined to their own homes for weeks or even months than were actually alive on the planet during the years of the Second World War.[6] Each of these 2.8 billion people was forced to rely 100 per cent on digital channels for their work, communication and entertainment. There was no other choice. Even the biggest sceptics about e-commerce suddenly discovered just how easy to use these services really are. During this period, even my own parents started up on FaceTime, since it was the only way they could see their grandchildren. As a result of corona, the barriers to the use of e-commerce and tools for digital communication have been significantly reduced – and will never return. People discovered like never before that these things were easy, useful and convenient. What was there not to like?

One of the few shares on the stock market that rose in March 2020 was Zoom Video Communications. Zoom had already been the most popular cloud solution for virtual meetings for quite some time. During the lockdown, digital meetings suddenly became the only acceptable form of meeting, so the use of Zoom began to skyrocket exponentially from one day to the next. In March 2020, Zoom had 200 million daily users, in comparison with 'just' 10 million before the start of the corona crisis.[7] In the meantime, digital meetings have become a normal part of our daily business and private lives.

In May 2020, Jack Dorsey, the CEO of Twitter, announced that henceforth the company's employees would have 100 per cent flexibility in choosing their place of work. If they preferred, they could still come to the office, but it was no longer necessary. Working fully from home was perfectly acceptable. The decision was entirely up to them.

> *There was no other choice. Even the biggest sceptics about e-commerce suddenly discovered just how easy to use these services really are.*

Looking back, it is a good thing that this quarantine period happened in 2020. Imagine what quarantine would have been like – above all, how less bearable it would have been, both privately and professionally – if the crisis had hit before all these digital aids were available. However, the recent massive use of digital tools has further increased pressure on the need for user-friendliness. Within a matter of weeks, everyone now knows which interfaces work well and which ones are less simple to operate.

The new minimum goes beyond digital interfaces

It is important to realise that the new minimum in customer experience goes much further than the technical interface. That is merely one aspect of the story. In recent years, smart retailers have also ensured that store workers have become friendlier, better informed and more empathic than ever before. These are benefits that you simply cannot find with the majority of e-commerce dealers. Or that, at least, used to be the case.

In my third book, *When digital becomes human* (2014), I described the future need for collaboration between technology and people. The core of my thesis was as follows: computers make it possible to automate processes, so that people will have more time to focus on the emotional side of the customer relationship. There was a growing understanding – in B2B sales, in the service departments of telecom companies and even in small self-employed businesses – that people could still make the difference. As a result, in the intervening years some companies have so dramatically improved the quality of their human service provision that the bar for the physical customer relationship has now been set extraordinarily high.

The corona crisis certainly gave a boost to the use of digital tools, but also led to the realisation of how much we enjoy being in the 'real' world. After just a matter of weeks, a lot of people were starting to miss the physical world. Conclusion? Online must be good, offline must be good, and, preferably, both channels must be capable of seamless integration with each other. This is what we now know as omnichannel.

Omnichannel, empathic personnel, perfectly performing and super-simple digital interfaces, dynamic offline shopping outlets, personalised services… These are the key facets of the new minimum in customer experience. The companies that in recent years have failed to set the bar sufficiently high will find it difficult to attract and keep customers. In contrast, the companies that in recent years have invested seriously in the broad diversity of new expectations will soon be able to comply with tomorrow's ever-changing norms.

Starbucks, mobile commerce and China

Starbucks has a strategy by which it hopes to excel beyond the new minimum. The next phase of the company's growth will be achieved through fast and personalised deliveries. In the very near future, people will be able to phone up to order their favourite Starbucks drink and have it delivered to their present location.

If you buy a drink at Starbucks, you know it is going to be either piping hot or freezing cold. Neither of these options fits in well with the 'order before midnight, delivered tomorrow' concept. With this kind of product, what you are really looking for is the magic of ordering by phone and getting your drink, still either hot or cold, just 5 minutes later, wherever you might be.

> *Kevin Johnson, the CEO at Starbucks, has said literally: 'We are going to apply to the United States what we have learnt in China.'*

To make this service possible, Starbucks works in the West with companies like Uber Eats and in China with Alibaba. At the present time, Uber Eats and Deliveroo are currently optimising these kinds of services in most western markets, although Kevin Johnson, the CEO at Starbucks, has said literally: 'We are going to apply to the United States what we have learnt in China.'[8]

Every observer can see that the Chinese market is now already very mature in terms of fast deliveries, not only of food but also of other products. In China, the new minimum is currently a delivery within 29 minutes, with the product being delivered not to your home but to wherever you happen to be at that particular time.

During my last visit to JD, the second largest Chinese e-commerce company after Alibaba, I was first introduced to the concept of the 'lightning delivery'. In 2019, their average delivery time did indeed amount to 29 minutes. But in the coming years they plan to reduce this to just a few minutes, with a target of a maximum of five. And when you visit the company, you get the impression that each year they will get closer and closer to achieving this goal.

In a similar fashion, Starbucks want to build up a lead over the new minimum. It wants to ride ahead of the pack. Its ambition for the period 2019 to 2022 is to open a new physical location in China once every 15 hours.[9] Of course, these will all be sales points where people can pop in to buy coffee directly, but at the same time it also allows Starbucks to build up an excellent logistical network throughout the country. The intention is that this tightly meshed network will make it possible in the not-too-distant future to deliver hot or cold drinks within 5 minutes in cities like Beijing and Shanghai.

Meituan Dianping

Each year the American media brand FastCompany issues a list of the most innovative companies in the world. In recent decades, the top three places usually went to the big names from Silicon Valley: Apple, Amazon, Uber, Facebook and Tesla. It was the same story, year after year. When I received an email in January 2019 telling me that the new list had just been published, I quickly surfed to the FastCompany website. I was curious (as always) to see which of the American giants had carried of this year's top spot. Imagine my surprise when I saw that the most innovative company in the world for 2019 was Meituan Dianping.[10]

This was the first time that an Asiatic (non-American) company had topped the listing and I am fairly certain that 90 per cent of people in the West have never even heard of them. During my lectures in Europe and the United States I regularly ask my audiences what they know about Meituan Dianping. In most cases, the answer is stony silence. It is only when there are a few Chinese faces in the auditorium that a hand or two is occasionally raised.

Be that as it may, Meituan Dianping is certainly a company worth keeping an eye on. It adjusts its norms for customer experience at an astonishing speed. The new minimum is getting more and more demanding each year and Meituan Dianping is one of the leaders in this trend. Meituan was founded in 2010 as a kind of Chinese version of Groupon, which made it possible for consumers to benefit from interesting discounts through group purchasing. In 2015, Meituan merged with Dianping, and that is when things really started to take off.

The core of their business model is no longer based on group purchasing and discounts. Instead, the company now wants to be a kind of Amazon.com for services. Via Meituan Dianping you can order meals, book hotel rooms, reserve tables at restaurants, buy tickets for the cinema, and so much more. The aim is to offer all aspects of local service provision to its more than 400 million active users.

In 2018, the company delivered meals worth a total of 33.8 billion American dollars. This is equivalent to the ordering of 178 meals per second. Their system works as follows. Local traders and restaurants offer their products on the Meituan platform. The customers choose what they want. Meituan couriers then deliver the order to the customer, wherever he or she might be, within a time limit of less than 30 minutes.

In the years ahead Meituan intends to invest in even faster delivery times. To make this possible, Xia Huaxia, Meituan's chief scientist, is developing new algorithms that can more accurately chart the behaviour of the company's customers. 'Our 400 million active users all have a certain pattern of behaviour. Once we understand that pattern, we can predict what people need and provide it to them with ever increasing speed.'

This reasoning is sound. We human beings are much more creatures of habit than we like to admit. Many of us display the same recurring pattern in our use of services and in the meals we like to eat. And the Chinese are no different. During a new customer's first weeks of use, Meituan maps out his or her consumption pattern. After that, the algorithms take over and do what they are best at: predicting what is likely to happen. The final step then involves offering the customer a tailor-made range of meals from which to choose. In the long term, Meituan hopes to be able to predict exactly what the customer wants to eat, so that the meal can be delivered even faster.

When JD talks about 'lightning delivery', the philosophy is precisely the same: 'If we want to be able to deliver a product or service within minutes, we need to know perfectly what people want, even before they actually place the order.'

But Meituan uses artificial intelligence to do much more than simply predict customer behaviour. That is just one side of the story. In order to offer lightning-fast service, the logistical side of the operation also needs to be optimised. At the moment, Meituan uses some 600,000 personnel to carry out its deliveries. You can easily recognise them by their flashy yellow jackets, as they race through Chinese cities on their electric scooters. The Meituan Dianping algorithms continuously study the routes of their couriers and combine this with an analysis of the real-time traffic situation on the roads, so that the deliveries can be routed as quickly – and as efficiently – as possible. As a result, these smart algorithms can make it feasible to complete deliveries for up to ten customers during a single delivery ride. This logistical optimisation has cut delivery times by 30 per cent.

This kind of innovative approach has opened up a whole new world for Meituan customers. In the space of just a few years, they have been given access to a platform offering them all the products and services they require for their day-to-day lives, which are then delivered to them in record speed without any need for effort on their part.
The company has built up a culture based on the slogan: 'Order on your smartphone and we will do the rest'. In keeping with this culture, hundreds of shops and restaurants have been transformed into what are effectively logistical centres, where Meituan personnel come to collect and distribute their products.

The new form of disruption: good quality, low price and direct delivery to the end user

In the past, things were simple. Markets were dominated by the big companies, which competed with each other for a few extra percentage points of market share. Disruption occurred whenever a new player appeared on the scene, who offered the same products at a lower price and usually also of a lower quality. These new players were often laughed out of court by the market's established names. At first.

In the past, things were simple. Markets were dominated by the big companies, which competed with each other for a few extra percentage points of market share.

The classic example of this kind of short-sightedness is Intel, a company that had achieved world leadership in the production of fast and powerful computer chips. When another company started to produce much cheaper but also much less powerful chips, nobody at Intel was particularly worried. The rival chips had a different architecture, which the engineers at Intel regarded as 'inferior'. But when the smartphone hype exploded just a handful of years later, it soon became apparent that the smartphone manufacturers were more interested in these cheaper chips than in their more expensive Intel counterparts. Intel had failed to spot the movement in the market and was caught with its trousers down.
And it was much the same story when Toyota first launched its cars onto the European market. Many of the engineers at BMW, Audi and Mercedes looked down their very long

noses at what they regarded as small and sub-standard Japanese models. 'Who on earth would ever want to drive a car like that?!', you could almost hear them ask. Even so, within in a few years these prestigious brands were forced to bow to the inevitable and bring out their own versions of smaller and (slightly) cheaper cars, since the market had clearly started to embrace the Toyota offer. This type of disruption was annoying for the existing players, but at least they had time to adjust to the changing circumstances. In most cases, the new kid on the block only gained market share relatively slowly.

Times, however, have changed. At the start of 2020, an article appeared in the *MIT Sloan Management Review* with the title 'The new disrupters'. This was about today's new kids on the block, who bring products and services to market that are by no means inferior in terms of quality to the existing offer. On the contrary, they are often better – and so are their prices and their customer service. In short, they have a much more customer-focused business model.

The Dollar Shave Club is a good example of this kind of disruption. Their razors are of good quality and are delivered direct to the end user at a price that is much lower than what you would pay for market leader Gillette. When they launched their product, the Dollar Shave Club focused on two key aspects: quality and price. Their message was clear: 'Do you really want to keep on paying 20 dollars a month to Gillette, 19 dollars of which goes to Roger Federer? Or would you prefer to pay significantly less for a razor that is every bit as good?' The company enjoyed a spectacular period of growth, forcing Gillette to lower its prices, before finally being sold to Unilever for a billion American dollars.

Subscription services can have a similar disruptive effect. As a consumer, you are given access to certain products at a lower price and with a lower level of risk. What's more, nowadays you can find almost every product within some kind of subscription scheme: music, food, clothes, flowers, art, toys, even pets. If you can name it, you can probably buy it on subscription. Moreover, this kind of 'direct-to-consumer' model often wins a serious portion of market share in double-quick time. The classic examples are Uber, Spotify and Netflix.

All these new players make grateful use of the possibilities offered by new media and influencers to boost their name familiarity and brand identity at top speed. They are often able to do this in a manner that people think is 'cool', so that consumers quickly develop a degree of sympathy for the fresh-faced newcomers. If these newcomers can then capitalise on this sympathy by offering services of good quality, an avalanche of word-of-mouth will explode in their favour. When this happens, the classic companies can do little more than look on in astonishment.

In recent years, many companies have pinned their disruptive hopes on digital transformation. Their main aim was to convert their analogue processes into digital processes. This cost them a small fortune and was often implemented successfully. However, these companies are now learning the painful lesson that this was not enough.

In many cases, the biggest mistake was a failure to take sufficient account of the changing wishes of their customers. The most successful newcomers owe their success to much more than just the simple use of digital channels. They were smart enough to see that these channels needed to be used to completely rethink and redesign their service provision. As a result, many of these new disrupters have helped to shape the contours of the new minimum in customer experience.

Excellent service is the new commodity

It is really quite odd. By continually increasing their level of customer service, companies are actually finding it harder and harder to differentiate themselves from their rivals. Outstanding service is now the norm everywhere, the new minimum. If you have ever been on a marketing training course, at some point you will have learnt about the USP of a company or product. What is your unique selling proposition? What unique aspect of your business model convinces customers to buy from you?
The USP theory says that if you are able to excel in one particular aspect, then an average score is sufficient for all the remaining aspects. In other words, a nine out of ten for something is enough to compensate for six out of ten for everything else. If you are in retail, you might be able to beat the competition by virtue of your excellent location or by having the lowest prices or the friendliest service. Excellent service can sometimes compensate for a higher price and a poorer location. In the same way, a brilliant location can again compensate for a higher price or a limited offer. Or that is the way it used to be. Today, I am increasingly seeing that consumers demand both good service and a competitive price. The new disrupters try to achieve good scores for every aspect of their operation. The Dollar Shave Club was cheap, of good quality and marketed with a cool communication strategy, all of which made location of minimal importance. They beat Gillette by scoring well across the board.

The idea of being good at all aspects of your service provision was first promoted by the tech giants. Companies like Booking.com or Amazon have a limitless range, competitive prices, a level of service that is better than the market average and a business model that makes location irrelevant.
An analysis of the screen time of the average consumer reveals that more than 80 per cent of it is spent on the websites of the big digital companies, which means that these companies have an increasingly important impact on the setting of customer expectations.
It is clear that all the 'classic' elements in the customer offer will no longer be enough to make the difference. Perhaps the only way to beat this conundrum is to offer customers a truly unique product, but how many companies are able to do that? Most aspects of service provision have now become hygiene factors: if you have them, great; if you don't have them, you will find it harder than ever to win.

Even possession of an effective digital interface has become a norm. Customers have already developed a zero-tolerance for online sites and applications that are anything less than perfect. Just examine your own behaviour. If you download a new app, how many chances do you give it to do what you expect? Nowadays, almost everyone will answer 'one'. New apps are seldom given a second chance. And how long does that single chance last? If you answer 'two minutes', you must be a very patient person. Most people have had enough after just 30 seconds. Half a minute is all they need to make their judgement. If the new app fails to meet the new minimum in terms of ease of use, it is immediately re-moved or else consigned to a lonely existence on the seventh screen of your smartphone.

What does this show? It shows that a good functioning app or digital interface is no longer a differentiating factor. It has become a minimum condition for staying in the game. Ease of use is the newest commodity. And the continuing evolution in this direc-tion is not going to make things any easier in the future. Commodity or not, there is still plenty of room for new possibilities and further improvement. E-commerce has already made it easier for consumers to buy products, but we are now moving into a new phase of voice technology that will make it easier still. Soon, we won't even need to click on a mouse; a vocal command will be enough. And before long even that won't be necessary, when, for example, my printer is able to automatically order new toner cartridges without my intervention.

We have evolved from complex to simple interfaces. In the years ahead, we will evolve from simple to invisible interfaces. This ongoing (r)evolution makes it necessary to con-tinue investing in new interface technology, even though its differentiating potential is decreasing all the time.

Me and the world

In the decades ahead, customer expectations will go much further than the demand for ease of use and outstanding service. This prospect leads to an obvious question: if these matters are taken for granted, how will companies in the future attempt to convince their customers to buy from them? My research for this book suggests that many companies will focus on two other key aspects of customer expectations.

1. Satisfying the hopes, dreams and ambitions of the consumer

Nowadays, many people have a bucket list: a list of often exotic destinations they still want to visit, or personal challenges they wish to attempt, or wonderful moments they hope to

experience with their families. At the other end of the social spectrum, many people are still struggling each month to make ends meet. Some young families invest heavily to buy their own home, and as a result are faced with a long period of financial stringency. Single parents often need to be creative to keep their head above water.

Every consumer has in his or her mind a film of how life should be. This gives companies an opportunity to respond positively and empathically to this film. As a company, you can become a partner in the life of the consumer, by focusing less on your own products and services and more on the dreams and concerns of your customers. How can you help to make their dreams come true? How can you give them new hope? How can you ease their worries?

2. Tackling the challenges of the world

Every study confirms it: more and more people, particularly young people, are anxious about the effects of climate change and its impact on the planet. The world is facing a series of major societal challenges. Customers like to work with companies that take a responsible attitude towards these challenges, in the hope that together they can make a difference. The outbreak of the coronavirus in the first half of 2020 has demonstrated just how ill-prepared to meet unexpected crises our world really is, even though scientists have been warning us for years that good advanced planning and the development of a reaction plan are crucial success factors. What's more, when a critical situation does arise, the world's politicians are often unable to provide the strong leadership that will help to relieve people's anxieties. This political inadequacy offers yet another opportunity to companies. They can fill the resultant vacuum by making a positive contribution and giving a positive signal which shows that they understand people's fears.

During the great lockdown the essential nature of the large distribution companies like Amazon and Walmart became clearer than ever before. And it was not simply that they made sure we all had enough toilet paper! Just try to imagine the chaos that would have ensued if their massive distribution networks had collapsed during the lockdown. It doesn't bear thinking about. Tech giants Google and Apple were also keen to make a contribution, announcing early on that they would work together to develop tracer software to help limit the spread of the pandemic. And these are only a few examples of the desire of the business community to ease the worries of their customers at a moment when the politicians seemed powerless to do so. Today's consumers expect more social leadership from companies than in the past and this is a trend that looks set to continue.

As a result, the pressure on customer experience is unlikely to decline in the years ahead. Quite the opposite, in fact. Expectations in terms of classic service provision are already at an all-time high, but increasing pressure on individuals will continue to be transferred to the companies in the form of even higher corporate expectations. In both their personal and professional spheres, people expect a great deal of themselves and it is costing them more and more energy to give substance to the film of their life. For this reason, they need all the help they can get to make their lives easier – and this is where the companies can step in. It is a massive opportunity.

Societal pressures will also continue to increase. The climate problem, for example, is not a short-term problem that will disappear anytime soon. Indeed, the urgency of this kind of world emergency is predicted to become greater with each passing year. This too presents opportunities for smart companies.

Hopes, dreams and ambitions

How can you help to realise the hopes, dreams and ambitions of customers? How can you really take away people's worries? Do you have a sufficiently good understanding of the film of their lives to make this possible?

Everyone is seeking to fulfil a goal in life. For some people their work is the most important thing. For others it is their family. Some people dream of letting their children see the world. Others want to teach them how to grow vegetables in their own garden. Everyone is different. Everyone has his or her own film, and each one is unique. But amidst all this diversity there is one common denominator. Everyone has need of hope in difficult times. Everyone dreams of good things and better days ahead. Everyone has certain ambitions for the future. The key question is therefore: as an organisation, how can you gain greater insight into these hopes, dreams and ambitions, so that you know how best to respond to them?

> *Everyone is seeking to fulfil a goal in life. As an organisation, how can you gain greater insight into these hopes, dreams and ambitions, so that you know how best to respond to them?*

Perhaps companies like Aldi and Lidl are more than just hard discounters, who win by having the lowest prices. Perhaps Aldi and Lidl are companies that make it easier for some people to make ends meet until the end of the month. In this way, these supermarket chains are actually a kind of financial partner, helping people to make the best of their meagre resources until the next pay cheque comes in. Or perhaps Aldi and Lidl make it possible for consumers to buy one or two luxury products for the Christmas and New Year festivities, which otherwise they might not have been able to afford. Easing worries and making dreams come true – even if they are only dreams of a slap-up Christmas dinner – are different ways in which companies can play an important role in the lives of their customers. You can apply this same philosophy to Ryanair. In strategy lessons, we refer to Ryanair as a low-cost player. Which, of course, they are. But from the perspective of some of their customers Ryanair is a company that makes it possible for them to enjoy a city trip each year. Thanks to Ryanair, they can cross Rome, Prague or Berlin off their bucket list, while the tickets to these destinations with the traditional airlines might have been beyond their means.

As a company, how can you help your customers to realise their hopes, dreams and ambitions? To make this possible, it is no longer enough to look at their customer journey. You need to look at – and understand – their life journey.
You won't find this understanding in the frictions of your company's processes; you can only find it in the frictions of your customers' lives. Some of these frictions deprive them of hope or make it difficult for them to achieve a particular dream. So how can you remove these frictions? How can you become your customers' life partner? The secret lies in providing not just transactional convenience, but also emotional convenience.

The paradox of modern society

Lots of people are worried. The majority think that things are going badly wrong with our world. Gloomy though it sounds, this too offers opportunities for companies. Organisations must seek to make worthwhile contributions to society in a manner that will allow them to dispel some of this gloom, whilst at the same time improving their perception in people's minds.
In an ideal world companies will create value for society in ways that reflect the hopes, dreams and ambitions of consumers. Whenever that is possible, the companies' efforts in the social field will generate a flywheel effect, exponentially increasing their popularity thanks to the additional commitment and appreciation of their customers.

The need for companies to invest in society is great. The world is facing a number of major challenges and many people are concerned about what the future might bring. There is, however, a paradox in this situation: people are getting more and more worried about the world at a time when many aspects of that world have never been as favourable as they are today!
One of my favourite books is *Factfulness*, written by Hans Rosling. In my opinion, it is a work of genius. The book uses data obtained from the United Nations in an attempt to convince people in an objective manner that the world has never had it so good. In one of the early chapters, Rosling sets out a test with twenty questions. These ask about the current status of matters such as hunger, poverty, climate, population growth, etc. at a global level. Most people answer fewer than 15 per cent of the questions correctly.

Rosling pours scorn on this poor performance, commenting that a group of chimpanzees would perform better than 85 per cent of human beings! The questions in the test each have three possible answers. This means that by the law of averages a chimp would score at least 33 per cent, whereas the majority of humans cannot manage even half of that total! This demonstrates conclusively that the bulk of the population around the world has a completely distorted view of the actual evolution of our planet.

Here are some examples. 88 per cent of the world's babies are now vaccinated during the first year of life. As a result, infant mortality has fallen by more than half since 1990. At the opposite end of the life cycle, average life expectancy has increased from 29 years in the early modern era to 73 years in 2019. 90 per cent of girls now attend school, in contrast with just 65 per cent in 1970. In consequence, the number of children per family has plummeted and in the medium term the number of people on the planet will also rise more slowly. In the year 1800, 85 per cent of the world's population was poor (meaning an income of less than two dollars per day). By 1966, this figure had been reduced to 50 per cent and by 2017 it had been slashed to just 9 per cent.

Many people currently have the feeling that the world is threatened by an increasing number of natural disasters. Indeed, such disasters do still occur and with disturbing frequency. But the number of people dying as a result has dropped dramatically in recent times. In the 1930s, an average of 971,000 people died each year from causes related to natural disasters. In the first decade of the 21st century, the comparable number of deaths was just 72,000. Of course, this is still 72,000 too many, but it is thirteen times less than a hundred years ago, while during that same period the world's total population has more than tripled. Yes, reading Hans Rosling's book really makes me feel optimistic!

That being said, Rosling's work still leaves room for nuance and criticism. Above all, he looks at problems and evolutions almost exclusively from the perspective of the past. For example, it is only in recent years that the climate problem has come to the forefront of people's thinking, but this fails to get a mention in the book – although in this case it is clear that the situation is much worse than it was a hundred years ago.

Is everything in our world perfect? Of course not! Do we have many serious problems to confront? Undoubtedly. But is the world a better place than it was 30 years ago? You bet!

As I am writing this book in the middle of the corona crisis, this may seem a strange claim to make, even for an optimist like me. The year 2020 will create a new peak for deaths resulting from illness and disease, as was the case earlier in the century with swine flu and, before that (but to a lesser extent), with the SARS virus. Even so, the underlying trend will continue to be downwards. The number of victims of terrorism also spiked in 2001 as a result of the 9/11 attacks, but has been falling steadily ever since. By now, the overall message should be clear. No matter how difficult the world situation might seem in 2020 and no matter how sad it is that hundreds of thousands of people are dying from COVID-19, life on our planet, viewed from an evolutionary perspective over the long term, is significantly better for the vast majority of its inhabitants than it was just decades ago. In short, we are making progress. Sadly, however, there is a caveat to this good news story: the corona crisis means that for the first time since 1998 the total amount of world poverty will increase, with an estimated half a million people being pushed back below a basic level of subsistence.[11] Yet another terrible consequence of this terrible virus.

The majority of people have a misguided view about the actual condition of our world. And his view is not just a little bit misguided; it is an awful lot misguided.

There is, of course, a difference between reality and perception. Even if things in general are improving, the 2020 crisis created a worldwide panic, so that confidence amongst the world's population is at a lower level than it was in 2019. And it wasn't at a brilliant level then, since even before the pandemic a growing number of people, rightly or wrongly, were becoming increasingly worried about the status of the world.

A global study entitled *Our world in data,*[12] carried out by Ipsos, has revealed (as did Hans Rosling's book) that mankind in general has a mistaken impression about the current state of our planet. 52 per cent of the people questioned thought that poverty is increasing, with this misconception being most strongly rooted in the traditionally 'rich' lands of Europe and North America. 61 per cent thought that a growing number of children continue to die at an early age, with the prosperous West again overestimating the gravity of the situation. In contrast, people in Africa assessed the situation more or less accurately, since they have had the benefit of seeing the proof with their own eyes.

This is yet further evidence, if any was needed, that the overwhelming majority of people have a misguided view about the actual condition of our world. And this view is not just a little bit misguided; it is an awful lot misguided. Most of the statistical curves for the unpleasant things in life are falling rapidly, whereas billions believe they are moving equally fast in the opposite direction!

Hans Rosling made it his life's work to try and correct this distorted perspective. Sadly, he died a few years ago and, notwithstanding his superhuman efforts, I fear that he failed in his mission. The reality is that people are still worried about the evolution of the world. In their mind's eye they can still see an increase in armed conflicts, criminality, terrorism and many other things that cause them sleepless nights, even though none of this is true.

How is this possible? Part of the problem is that the evolution of (social) media in recent years has provided us all with 24/7 access to news, whether we want it or not. As a result, we are seeing more unpleasant things on our screens than ever before, and so we assume that more of these unpleasant things must be happening. In the past, most people glanced through the daily paper over breakfast and then watched the television news in the evening. This meant that news editors needed to be careful to confine their selection of what to report to matters that were of wider importance. Today, we are bombarded with tweets and push messages from mobile news apps almost every minute of the day, so that we can no longer see the wood for the trees.

This flood of news messages, most of them irrelevant, negatively colours our perspective of the world. Nowadays, if something 'bad' happens, we have a seat on the front row and can follow events as they unfold in all their gruesome technicolour detail. The terrible bushfires in Australia seem to confirm our worst fears about climate change and the coronavirus reinforces our belief that society is ill-equipped to deal with the major challenges it faces.

This is an interesting paradox. In many ways, the world has never been in such good shape or so kind to its inhabitants as it is today. But that is not how the majority of people see things. If a company were to attempt to change this perception, in my opinion it would be fighting a losing battle. The only option is to latch on to the themes that concern your consumers and try to make a positive contribution towards them. That is where the real opportunities for the future are to be found. In particular, three concerns stand head and shoulders above the rest: climate, technology and health.

Concern 1: climate

In recent years, the climate problem has occupied an increasingly prominent position in the mindset of the average consumer. In the most recent Young Shaper[13] study, climate was by far the biggest source of concern for the younger generations.

But it is not just young people who are worried. Many companies also recognise the seriousness of the situation. The World Economic Forum calculated that 44 trillion American dollars of economic value, equivalent to half of the world's total GDP, is dependent on the natural environment.

The most vulnerable sectors are construction (4 trillion American dollars), agriculture (2.5 trillion American dollars) and the food industry (1.4 trillion American dollars). A concrete example: 60 per cent of the world's production of coffee beans is threatened by climate change. This can have major consequences in a sector that is worth 83 billion American dollars.[14]

Statistics of this kind mean that every company is now in the sustainability business. As a result, there is a risk that sustainability will soon come to feel like a commodity. The trick is to find a way to promote sustainability in a way that allows your company to differentiate itself.

MAX Burgers is climate neutral

Since Greta Thunberg put awareness of the climate problem more firmly on the map than ever before in 2019, no company or organisation can afford to ignore the situation. They need to act with concern about the climate at the forefront of their thinking. First and foremost, because it is the right thing to do. But also because of growing pressure from the market.

More and more studies are linking economic value to positive societal behaviour. A study by McKinsey[15] has demonstrated that 70 per cent of consumers are prepared to pay 5 per cent more for a green product, provided that the product matches the same quality norms as the non-green product.

People get a good feeling when they believe they are helping to make the world a better place, but they expect something in return. The products they buy must be at least as good and the standard of service provision must be superior to the new minimum.

MAX Burgers is the oldest hamburger chain in Europe. It opened its first restaurant in Sweden in 1968. Their burgers are delicious and I am a big fan! Some time ago I meet Kai Török, who is responsible for the company's sustainability strategy, at an event in Stockholm. At the start of his presentation, he asked the audience if they could remember what it was like to eat a tasty burger.

Not surprisingly, everyone could. But then he asked us: 'And now think about the tastiest hamburger you have ever eaten. For how many of you was it a burger without red meat?' I looked around the hall and only saw a dozen or so raised hands among the thousand or so spectators. Almost everyone was thinking of a juicy beef burger. Including myself, if I am honest. MAX Burgers wants to be climate positive. To make this possible, it will need to sell one out of every two burgers without the red meat that has such a negative impact on the climate, as a result of the need to breed cattle. This left the company with only one real alternative: to make delicious burgers that replaced beef with chicken, fish or vegetable alternatives. Of course, you also need to do much more than simply add these new burgers to the range. You need to make sure that the quality is super-good and you need to persuade people to buy them. And they did!

The hamburger chain launched its first 'climate-positive' menu in 2018. Climate-positive means that the company compensates for its negative emissions and then adds a little bit extra. MAX Burgers wants to ensure that in total it generates more positive effects than negative effects. To achieve this, it takes the following concrete actions:

1. It measures the negative emissions linked to its products. This means all emissions, from the farmer's field until the product is placed in the hands of the customer. It even includes the distances travelled by MAX Burgers employees to get to their work. Last but not least, the effects of waste disposal are also analysed, so that the entire production process from A to Z is covered.

2. Within this process, the company does everything possible to lower the level of its emissions. Selling as few beef products as possible is an important part of this strategy. For example, its own variety of veggie-burger is really very good. In recent years, MAX Burgers has seen a growth of 100 per cent in this product category. By working closely with all its suppliers and by critically re-evaluating its own operational practices, the chain has succeeded in significantly reducing its emissions.

3. Nevertheless, some emissions remain, for which the company takes full responsibility. To compensate for this, MAX Burgers plants new trees that will help to reduce an equivalent of 110 per cent of these emissions, so that the company can justifiably claim that it is 'climate-positive'.

In recent times, MAX Burgers has enjoyed a consistent growth of more than 20 per cent each year and is now the most profitable hamburger chain in Sweden.[16] Its non-beef products are truly fantastic – if that was not the case, their strategy would never work – so that more and more customers are encouraged to help MAX Burgers to fulfil its mission.

Together with these customers, the chain wants to make the world just that little bit better, but without robbing its burger fans of their scrumptious taste experience. This certainly sounds like 'an offer people can't refuse', don't you think?

Concern 2: technology

Society as a whole is currently undergoing a massive digital transformation. This inevitably involves facing new challenges and dealing with new tensions. The studies carried out by the British-Venezuelan researcher Carlota Perez[17] have revealed the impact of the five most important technological revolutions in the history of the world.

The first crucial technological revolution was the industrial revolution (1771). The major breakthrough was first made in England. The steam age began in the early 1800s, characterised by the introduction of the steam train. By the end of the 19th century, a large-scale iron and steel industry had emerged, with Germany and the United States leading the way. 1908 saw the start of a new era of oil and mass production, of which the car industry was perhaps the most prominent example. Today, we are currently in the middle of the fifth technological revolution: the digital revolution.

The four previous revolutions have all followed the same broad pattern:

1. **The installation phase:** this phase is characterised by the disruption of the market. Current methods of working are called into question and 'attacked' by the new technology. Amazon, for example, turned the retail market upside down. The arrival of Netflix put Blockbuster out of business. Nokia was torpedoed by the smartphone. Buying music on CD was replaced by digital alternatives: first iTunes and then Spotify. There are dozens of examples.

   This first phase is also characterised by the emergence of organisations that want to use the new technology and know how best to exploit it to their own benefit. During the era of mass production, the Ford motor company was the classic example. Horse traders and coach makers were not exactly Henry Ford's biggest fans!

   As a result of these developments, an inequality is created in the market. A handful of people become very rich, but usually at the expense of everyone else. This is the phase of big winners and even bigger losers, leading to dissatisfaction and uncertainty in the marketplace. After a time, everyone wants to jump on what seems to be a highly profitable bandwagon, blinded by a naive belief in the invincibility of the new technology. This can lead to dangerous financial bubbles.

2. **The turning point:** this is not the most pleasant phase of the revolution. During the first four technological revolutions there always came a moment when the market was plunged into deep recession, as was the case, for example, with the Great Depression of the 1930s. During this phase, people discover that their expectations of the new technology are not being met, as a result of which serious financial losses are incurred, often followed by a stock market crash and general disillusionment in society as a whole. The recession and disappointments of the 1930s ultimately led to the Second World War. The turning point is usually a difficult time for everyone and everything.

3. **The deployment phase:** no matter how sombre the turning point might be, the situation eventually improves. The years after the Second World War were years of

economic prosperity, during which almost everyone was able to enjoy the benefits of the new technology. In this phase, the technology is no longer used to make just a few people fabulously wealthy, but to serve the interests of a much wider target group, resulting in general societal satisfaction with 'progress'. Carlota Perez describes these phases in the four previous revolutions as the 'golden ages'.

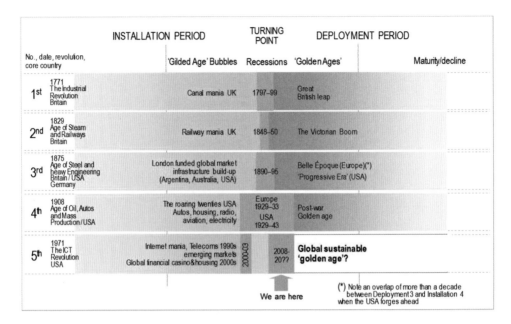

No., date, revolution, core country	INSTALLATION PERIOD		TURNING POINT	DEPLOYMENT PERIOD	
	'Gilded Age' Bubbles		Recessions	'Golden Ages'	Maturity/decline
1st 1771 The Industrial Revolution Britain	Canal mania UK		1797–99	Great British leap	
2nd 1829 Age of Steam and Railways Britain	Railway mania UK		1848–50	The Victorian Boom	
3rd 1875 Age of Steel and heavy Engineering Britain / USA Germany	London funded global market infrastructure build-up (Argentina, Australia, USA)		1890–95	Belle Époque (Europe)(*) 'Progressive Era' (USA)	
4th 1908 Age of Oil, Autos and Mass Production/USA	The roaring twenties USA Autos, housing, radio, aviation, electricity		Europe 1929–33 USA 1929–43	Post-war Golden age	
5th 1971 The ICT Revolution USA	Internet mania, Telecoms 1990s emerging markets Global financial casino&housing 2000s	2000–03	2008– 20??	**Global sustainable 'golden age'?**	

We are here

(*) Note an overlap of more than a decade between Deployment 3 and Installation 4 when the USA forges ahead

This same pattern can be discerned in each of the major technological revolutions. Our society is currently in the middle or turning point phase of the fifth of these revolutions, typified by high unemployment, populism, growing inequality, social unrest and anger. The sense of disruption and the feeling of disenchantment with the exaggerated power of the big technology players in China and the United States are almost palpable.

This turning point phase can last for a number of years, even decades, and often goes hand in hand with one or more financial crises. The first was the banking crash in 2008. The second (and much heavier) is the corona pandemic.

The key question then becomes whether or not the time has now arrived to invest in structural change, in the hope that we are approaching the start of our own 'golden age'. In 2030, will we look back at 2020 as the moment when we turned the corner to brighter and happier times? Today, this question is the cause of a great deal of uncertainty and frustration among large segments of the population.

Carlota Perez remains positive. She believes that the climate and environmental problems we are currently facing must be seen as an opportunity to develop a strong economy driven by commercially interesting innovations that aim to solve precisely those problems. She calls this Smart Green Growth.

The Digital Dark Side

In recent years, new technologies have added considerably to customer experience. At the same time, however, the world has also been confronted with the dark side of technology. In her book *The age of surveillance capitalism*, Shoshana Zuboff[18] pleads for a new form of capitalism. Today, a handful of organisations make use of an ocean of consumer data to earn astronomical sums of money. The price that society pays to make this possible is the manipulation of our way of thinking and of living by algorithms. More and more people are starting to feel uncomfortable about the impact of Big Tech. For the companies forced to compete against these tech-giants the competition often feels unequal and unfair. In certain domains the power of these dominant players feels almost threatening. To make matters worse, the possibilities open to other less visible players who have genuinely bad intentions are potentially even more threatening.

This 'dark side' is a problem in every part of the world. In the West, there is already clear evidence that these dark forces have attempted to undermine the democratic process. The saga of Cambridge Analytica and the manipulation of content by Facebook leave little room for doubt. Social media are fantastic, but for people with less than honourable motives they have become a kind of 'weapon of mass influence'. The lack of transparency and the unwillingness to take decisive action displayed by the Facebook leadership led to a significant loss of confidence in the company. Even so, almost everybody (now totalling almost 2.5 billion people) continued to use the platform, simply because there is no real alternative. The consumer had no choice – and that is not always a pleasant feeling.

At a different level, the government in China uses social media to monitor its population. When a number of Chinese scientists used their social media outlets during the first weeks of the corona outbreak to talk about a new and dangerous virus, they were quickly

silenced. Big Brother in Beijing was watching them and took immediate steps to make further communication with the outside world impossible.

Companies – even foreign companies – have been subjected to the same treatment. A few years ago, the Marriott hotel chain made a serious error of judgement in referring to Taiwan as a separate country on its Chinese website. Within a matter of hours, the site was unilaterally taken offline by the Chinese authorities and only restored several weeks later. During that period, negative propaganda was also spread about Marriott, with the clear intention of causing the group economic damage.

The idea that someone somewhere is looking secretly over our shoulder makes most of us feel uncomfortable at the best of times. In the worst of times, this can lead to dramatic changes in behaviour. During the anti-Beijing demonstrations in Hong Kong (2019-2020), it was clear to see how many of the protesters were 'armed' with umbrellas or laser lights. The umbrellas did not serve as protection against the rain or the sun, and the laser lights were not intended to add a little carnival atmosphere to the proceedings. Both were tools to prevent identification by the thousands of government security cameras fitted with face recognition technology. This same fear of the digital watchdog also led to a significant reduction in mobile payments. The choice between convenience and privacy was suddenly presented in very stark terms. In most parts of the world the majority of people put convenience before privacy on an almost daily basis, since time is a precious and limited resource. But in Hong Kong the balance has shifted radically in the opposite direction. During the past two years, privacy has become the greatest good. Convenience is no use to you if you are locked up in a Chinese prison.

Sadly, it seems likely that the digital dark side is only at the start of its development.

> **_Good old-fashioned bank robbery has now been superseded by the digital plundering of individual bank accounts._**

Good old-fashioned bank robbery has now been superseded by the digital plundering of individual bank accounts, using methods that are becoming increasingly sophisticated with each passing month. In the near future it is possible that you will receive an e-mail from your partner asking you to make a small bank transfer payment, because he/she doesn't have the time. The amount in question will probably be relatively small and the email will seem to come from your partner's address and be written in his/her style. As a result, there is a good chance that you will make the payment.

However, the email address making the request and the real email address of your partner will be ever so slightly different, but this difference will be so miniscule that you will only notice it if you are using maximum concentration. Moreover, the sender of the false message will have been monitoring your email correspondence for days via artificial intelligence, so that they know exactly how your partner would make this kind of request and can imitate it perfectly.

Imagine that a cybercriminal can send ten thousand or so of these emails each day. Even if only 10 per cent of his targets fall for the bait, that is still a pretty lucrative day's work. With that kind of success rate, who is crazy enough to still want to rob a bank?

In January 2020, the Belgian company Picanol was attacked by hackers. The company's entire computer system was immobilised. As a result, the factory where the company manufactures looms was forced to close down production. Most of its large workforce was made temporarily redundant and Picanol shares were suspended on the stock market to prevent their price from hitting rock bottom. The economic damage was immense. What happened to Picanol is terrible, but it is only the tip of the iceberg. What if hospitals or nuclear power plants were ever to be targeted in the same way? The digital dark side is a concrete threat and a new form of criminality that rightly has many people worried, especially since it is becoming increasingly clear that companies and government authorities are still ill-prepared to meet the danger.

I have said it before, but it bears repeating: most things in the world are better than ever before, but people are still more worried than they have ever been. They question society's ability to deal with the challenges facing us and therefore, as far as technology is concerned, focus on the (negative) consequences of the digital revolution in which we are engaged.
Of course, it has to be admitted that this revolution is complex and is taking place at lightning speed. Even so, everyone recognises the advantages that technology can bring and the vast majority of us could no longer imagine our lives without the new possibilities it offers. At the same time, people are anxious about the potential impact on business, society and their own personal opportunities in the future. What does the current revolution mean for me and how can it benefit the community as a whole? These are the key questions on everyone's lips.

Concern 3: health

I began to write this book in March 2020, as the corona crisis was strengthening its grip on Europe and the United States. Dozens of prestigious events were cancelled, such as the South by South-West festival in Austin, the Indian Wells tennis tournament, the European football championship and even the Olympic Games in Japan. Every now and then, the world is rocked by an event that we never imagined could be possible. Before September 2001, no-one ever thought that aeroplanes packed with innocent passengers would be used as guided missiles against skyscrapers. In 2007, no-one believed that the banking system was on the point of collapse. A virus that could cripple the world economy? That kind of thing only happens in Hollywood movies, doesn't it? No, it doesn't. From 2020 onwards, that is our new reality.

Every company is becoming a healthcare c✱mpany

Steven Van Belleghem

As a result, since the start of 2020 every company has become actively engaged in health care. There is no alternative to introducing strict hygiene rules to protect both customers and employees. For quite some time to come, we will no longer be able to take good health for granted. And when we wish someone 'good health' on 1 January 2021, we will probably mean it more than we have ever meant it before. As a concomitant of all this, companies will need to look seriously at how they can also make a meaningful contribution to public health.

The large technology players have already been knocking on the door of the health industry for quite some time. Amazon, for example, has set up its mysterious 'Gesundheit' project, which intends to find a remedy for the common cold. This is taking place within the framework of the Amazon Grand Challenge research group, which is charged with finding solutions to problems that have a major impact on society. That is certainly the case with the common cold. The University of Michigan has calculated that colds cost the American economy roughly 40 billion dollars a year in medical care costs and lower pro-ductivity. Scientists have been trying to find a vaccine since the 1950s, but so far without success. Perhaps Amazon will do better.

Google has also launched a number of initiatives in the health field, like its collaboration with Novartis or the setting up of its own medical company Calico, which hopes to reduce the effects of ageing.

In future, every sector will need to be involved in health care. COVID-19 has made the world afraid. If a pandemic can happen once, it can happen again. In order to reduce this risk, people will expect new hygiene regulations to be enforced in all walks of life. Armies can destroy buildings and aircraft with remarkable precision. From now on, society will demand this same precision when targeting harmful viruses. Customers will insist that the companies they buy from think seriously about these matters and introduce measures that will benefit the health of us all. Our health, which has suffered so grievously in 2020, is now at the absolute summit of the Maslow pyramid. The focus will switch from making sick people well again, to making sure they don't get sick in the first place. In other words, prevention rather than cure. This is something that every consumer and every company can work at.

The Offer You Can't Refuse

Our own reaction to the corona crisis illustrates perfectly the new expectations of today's modern consumers. By analysing this reaction, we can better understand the changes in these expectations.

The corona crisis has strengthened my conviction that this is the direction in which customer experience will evolve in the years ahead.

Most of the people I know asked lots of questions about the impact of the virus. In the first instance, almost everyone thinks about themselves and their family. 'Hopefully, we won't get sick and nobody we know will die.' The next set of questions then go further than our immediate health. 'What about our holiday plans?' 'Will our friend's wedding still be able to take place?' 'What will be the effect on my job and our savings?' After these initial (and largely personal) reflections, people move on to express their concern for others and for society in general. 'It must be terrible to live in Italy, where so many are dying is such distressing circumstances.' 'How long will it take the economy to recover?' 'When will the pharmaceutical companies find a vaccine?' We tend to look at crises like the corona crisis with a kind of double feeling: we think first about how the crisis hits us, and only then about the way it hits the wider world.

I began to develop the concept for The Offer You Can't Refuse model in September 2019. The key questions I asked myself were these: 'What personal needs of the customer must be satisfied?' and 'Which of the customer's wishes for the improvement of society must also be satisfied?' This double way of thinking forms the basis for my theory in this book. The corona crisis has simply strengthened my conviction that this is the direction in which customer experience will evolve in the years ahead.

How can you win and keep your customers in a world where ease of use and good service have become commodities? That is the question I intend to answer in the following pages. The challenge is to formulate an offer for your customers that gives them no real reason not to accept what you are proposing. In short: *Make them an offer they can't refuse!* If, as a company leader, you look out of your office window, you can only see a very small piece of the world. But the invisible digital segment of that world is getting bigger and more important all the time. Nowadays, it is everywhere, and the difference between online and offline is becoming increasingly blurred. In fact, we are really living in a hybrid world, where all our offline interactions have a digital component. Investing in a strong digital presence is an important part of The Offer You Can't Refuse.

Understanding what concerns and motivates the person behind the customer will allow you to move beyond mere technological improvements. Most of today's investments in digital technology result in outstanding digital ease of use: in other words, transactional convenience. But once you understand the person behind the customer, you can try to offer them something more: emotional convenience. By responding to these deeper sources of inspiration, you can become a partner in the life of your consumers. Investing in emotional convenience is therefore a second element of the strategy. Last but not least, it is important for companies to accept their responsibilities towards the wider society in which they operate. Nowadays, the market is looking to companies rather than to governments to take the actions that will have a positive impact on the community as a whole. This is the third element in The Offer You Can't Refuse strategy.

Hybrid

Every part of the offline world will have a digital layer!

the offer you can't refuse model

Surprising that Spotify made it!

At the end of 2019, some 271 million people were making use of the Spotify music service.[19] These millions of consumers now regard the availability of millions of songs for a limited monthly cost as the most normal thing in the world. It doesn't take long to get used to top-class service provision. Spotify was founded in Sweden in April 2006 by Daniel Ek and Martin Lorentzon. In 2006! Perhaps some of you can still remember what it was like back then. In 2006, more than 40 per cent of music-lovers in the Western world went in search of 'illegal' downloads to satisfy their musical needs.[20] Downloading music in this way was not strictly speaking allowed, but it had become more or less normal behaviour. And it was precisely at this moment, when the rage for illegally downloading music was at its height, that Spotify decided to launch a paying model! On paper, this seemed like a suicide mission. But that is not the way things turned out. At the start of 2020, Spotify is now valued at 25 billion American dollars. So how did they manage it?

The first step was the digital interface. When someone wanted to download a song illegally in 2006, it could take several minutes. You had to sit and wait before you could listen to your music. With Spotify, you simply clicked on the song you wanted and it immediately began to play. The first users had a magical feeling, almost as if the songs were actually loaded on their own hard drive. People clicked and music filled the air – instantly. Today, it seems self-evident, but back then it was a breakthrough. The speed of the Spotify interface was the first differentiator in comparison with the illegal model. By 2008, there were already 50 million tracks available on Spotify and the company decided to launch its famous playlists. In this way, Spotify began to offer its consumers voyages of musical exploration, ranging from new sounds to forgotten classics. In fact, that is where the name 'Spotify' comes from. It is a combination of two words: 'spot' – rediscovering a number

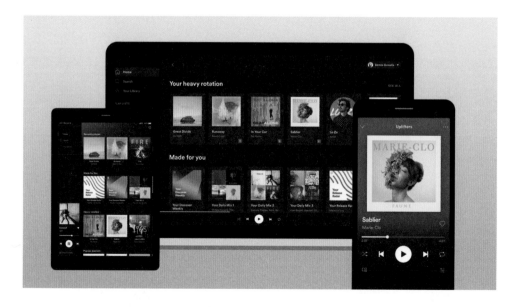

you had forgotten – and 'identify' – being able to put a name to that number. With the playlist, Spotify became a partner in the life of the modern music-lover. And with the help of the Spotify algorithm, people were even able to compile their own playlists, which they could then share with their family and friends. In other words, Spotify helped them to share their musical passions.

Notwithstanding the serious criticism sometimes levelled at Spotify, mainly as a result of the limited payments it makes to artists, the company has helped to remove digital music from the stigma of illegality. For some people, Spotify was a way to ease their conscience. Thanks to Spotify, millions of music fans were able to listen to their favourite numbers efficiently, intelligently and honestly. In short, it was simply an offer they couldn't refuse.

The Offer You Can't Refuse

The quote 'Make him an offer he can't refuse' was made world-famous thanks to *The Godfather* series of films (from 1972 onwards). In one of the most legendary scenes, Mafia boss Don Corleone (Marlon Brando) is visited by his godson, Johnny Fontane (Al Martino). Johnny has been a well-known singer, but now hopes to get a film role to breathe new life into his fading career. The head of the film studio has already turned him down for the role, which is not to the liking of Don Corleone. He tells Johnny to leave the matter with him. It is then that he speaks one of the most famous one-liners in Hollywood history: 'I'm gonna make him an offer he can't refuse.' In *The Godfather* films, this expression meant accept the deal or accept the consequences – which was usually death. Let's be clear on this: I am not proposing that you liquidate your customers if they refuse to buy with you! No, I am suggesting something more in keeping with the original meaning of the quote, which was first made in the film *Burn 'Em Up Barnes* (1932), where it more literally meant making someone such an attractive offer that it is impossible to reject.

The trick is to make your customers an offer that contains all the elements they find important. You must learn to understand the needs of contemporary consumers and respond to them effectively, so that you make them an 'offer they can't refuse'. You must ensure that all the meaningful reasons for not buying from you no longer apply. This means giving them value at different levels, so that the reasons for buying from you become irresistible.

That is how Spotify built up their amazing success: they provided a perfect interface, became a partner in people's musical lives and solved the problem of illegal downloading. What more could any music-lover want?

Four strategies for building
The Offer You Can't Refuse

The Offer You Can't Refuse model builds further on the customer expectations referred to in the first chapter. In particular, a combination of four specific elements will help you to develop an offer that no-one will want to turn down.

1. **Quality products and good service for a good price**

   This, of course, forms the basis for every good customer relationship. The product and the service provision must be first-class. And the more unique your product, the stronger your selling proposition becomes. But let's be honest: nowadays, there are very few truly unique products. Most of today's companies find themselves with products that put them in what is effectively a commodity situation. Even so, the basic 'quality-service-price' rule remains valid. You can have the most advanced customer-experience strategies in the world, but if the fundamentals are wrong you will never succeed. This is the absolute minimum condition for every company. For this reason, I will not be discussing this aspect of the strategy any further in this book. It is so basic that everyone should know it. And if you don't …

2. **Transactional convenience**

   Ease of use is the new commodity, but this does not mean it will disappear or that its importance will decrease. Quite the reverse. Optimal ease of use is now the new minimum. Time will continue to be the most precious resource of the modern consumer. Saving customers' time will therefore continue to be a major priority for companies. In the years ahead, digital ease of use will continue to evolve. This trend is already

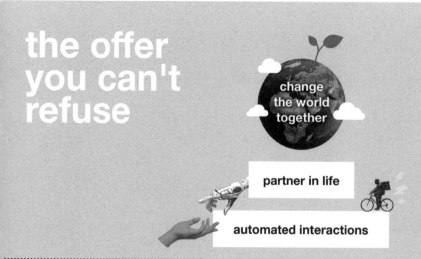

the offer
you can't
refuse

change
the world
together

partner in life

automated interactions

 good product / service & price

clear: the effort that a customer needs to make to perform a transaction will decline further. The next step in this evolution will be the development of invisible, automatic transactions. The interfaces that will make this possible will reduce interaction with the customer to virtually zero. The transaction will still be made in accordance with the customer's wishes, but without any effort on his or her part. The coming decades will see the further evolution of convenience. Paradoxically, however, the more ease of use improves, the less differentiating it will become. Because as I have already said: it is now the new minimum – for everyone.

3. **Partner in life**

   People are searching for hope. They have dreams and ambitions. How can you help them to fill in the film of their life in the best possible manner? If you can make it possible for consumers to realise their dreams, you will provide them with a unique experience that will allow them to cope more easily with the difficult things in their lives. Smart brands will succeed in eliminating key concerns from the daily lives of their customers. They will help them to complete their daily tasks more efficiently. This strategy is not about removing the frictions from your company's sale process. No, it is about removing the frictions from the day-to-day existence of your customers. It has nothing to do with the customer journey; it has everything to do with the life journey.

4. **Save the world**

   How can you (together with your customers and your personnel) create societal added value? People have many different worries about the future. As a company, you must be seen to take your responsibility and make a contribution towards relieving one or more of these worries. In this way, you will be helping to make the world a better place and will reap the rewards that this brings with it.

At last! A smart fridge

A smart fridge! I wrote about this for the first time in 2010. Back then, the internet of things was just an abstract theory, but the magical idea of a smart fridge continued to linger in our collective brain. Now, of course, such a fridge exists, but many have come to see it as the latest in a long list of gadgets that the world does not really need. But that is not how it has to be. A truly smart fridge is capable of being developed into an 'offer you can't refuse'.

How? By providing its owners with the ultimate in convenience. When your last bottle of milk has been used, the fridge can automatically put 'milk' on your next shopping list. At the end of the day (or, say, twice a week, depending on the settings), this list is mailed automatically to your favourite supermarket. A short time later, the products on the list are delivered to your front door. This is a perfect example of a perfect interface, where the input and effort of the customer are reduced to zero.

The most recent Samsung fridge has succeeded in becoming a partner in life for the consumers who use it. The fridge scans its contents to see which products it contains. This information is linked to a database with recipes. As a result, the fridge can suggest particular meals, based on the ingredients on its shelves. If one or two of the ingredients for a particular recipe are missing, the fridge automatically adds them to your next shopping list. In this way, the fridge owner is assisted to prepare the family menu for the following day. At the same time, the fridge also has the ability to select the ingredients that are nearest to their sell-by date, so that these can be used before it is too late. In other words, the fridge is a partner both in setting the family diet and in reducing expensive and environmentally unfriendly food wastage.

This last application has a positive impact for the planet. The average American family throws away 43 per cent of its food, because the sell-by date has expired.[21] If smart fridges can assist families to use these ingredients before the sell-by date is reached, the amount of food wasted would be dramatically reduced. In this way, Samsung, working together with its customers, can help to tackle a major social problem that cannot fail to benefit both society and the environment in the long run. All the elements of The Offer You Can't Refuse model – good product quality, transactional convenience, a partner in life and saving the world – are present.

Aladdin's lamp

I assume that most of you will know the story of Aladdin and his magic lamp. As a big Disney fan, I must confess that *Aladdin* is one of my favourite films. If you haven't seen it, the story is fairly easy to summarise. Aladdin finds a dirty old lamp and gives it a polish. A genie appears from the lamp and promises to fulfil any three wishes that Aladdin might have.

What would you do if you had the good fortune to find a lamp like that? Before you let your enthusiasm run away with you, there are one or two rules you will need to observe. You cannot ask for more than three wishes. And you cannot ask the genie to make someone fall in love with you or to bring someone back from the dead. Other than that, you are free to fulfil any of the many dreams you might have, up to a maximum of three. Just imagine it! You find your lamp, you give it a quick rub and a genie appears with the wonderful news that you have three wishes. So what would you choose? What would be your first wish?

During the past year, I have asked thousands of people this question during my presentations. People from every continent, every level of the management ladder and every age group, from sixteen to sixty. But no matter where I ask the question or who I ask it to, the answer for everyone is nearly always the same.

And you? What would it be, that first wish?

Something for yourself?
Something for your family, friends or children?
Something that solves one of the world's major problems?

The results of my real-life research were conclusive: roughly 95 per cent of people would choose something for themselves or for their family, friends or children. Just 5 per cent want to solve a major world problem as their first priority. I am fascinated by this outcome. Everybody is always talking about the challenges facing the world and how we all need to contribute towards solving them. But once the genie is out of the bottle, we all seem to develop instant amnesia. We could solve all the world's health problems. We could end the famine in Yemen and the war in Syria. We could eradicate world poverty. But no, as soon as we have the choice we opt for something that has a more direct impact on our own little lives. Not that there is anything wrong with that, of course. That is just the way people are. We think first about ourselves, and only then about the world.

Work your way up!

The Offer You Can't Refuse model only works in a single direction: bottom-up. If you want to be successful, you first need a perfectly functioning interface. After that, you can start thinking about the life of your customers. And after that, you can start thinking about saving the world. This can be frustrating for many of the NGOs. People who work for these organisations often say to me: 'But Steven, we are trying to improve the world, we are at the very top of your model. So why are things not working the way we hoped?' The answer to this question is to be found at the bottom of the model: 'You make it too difficult for people to donate money to your organisations. The effort required from potential donors is just too great. As a result, you only attract donors who are truly motivated by your work. All the others drop out. For them, it's just too much bother.' In other words, doing good for the world is not enough; the other levels of the model are equally important. This reflects the fact that there is always a huge gap between what people say and what they do. In recent years, many people in all walks of life have talked about the importance of the climate debate. But in reality, not everyone has made the same effort to try and make a positive contribution. We all know that flying is bad for the environment, but our personal freedom (particularly if it means a holiday in the sun) is also important to us.

During the corona lockdown international air traffic was grounded, so that we were no longer able to fly. Everyone could see how nature benefited, once the level of human pollution was reduced. This positive effect was noticeable very quickly. Once the epidemic had started in China, the number of airline passengers fell dramatically, even though at that time planes were still flying in many other parts of the world.

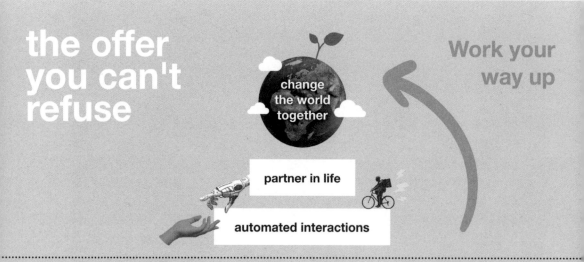

the offer you can't refuse

change the world together

Work your way up

partner in life

automated interactions

:) good product / service & price $

Conclusion? Before the corona crisis, mass communication about the climate and the harmful role played by air travel had not the slightest impact on our behaviour. But once there was a risk to our own personal health, people started to change their behaviour almost overnight. I repeat: we think first about ourselves, and only then about the rest of the world.

Centraal Beheer: NPS +50

Centraal Beheer – the name translates as Central Management – is one of the largest and most popular insurance companies in the Netherlands. It was founded in 1999 as part of the Achmea insurance group and is based in the Dutch city of Apeldoorn. In the Netherlands, the company is famous for its now legendary advertising slogan: 'Just call Apeldoorn'.

In 2016, I was able to give a lecture at this excellent company for the very first time. It was one of those occasions that I will always remember. Before I got up to speak, the then CEO, Pieter Louter, wanted to say a few words to his people. His message was not particularly cheerful: 'Dear Colleagues. We have a fantastic company, but our customers are not really all that happy with us. We all work very hard, but we still have a negative Net Promoter Score.' The Net Promoter Score is the difference between the number of people prepared to actively recommend a company to others and the number that give a negative recommendation. In other words, back in 2016 there were more people telling family and friends not to use Centraal Beheer than there were encouraging them to sign up. Some of the reactions to this situation from the CB audience bordered on indifference: 'Yes, we know that. But we are still the best insurance company in the Netherlands, aren't we? Besides, it's almost impossible to get a positive NPS in the insurance sector. People just don't like our industry.' I looked backwards and forwards between the director and his team, curious to see what would happen next. 'Of course, you are right,' said Pieter. 'We are one of the best companies in our sector, but that simply means that we are the best of a bad bunch. A negative NPS is still negative, even if you are the best of the sector. And to be honest: I am sick and tired of it.'

Sustainable living by Centraal Beheer

I could feel the tension rising in the room and one or two people began moving nervously on their chairs. But Pieter wasn't to be stopped. Now that he had started, he intended to finish what he wanted to say: 'Look, I want to give us a new ambition. I want us to achieve an NPS of +50 as quickly as possible.' A gasp of disbelief was followed by stunned silence. An NPS of +50 is exceptional, something achieved by only a very small minority of organisations. For me, giving this kind of message just before my presentation was super. I couldn't have hoped for a better introduction. Pieter had crossed the ball; all I needed to do was knock it into the goal.

When I looked into the room, I could see that people were in two minds. Half clearly thought that the CEO had lost his mind and was no longer fit for the job. No-one in the sector had ever achieved an NPS of +50! But the other half seemed cautiously enthusiastic. You could see them thinking: 'At long last, maybe we can change something fundamental about the way we work.' In other words, they would finally be able to concentrate on what really matters to any company: customer satisfaction.

'Small Dents' Days, outstanding digital interfaces and a 'royal goodbye'

During the past few years Centraal Beheer has made it super-easy for customers to take out a new insurance policy and to settle claims.

We are now four years further. Has Centraal Beheer achieved its ambition of an NPS of +50? During the research phase for this book, I had a conversation with Albert Spijkman, the company's director-general. You can view this conversation in full on my YouTube channel.

'No, we have not yet reached the target of a general NPS score of +50,' explains Albert, 'but we have had scores of +50 and often a lot more for many of our interaction moments.' During the past few years Centraal Beheer has made it super-easy for customers to take out a new insurance policy and to settle claims. This has been the basis for their success.

In addition, the company has also developed numerous new interactions, all of which are designed to improve its relations with its customers. One of the main disadvantages of being an insurer is that you almost never get to see or speak with your customers, unless something has gone wrong. Centraal Beheer has tried to change all this with the introduction of its 'Small Dents' Days. During these days, the company's customers can go to a number of garages spread across the Netherlands to have a maximum of three small dents removed from their vehicles free of charge. Centraal Beheer also makes sure that the atmosphere in these garages is friendly and welcoming, so that the customers return home feeling good about themselves, their car and the company. It is also an excellent opportunity for the insurer to meet its customers in a 'real life' setting.

Centraal Beheer continues to conduct research to establish in which phases of the customer journey it still needs to do better. One of the moments in that journey that most companies overlook is the moment when the customer decides to end the relationship. In contrast, Centraal Beheer decided to introduce a 'royal goodbye' for customers who intend to terminate their policies. They are thanked for their years of loyalty and told in glowing terms that they will always be welcome to return. As a final element in this 'farewell' communication, the company also sends the ex-customer a packet of flower seeds: forget-me-nots! It is a brilliant and very cheap idea, but one – like many of Centraal Beheer's other small initiatives – that has had a huge impact on customer satisfaction.

Partner in living

Once the foundations for greater customer satisfaction had been laid, it was time to move on to the next phase. Albert Spijkman describes the new strategy as follows: 'Centraal Beheer is in the process of transforming itself from a seller of insurance products to a service company that helps people to live comfortably and sustainably.' Instead of selling people insurance policies, the company now wants to take some of the worry out of people's lives. One of their first innovations was the Handyman app. This is a kind of Uber for odd-job men. If you have a job that needs doing around the home, whether great or small, the app will help you to find the tradesmen you need. If you are prepared to make a small extra payment, you can even benefit from a same-day service. To make this possible, Centraal Beheer makes use of its network of technical experts in many different fields. They have been working with these experts for years for repairs carried out in connection with insurance claims. Now the skills of these craftsmen are being exploited to create an added value that has nothing to do with insurance. And the really good thing about the handyman app is that anyone can use it: you don't need to be a Centraal Beheer customer. After just one year, the app has some 25,000 users, of whom more than 60 per cent do not currently have insurance policies with the company. But in the future, who knows?

This service is still very much in its infancy, but it is already providing a concrete flow of income. This shows that for Centraal Beheer the transformation from insurance seller to service provider is more than just a PR gimmick. The intention is to develop a profitable and sustainable business model.

'Finally finish all those odd jobs!', Odd-job help by Centraal Beheer

In 2021, the introduction of smoke detectors in people's homes will become compulsory in the Netherlands. Most insurers will send their customers an email or letter with the message: 'Dear Customer. In order to comply with the law, you will need to install type X smoke detectors by no later than 31 December 2020.' But Centraal Beheer plans to take things a step further. The company will not only provide all necessary information to its customers, but will also come and install the detectors for them. This paid service has the double advantage of making things as carefree as possible for the customers, while also earning money for Centraal Beheer. Yet another instance of win-win

Centraal Beheer: an 'Offer You Can't Refuse'!

Developing a sustainable energy policy is one of the answers to the challenges presented by climate change. One of the possibilities in this respect is an increase in the installation of solar panels for domestic use. Until now, the problem has always been that many consumers find the installation process complex and cumbersome. However, Centraal Beheer saw this problem as an opportunity. As a result, at the start of 2019 the insurer decided to start selling and installing its own solar panels. Via the company website you can now buy panels in a quick, easy and user-friendly manner. You just type in your address and an online scan assesses in seconds whether or not your house is suited for panel installation. If it is, the software calculates the number of panels required and sends you a price quotation by e-mail. Everything is done with the same digital efficiency as the tech-giants, which is what people nowadays have come to expect. And because it will be an insurance company doing the installation, people are reassured that everything in terms of quality

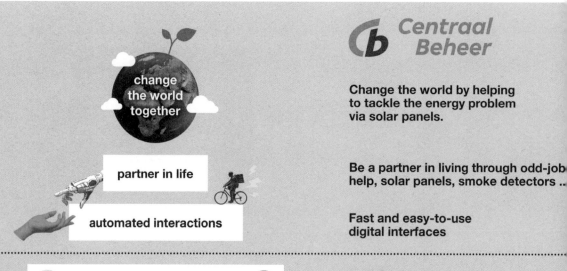

Cb Centraal Beheer

change the world together

Change the world by helping to tackle the energy problem via solar panels.

partner in life

Be a partner in living through odd-job help, solar panels, smoke detectors ..

automated interactions

Fast and easy-to-use digital interfaces

 good product / service & price

Good insurance products

and safety will be 100 per cent in order. Perhaps some of you are wondering why a success-ful insurance company should suddenly want to start selling solar panels. But it is not as strange as it might sound. It is actually a field in which insurers already have a consider-able amount of knowledge and expertise. For example, Centraal Beheer has already dealt with more than 5 000 damage claims involving solar panels. As a result, they know exactly what can go wrong and also which makes of panel are the most reliable.

Centraal Beheer launched its solar panel initiative via its website as a trial. There was no marketing of any kind. Even so, within the first few months over 300 customers placed orders, which resulted in the installation of more than 4 000 panels. During 2020, the service will be given commercial support and transformed into a full service within the company's range. Once again, an important double function will be fulfilled: it relieves the customer of the burden of a complex purchase process, whilst at the same time con-tributing to the solution of an important societal challenge.

Taking all these elements into account, it is easy to see that Centraal Beheer is already well on the way to making its Offer You Can't Refuse strategy as concrete as possible. The core objective is to make customers super-satisfied (NPS +50). To achieve this the insurer makes use of the very best digital interfaces, while simultaneously becoming a partner in living for its customers and developing a range of services that will create societal added value to the benefit of us all. It is a golden recipe for success.

Restaurant Addo in Seattle

The Offer You Can't Refuse model is not only for large organisations. The philosophy can be applied in every enterprise, whether great or small. During the corona lockdown of March 2020 many thousands of restaurants worldwide were forced to close. In the United States, that immediately led to a wave of unemployment amongst staff, while the restau-rant owners struggled desperately to keep their heads above water.

Chef Eric Rivera runs Addo, a popular restaurant in Seattle where he offers both cheap dishes in a Puerto Rico style, as well as extensive high-end menus with appropriate wines. Even though his physical restaurant was obliged to close, during the first two weeks of the lockdown he was able to double his turnover in comparison with March 2019. And instead of having to lay off his personnel, he actually needed to employ twice as many new ones. So how did he do it?

The first step in Eric's strategy was to use a good digital platform. He opted for Tock, one of the less well-known restaurant platforms. Most restaurateurs work with the more fa-miliar names in the sector, like OpenTable, but in times of crisis Tock is more interesting. Via Tock, customers can place their orders and pay for them with just a few clicks. The customer benefits from maximum ease of use, while the restaurant manager benefits from guaranteed payment for his services.

The second step in Eric's strategy was to try and better understand how consumers think about food during a major health crisis. In the first place, they expect a high-quality service and safe delivery. Second, they don't want to eat the same thing every day, even though the crisis meant that most restaurants' take-away menus were now much more limited than before.
Eric Rivera understood these expectations. As a result, he decided to offer an entirely new menu each day. But he also kept the range of options that people were used to from his restaurant in normal times. You could order food bowls for just nine American dollars, but you could also get more extensive meals with a bottle of wine for over a hundred American dollars.
Last but very definitely not least, Eric then took a crucial strategic decision, which benefited both himself and his customers.

He decided not to work with companies like Uber Eats, but opted instead to work with his own staff for the delivery of the meals. In this way, he could guarantee his customers safe and high-quality delivery, without losing a significant portion of his financial margin to expensive partners.

He decided not to work with companies like Uber Eats, but opted instead to work with his own staff for the delivery of the meals.

This third step in the strategy also allowed Eric to make a societal contribution. In addition to ordering their own meals, people were given the opportunity to donate a nine-dollar food bowl to Seattle's homeless community. After just two weeks, more than a thousand bowls had been donated.

I regard this as a wonderful example of how a small entrepreneur can develop all the steps of The Offer You Can't Refuse model – a good (tasty) product, transactional convenience, partner in life (food and drink), and societal added value – into a successful customer proposal.

And in my industry? Do I really have to do everything?

'Is it really necessary to go so far in every industry?' That is a question that I am frequently asked by tired managers and worried business owners. In recent years, companies have been forced to try and keep up with an avalanche of changes and innovations, as well as fighting off recurrent crises. When they now hear that customer expectations are already in the process of changing yet again, this discourages some of them. Their question is a valid one. Many successful companies do not offer every aspect of The Offer You Can't Refuse model. Amazon.com is one of the most successful companies on the planet, but you can hardly say (in my opinion, at least) that they are doing much to make the world a better place. Of course, they do possess a perfect digital interface and they are also partners in the lives of many of their customers. But that is where it stops. So must every company climb all the way to the top of The Offer You Can't Refuse ladder? No, I don't think so. Not all steps of the model are necessary in all circumstances. It is important to look at the benchmark in your own sector.

If you are working in a sector where product and price are all that matter, count yourself lucky. And the more conservative a sector is, the easier it becomes to make the difference. In that case, all you need to do is ensure that your transactional convenience is 10 or 20 per cent better than that of your competitors. This will provide you with all the difference you need. If you are active in a sector where most of the companies already offer good transactional convenience, you can make the difference by becoming a partner in your customers' lives.

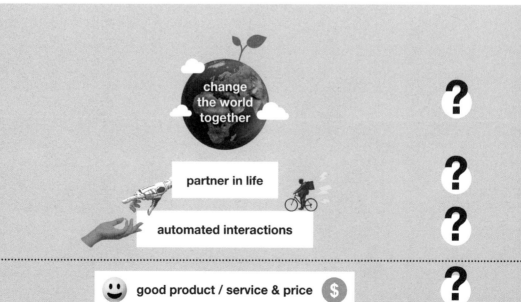

In this respect, the retail market is an interesting market. Of course, product and price have been crucial in this sector for decades, but in recent years many retailers have done their best to implement performant digital convenience. As a result, the battle for differentiation is now taking place at the higher levels of The Offer You Can't Refuse model. In September 2019, I had the pleasure of meeting Jamie Oliver at an event in Amsterdam. He told me about his partnership with the British Tesco chain. Their shared objective was to help children in the United Kingdom to eat more healthily. In this way, they hoped to become a partner in life for parents, whilst at the same time doing something to improve the health of future generations – in other words, respond to the two highest levels of The Offer You Can't Refuse model. Jamie made a series of fun videos and in the supermarkets you could find recipes with all the necessary ingredients on the adjoining shelves. If there was a healthy alternative for a particular product, Tesco positioned it next to the less healthy product, with an appropriate explanatory text. The supermarket also ensured that the healthiest product was the cheaper of the two.

A decade ago, retail was a product/price industry. However, the arrival of online commerce has meant that digital interfaces have become increasingly important and we are now seeing more and more initiatives to which 'partner in life' and 'save the world' strategies are being added.

Perhaps it feels comfortable to work in a sector where not all the steps of The Offer You Can't Refuse model are necessary. I would warn you, however, to be wary of falling victim to the 'fast snail' syndrome. You need to make sure that you don't become the fastest snail. You might possibly be performing well in your sector, but you may be evolving only very slowly in absolute terms and are therefore out of step with the evolutions taking place elsewhere in the world. This means you are the fastest snail, which can feel good, but in the long run it is more interesting to have the speed of a rabbit or even a leopard. When crisis hits or change is necessary, moving at the speed of a snail – even a fast one – may not be enough to save you. Remember that it is you, as a company, which sets the benchmark, not the sector. You always have the right to decide how fast you want to move.

Hopper solves a problem that consumers have been wrestling with for years

Hopper is a remarkable company. It was founded in 2007, but it was only in 2014 that it burst onto the world stage. For its first seven years, the company conducted research into the price curves of airline companies. Today, Hopper is one of the most popular travel apps in North America.

In October 2018, I met the founder of Hopper, Frederic Lalonde, during an event in Canada. He told me how the lack of transparency and the high volatility in the pricing of plane tickets had long been a thorn in the side of consumers. Worse still, most consumers thought they were getting a bad deal. Nobody knew when was the best time to buy a ticket. As early as possible? As late as possible? People could only guess – until Frederic and his team set to work.

Their algorithms can predict the price curve of plane tickets with great accuracy. If you want to book a flight using their app, at first glance it seems like any other travel app. You type in a date and destination, in response to which you are given a selection of flights from which to choose. Nowadays, most online sellers of air tickets have succeeded in offering their potential customers a user-friendly online interface – the second step (after price and product) towards The Offer You Can't Refuse.

But that is where the similarity with the Hopper app ends. Hopper wants to go further than its rivals, by becoming a partner in life for travel. At the moment when you want to book a flight with Hopper, there is a good chance you will probably receive the following message: 'Dear Customer. It is better not to book now. The price is still too high. Would you like us to send you a new message when the best moment to book arrives?' Of course, everyone answers 'yes'. A few days or weeks later, you then get a push message from Hopper: 'Dear Customer. Your ticket to New York is now 15 per cent cheaper than when you first looked at our site. This is the best price you will get.' Clever, don't you think? Hopper has grown dramatically without any form of classic advertising. It has all been based on very impressive word-of-mouth – and it is not hard to understand why.

The company's algorithms go even further in advising the customer. Imagine that someone from New York wants to book a trip to Hawaii in the winter. From New York that means a flight of more than 12 hours. The Hopper app may suggest that you might like to consider a trip to Florida instead. The weather there is also great during the winter, but it is only three hours flying time from New York and the tickets are usually a lot cheaper.

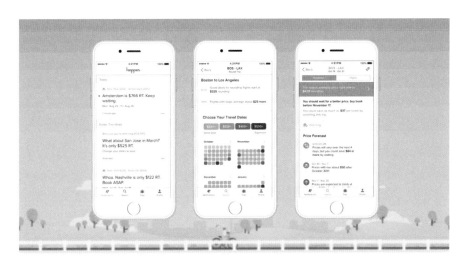

Frederic told me how many customers are happy to follow recommendations of this kind. In reality, the apps says the following: 'You don't really want to go to Hawaii. You just want to go somewhere warm and sunny during the cold winter months. I know this, because I can see that in recent winters you have always taken a trip to the sun.' In this way, people are helped with both their choice of destination and the optimisation of their ticket price. Clearly, Hopper goes much further than simply offering consumers a user-friendly interface. The company wants to be a partner in the travel life of its customers. This formula has seen Hopper grow dramatically, year after year. Competitors have been forced to recognise this success and are now starting their own climb up the ladder towards the higher levels of The Offer You Can't Refuse.

The next step for Hopper is to think about how it can make a positive contribution to the world. In future, the aviation sector will need to answer a growing number of questions about its environmental impact. This means that in the short term Hopper will need to find a 'save the world' added value, if it wants to keep its competitors at bay.
Markets continue to evolve. Just a few years ago, sites for the sale of plane tickets were all about having a good interface. Now, they are evolving towards a 'partner in life' role. In the years ahead, like Hopper, they will need to develop 'save the world' initiatives. The higher your competitors climb up The Offer You Can't Refuse model, the greater the need for you to climb higher still, if you want to differentiate yourself.

Suddenly it gets urgent

Look at your own sector and evaluate which phase of the model it is currently experiencing. If you can go one level higher than that current level, you will be able to make the difference.

But the question bears repeating: is it necessary in every sector to climb right to the very top of The Offer You Can't Refuse model? A few pages ago, I recommended that you should look at your own sector and evaluate which phase of the model it is currently experiencing. If you can go one level higher than that current level, you will be able to make the difference. However, I need to add an important caveat to this recommendation.
The situation today offers no guarantee about what the situation will be like tomorrow or the day after tomorrow. For this reason, it is also vital to evaluate the external factors that have the potential to change the existing situation. For example, is there a possibility that the pressure exerted by climate concerns might increase dramatically in your sector? Is there a danger that new technologies will radically disrupt the sector's business model? You need to be proactive in charting and investigating external factors that could transform the situation into one of urgency. Because when that happens, before you know it all the aspects of the model suddenly become urgent.

Verstraete IML: the story of a printing company in full transformation

I live in Knesselare, a small municipality in Belgium. As a child, I grew up in Maldegem, which is about ten kilometres down the road. When I started writing my management books a decade ago, I never imagined that I would one day use a case study from my own native village. But now I would like to tell you the story of Verstraete IML, because the company has succeeded in applying The Offer You Can't Refuse model in a sector where not so long ago price and product were everything, but where other criteria are now beginning to come to the fore.

Verstraete IML is a fast-growing SME, employing some 600 people. The company is the world leader in In Mould Labelling. IML is a decorative technique. A pre-printed label in polypropylene (PP) is placed in a mould. This mould has the shape of the end product; for example, a butter dish. Molten PP is then poured into the mould and blends with the label and takes on the shape of the mould as it hardens. The result is that the label and packaging become one and no further decoration of the product is needed.[22]

Verstraete IML was founded in 1975 by Geert Verstraete. The company began as a printer of labels, primarily for beer bottles and for the milk industry. At the end of the 1980s, one of their biggest customers, the Van De Moortele sauce company, asked if the printing house was prepared to invest in In Mould Labelling. It was during this same period that the second generation of the family, Koen and Griet Verstraete, also began working in the business. They decided to agree to the proposal and bought the first IML machines. After successfully meeting the requirements of Van De Moortele, more and more customers soon followed. Before long, the company stopped printing classic labels, so that it could concentrate fully on IML. This was when their growth really began to take off. Between 2008 and 2020 the number of employees doubled, from 300 to 600. Verstraete IML also opened a new production site in the United States. The company eventually grew to become the world leader in this niche market and in 2020 prints roughly 60 million labels per day.

War on plastic

Verstraete IML is unquestionably a successful growth story. In its early years, the innovative nature of the technique meant that IML experienced little competition. After a time, however, an increasing pressure on price began to make itself felt. The price war in the retail sector impacted on every phase of the supply chain, including the moulded products made by Verstraete IML.

In order to make the difference in this price-sensitive market, the company soon decided to adopt a 'partner in packaging' strategy. Koen and Griet Verstraete wanted to be more than just another printing firm. Instead, they now also wanted to give advice to their customers about their packaging. Teams from Verstraete IML collaborated actively with the packaging producers and marketing teams of P&G, Nestlé and Unilever to develop the most suitable and most attractive kinds of packaging. In this way, they added an extra value to their customer relationships and were able to maintain their top position.

Everything was going perfectly, until the 'war on plastic' broke out. The major climate protests of 2019 increased pressure on the sector to take action to combat global warming. Many of the producers of consumer goods made clear in their annual reports that they intended to use less and less plastic. The CEO of Unilever announced that by 2025 they would be using just half as much 'virgin plastic' (plastic that is used for the first time). This is great news for the planet, but less great news if you are running a factory specialised in the printing of plastic packaging. Until very recently, the ILM market was driven by the lowest level of The Offer You Can't Refuse model: product and price. The new trends meant that Verstraete IML suddenly needed to start thinking about the social impact of their work on the climate. And they needed to start thinking about it fast.

I discussed this challenge with Nico Van de Walle, product and circular economy manager at Verstraete IML. 'When the Ellen MacArthur Foundation was founded in 2016, for us that was the first signal that our market might soon be in for some serious disruption.' Ellen MacArthur is a British sailor, famous for her solo voyages and her participation in long-distance ocean races. During her many long journeys she was shocked time and time again by the amount of plastic she saw in the world's seas. To do something about it, she decided to set up the Ellen MacArthur Foundation, which led to the formulation of a new worldwide commitment to what became known as the New Plastics Economy, whereby 450 leading companies undertook to tackle the problem of plastic in the environment. 'Verstraete IML was a member of this group right from the very beginning. A company like ours has two choices: you can either be frightened into inaction by the "war on plastic" or else you can decide to participate in shaping the new future. We chose the latter option,' explains Nico Van de Walle. The group wants to see the transformation of the linear economy into a circular economy, by making plastic packaging 100 per cent recyclable, reusable or compostable. The solution for the 'war on plastic' is not a world without plastic, since that is virtually impossible and is also not the best option from the perspective of both our CO_2 footprint and food wastage. No, what we need to do is neutralise the problem that plastic today represents.

The holy grail

The ambition was therefore clear. Verstraete IML began, together with companies like P&G and Danone, to give new shape and form to the packaging industry of tomorrow. They referred to their joint efforts as the search for the holy grail. According to Nico Van de Walle, the solution lies in the intelligent manufacture of packaging. 'Packaging is a very complex whole, formed from many different component materials. To reach the ambitious objectives we have set, we need to ensure the better sorting and recycling of packaging. Sorting centres need better information about the different types of materials, so that the right used packaging can find its way into the right circular trajectory. We help to solve this problem through our use of smart packaging.'

Verstraete IML has started with the production of packaging onto which a Digimarc Barcode is printed. This Digimarc Barcode covers the full surface of the packaging in question and effectively adds a code to each individual item. The code is not visible to the human eye, but can be picked up and identified in the sorting centres by smart cameras and sensors, so that the packaging can be diverted into the correct recycling channel. This more accurate sorting of used packaging is essential if the ambitious targets of the New Plastic Economy are ever to be met.

In due course, all packaging will be marked with an invisible digital code of this kind. The proof of concept has already been approved and in coming years will be implemented with ever increasing speed. For me, it is fantastic that a company from the village where I was born can have such a huge impact on the war on plastic. Nico Van de Walle is also enthusiastic about the prospects, but remains realistic: 'It helps us to reach the climate objectives and that is really cool. But it will very quickly become a minimum require-ment, no more than that.'

With this in mind, Verstraete IML already has plans to use the Digimarc Barcode for more than simply the identi-fication of packaging in sorting cen-tres. In fact, the idea of intelligent and interactive packaging opens up a whole new range of possibilities. For example, you can potentially use your smartphone to make packaging come alive in many different ways.

One of the tasks of food companies is to educate their customers about the right way to recycle packaging. It is perfectly possible that in the near future you will be able to use an app to scan all you packaging, which then tells you the best way to recycle it. But it is much more than a question of straightforward functional content. If there is a cow depicted on your packaging, you will soon be able to make it talk. It might even be able to play games with your kids. What if a tube of toothpaste could play a song lasting two minutes, which is the length of time your children should be brushing their teeth? That would be a great aid to parents! Verstraete IML wants to differentiate itself through this kind of 'partner in packaging' strategy: thinking together with customers about the options opened up by new technology.

The speed with which the 'war on plastic' developed made it an absolute necessity for Verstraete IML to climb up all the different levels of The Offer You Can't Refuse model. Their industry has evolved in a very short space of time from a pure price focus to a focus on the need to be an essential partner in the battle against climate change. The slim and proactive choices made by this remarkable family company have ensured that it remains the world leader, even though the industry has been transformed from top to bottom. It is truly impressive that thanks to the 'war on plastic' (and their approach to it) they are now able to offer their customers and society more value than ever before.

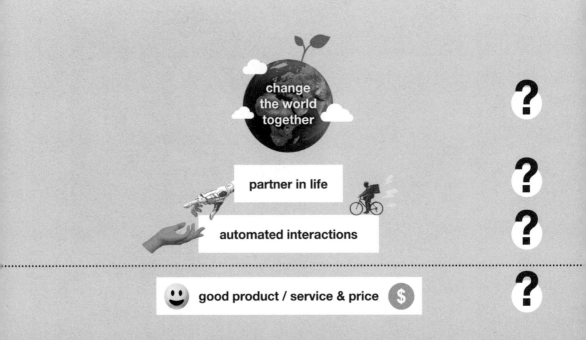

Where is your company?

My invitation to you is to think carefully about the position of your sector and your company in The Offer You Can't Refuse model. Are you working in a market where product and price are all that matter? If so, you are lucky: by focusing on ease of use you will soon be able to differentiate yourself from your rivals. Or are you working in a market where every aspect of the model is in play? In that case, you face a really serious challenge, because you will need to find a way to roll out your Offer You Can Refuse strategy in a credible and consistent manner – which is much easier said than done.

This is a fun discussion to organise with your colleagues over lunch. How far does the model apply to our sector? How far does it apply to our company? What do we need to do to get one step higher up the ladder? And will that put us on a higher rung than our competitors?

But the last and perhaps most important question in your brainstorming session is this: what external factors might change the current situation, so that it becomes a matter of urgency to implement all levels of the model as quickly as possible? What evolutions in our sector and beyond might trigger the need to develop a digital interface, or a 'partner in life' philosophy or added societal value, or even all three, not just as a matter of urgency but as a matter of survival?

A world with technology that goes much further than straightforward ease of use

Later in the book I will examine the details of the different strategies for the development of The Offer You Can't Refuse model. But before we look at strategies and cases, there is another theme I first wish to explore.

The implementation of the new customer model will be strongly influenced by technology. The coming decade will see the breakthrough of four new general purpose technologies: 5G, artificial intelligence, quantum computing and robotics. Each of these has the potential to revolutionise the customer relationship of the future. In the next chapter we will investigate each of these evolutions and the possibilities they open up.

PART

2

general purpose technologies

four
technologies
that go further
than
ultimate
ease of use

Complex challenges

Most people would probably agree with the following statement: 'In recent years technological progress has been spectacular.' Of course, this is perfectly true. No-one can deny it. Even so, a degree of nuance is necessary, since during the past two decades digital progress has largely been confined to solving relatively simple problems. During the next 20 years the problems to be solved will be much more complex.

> *During the past two decades digital progress has largely been confined to solving relatively simple problems. During the next 20 years the problems to be solved will be much more complex.*

Consider, for example, the world of mobility. During the past two decades we have all become familiar with navigation systems. I can still remember the first one I ever bought. It was back in 2001 and I was very proud to be the owner of the latest techno-gadget, even though the likelihood that the sat-nav would lead me to the right destination was only about fifty-fifty. In those days, I always used to print out a route from my computer at home, just to make sure. Today, I use Waze, with a hit rate of 99.99 per cent. I trust it blindly and, as a result, my life has become easier and less stressful, thanks to its near perfect navigation technology. In fact, I could no longer do without it. But during the next 20 years the mobility challenge will be to develop self-driving and climate neutral cars. This is a challenge of a completely different order, which will require the development of technology that is significantly more sophisticated than the technology needed to digitalise maps.

The same is true of health care. During the past two decades we have become familiar with all different kinds of health apps and gadgets, which monitor our sleeping, eating and sporting habits. And it was tech-giant Google that probably made the biggest impact on the entire health industry. If someone doesn't feel well or has an unexplained pain, nowadays they turn first and foremost to 'Dr. Google'. I am sure that most of us have consulted the online doctor before approaching a 'real' offline one. You all know how it works. You simply say: 'Hey Google, I've got a headache.' In response to which you get a whole list of suggestions for the possible cause, ranging from the most frightful tropical diseases to a glass too many of wine last night! We are all sensible enough (I hope) to realise that current online medical information needs to be taken with a very large pinch of salt. But that is set to change. In my opinion, we are only right at the very beginning of the possibilities for digital health care. During the past 20 years the focus was on self-measuring apps and the provision of general online information. During the coming 20 years the focus will switch to matters such as diagnosis by artificial intelligence and the editing of DNA. Within the next decade the partnership between artificial intelligence and human doctors will evolve into a minimum condition. How long will patients continue to trust doctors if they are not supported by smart computers when proposing forms of treatment?

Scientists are already investigating how DNA can be manipulated. The Chinese scientist He Jiankui recently manipulated the genes of IVF twins so that they could no longer be infected by the HIV virus – an illegal practice for which He is currently serving out a sentence in prison. Whatever the ethical questions involved, the case has at least shown that DNA can be altered before birth to eliminate the threat posed by certain illnesses and diseases.

It needs to be remembered that the use of this kind of CRISPR technology has by no means been perfected and it is not 100 per cent clear whether the experiment carried out by He will be successful in the long term. It is even possible that he might have created undesirable mutations.[23] But the potential of the method, once it has been refined, is massive.

At the moment, the weight of opinion still holds that these practices are illegal and unethical. But what will people think when the scientists tell us that that they can protect future generations of unborn children from countless deadly diseases? Will there come a time when such practices are regarded as standard or will society persist in its belief that it is morally indefensible to 'play God'? It is clearly – and will always remain – a difficult discussion, but it highlights the complexity of the new challenges facing the medical profession, in comparison with which our current counting of the number of our daily steps or the continuous measuring of our heart rate pale into insignificance. The easy years of digital evolution are behind us. Online communication, the ordering of products via the internet and the digitalisation of some services may seem as though they have changed the world, but they are nothing compared to the likely effects of the difficult challenges that lay ahead. During the coming decades we will be introduced to digital technology that has the potential to change society to its core. And the complexity of these changes will not be limited to the technology alone. A large part of what will soon be technically possible has huge societal and ethical consequences.

General purpose technologies

Which technologies have really changed the world in recent years? I can get very enthusiastic about the idea of a slightly faster plane or a robot that can make you a cup of coffee. I like innovations of that kind, but let's be honest: they are unlikely to catapult the world into a new phase of development. No, they are simply 'nice to have': incremental improvements of things that already exist. Netflix is great fun and I am a big fan, but it has not changed the world. True, we are now able to view amusing and exciting content in a non-linear manner, and that is good. But what we are doing remains the same. It is only the interface – the how we do it – that is different.

Fire, the wheel, agriculture, printing and the internet are examples of technologies that have moved human society into a new phase. We refer to breakthroughs of this kind as 'general purpose technologies'. Each of them genuinely did change the world. They fundamentally improved the daily lives of people who lived at the time. Whoever was born in an age when the wheel, printing or the internet already existed cannot imagine how people ever lived without them.

Today, we are standing on the eve of the breakthrough of not one but four general purpose technologies. Individually, each of these four technologies has the potential to change every sector. Together, they will generate a flow of new innovations, the like of which the world has never seen.

The technologies in question are:

- **5G:** the mobile network of the fifth generation, with an increased capacity for data transmission and fewer delays than with the 4G network.
- **Artificial intelligence:** a form of computer science in which machines are able to learn independently and even take decisions on the basis of data or impulses gathered from their environment.
- **Quantum computing:** a new generation of computers that makes use of the principles of quantum mechanics. A quantum computer has a computing power that is exponentially greater than a standard computer, so that it can tackle more complex problems.
- **Robotics:** the automation of tasks by machines has already been taking place for decades and most factories now make use of robots. The coming years will see a further refinement of this technology, so that more and more tasks will be capable of robotisation. In the future, robots will have sophisticated motoric functions, so that they can be employed, for example, in operating theatres or to automatically deliver products to your house.

General purpose technologies

Artificial Intelligence & Machine Learning

5G

Quantum Computing

Robotics

5G: more than just faster internet

5G is the next generation of mobile internet connection. Thanks to the first generation, 1G, we were able to talk to each other on our cell phones. The introduction of 2G added text messages to our range of communication tools. When 3G arrived, it became possible to use the internet on our smartphones. 4G opened up the possibility for high-speed data transfer, so that we could all enjoy the delights of video and streaming applications on our phones. And now we are standing on the threshold of 5G. By 2024, some 65 per cent of the world's population will have access to this new technology.[24] There are three major differences between 4G and 5G:

1. The connection is much faster, with almost real-time connections, as a result of which the level of reliability will also increase. This faultless real-time experience is necessary for applications such as self-driving cars and surgical operations at a distance.
2. 5G will provide faster uploading and downloading speeds. With 5G, a film of several gigabytes can be downloaded on your smartphone in seconds.
3. The network capacity is greater, so that more devices can make use of mobile internet at the same time. This capacity is crucial for the multiple applications in the internet of things. Moreover, if countless devices can communicate with each other, they will be better able to make accurate decisions, which is necessary for the proper functioning of smart cities.

Put simply, you could say that 5G is faster and more reliable than 4G. But that sounds too incremental, whereas in reality the changes 5G will bring are radical. Once the 5G breakthrough is complete, the long-awaited internet of things will truly take off. This additional connectivity will also transform many industries forever.

> *Once the 5G breakthrough is complete, the long-awaited internet of things will truly take off.*

Similarly, for the very first time cities will also become truly 'smart'. Traffic lights will be automatically adjusted to reflect the numbers of vehicles and pedestrians. Fast-working sensors in our phones and in our cars will ensure that a variety of services can be provided in the best possible manner. Sensors will also warn city authorities if acute problems arise, such as air pollution, extreme weather conditions or a traffic gridlock.

5G is likewise an essential component for the effective operationalisation of self-driving cars. One of the absolute criteria for allowing a car to drive itself is its ability to react perfectly to changing situations in real time. In traffic, decisions often need to be made in a matter of seconds. People are good at making these kinds of decisions, but the current telecom networks are insufficiently fast and too unreliable to make it possible for machines to do the same. 5G will speed up the necessary evolution in this field immeasurably.

In terms of customer experience, 5G will facilitate further improvements through the use of automated and invisible interfaces. If machines can talk, a huge range of purchases can be performed fully automatically. When this happens, the customer will no longer even be a part of the decision-making process. In this way, smart machines will take over the vast majority of routine purchases.

5G also has an important role to play in pushing open the door to 'mixed reality'. You can imagine this as a kind of virtual layer superimposed on a city. For example, as you walk through the streets of New York, you will be able to see instantly the Yelp feedback scores of every restaurant you pass. From time to time, personal advertising messages based on your profile and preferences will also appear. The 'mixed-reality' concept has already generated a number of interesting gadget-like applications, of which Pokémon GO is probably the most famous, but in future, thanks to 5G, this type of technology is set to become part of our everyday lives. As a result, the difference between the physical world and the virtual world will narrow. Today, we still speak of 'online' and 'offline'. During the next ten years, we will evolve toward a continuous mix of both: mixed reality.

The 5G applications will first be employed in industry or in well-defined locations. To make this possible, factories and hospitals will set up their own 5G hotspots. It will take a while longer, however, before the benefits of 5G become fully available for the consumer population, because 5G needs far more masts than was the case with 4G. Building this infrastructure will take a number of years. For this reason, the initial use of the new technology will be focused on specific settings.

5G hospitals

South Korea is one of the worldwide pioneers in the implementation of 5G networks. 5G first became available there in October 2019 and by the start of 2020 there were already 4 million users,[25] equivalent to just less than 10 per cent of the total population.

One of the first important South Korean projects to demonstrate the power of 5G was the construction of a 5G hospital in the city of Yongin, not far from Seoul. One of the advantages for the patients is that they can easily view their own content during their hospital stay. That, however, is only an incremental improvement.

The more radical changes are to be found in the hospital's new approach to diagnostics. If, for example, pieces of tissue are removed during an operation, there is nearly always a requirement for extra testing. In classic hospitals, these samples usually need to be sent to the other side of the hospital or even to a different hospital altogether. In an average Korean hospital, this first option means a walk of about 20 minutes. Thanks to 5G, it will now be possible for medical personnel to have access to real-time insights into the necessary data during the actual operation. As a result, the right treatment for the patient can be determined far more quickly, while the doctors also save precious time.

The hospital has further plans to make use of a number of autonomous robots, which can take research samples from one laboratory to another. This and other similar innovations are all intended to increase efficiency and quality of service. The 5G network will also have advantages for medical students. During their training, they normally follow operations live in the operating theatre. This means that there are often too many people in the theatre, which is not good for the concentration of the surgeon or the students, as well as being unhygienic. Moreover, in these circumstances not

every student has a good view of what the surgeon is doing. The 5G network will make it possible to follow an operation perfectly in real time from an adjacent classroom. This improves the quality of the operation and the quality of the teaching, which benefits patients both in the short term and in the long term.

During the corona crisis, China also equipped a number of its hospitals with 5G networks, in an attempt to free up extra medical capacity. When the number of infections in China began to increase exponentially in January 2020, there was a serious shortage of doctors to deal with the situation in the city of Wuhan, where the main outbreak was centred. Thanks to the use of 5G networks, it was possible to plan consultations with doctors in hospitals elsewhere in the country. Perfect real-time video streaming made it possible for these long-distance doctors to assess the patients' condition with a good degree of accuracy. As a result, more patients were processed quickly and efficiently, while the doctors themselves ran no risk of being infected.

Artificial intelligence

When I was ten years old, one of my childhood dreams came true. My parents took me to the Universal Studios in Los Angeles. In the studio park, I was given the opportunity to sit behind the steering wheel of my absolute hero: KITT. KITT was the world's first smart, talking, self-driving and obstacle-jumping car, used in the TV series *Knight Rider*.

For its time, *Knight Rider* was highly futuristic and I was one of its biggest fans. Especially of KITT. Everything that KITT did seemed to be impossible. Not anymore. I have already had the privilege of sitting in a real self-driving car, operated by speech technology. Some of KITT's functionalities are now the most normal thing in the world, such as in-car telephoning, smart navigation, voice controls and automatic parking. Sadly, today's cars cannot yet jump over obstacles in their path, but perhaps even this will be possible one day.

One thing is clear: science fiction is increasingly becoming science fact. Computers are getting smarter and smarter. They succeed in analysing bigger and bigger quantities of data, which they convert into increasingly accurate predictive behaviour.

In my previous book, *Customers the Day After Tomorrow*, I discussed the major breakthrough of artificial intelligence and its likely impact on the customer experience in some detail. In the meantime, we are three years further and the potential of AI is becoming ever more tangible.

Artificial intelligence has actually existed for decades, but the real tipping point moment came in 2016, when Google DeepMind humiliated the world champion in Go, the most complex board game in world. Some people compared this with the victory of the IBM computer Deep Blue over the chess grandmaster Gary Kasparov in 1996. But this does the computing ability of DeepMind an injustice.

The huge difference between chess and Go is the number of possible moves. Of course, the number of moves in chess is mind-bending enough for most of us, but they are theoretically limited, so that computer experts can programme all the potential next moves in advance. Once this has been done, a smart computer can quickly choose the best of these moves. That is how Deep Blue was able to beat Kasparov. But Go has exponentially more moves than chess, making it is impossible to pre-programme them all. So when DeepMind thrashed Lee Se-Dol, the world's best Go player, at the end of 2019, it could only mean one thing: the computer won using its own computing power and insights to defeat its human opponent. And it beat him not just once, but time after time. So much so, that Lee decided to give up the game in frustration. As he explained: 'Even if I am the best human player, there is still "something" else that is better than me – and that I cannot accept.'

In the meantime, every consumer has come into contact with artificial intelligence, whether they know it or not. Every time you open Facebook, algorithms decide what you get to see and what not. Likewise, if you log on to Netflix, artificial intelligence compiles a first initial menu of suggestions for you. What's more, 75 per cent of Netflix users opt to view films and series based on these initial suggestions.[26] Amazon uses the same process of historical data analysis to propose new products it thinks (or rather, knows) you will like. Smart passport scanners at airports check to make sure that you really are who you say you are. The Waze algorithm takes over control of your route planning every time you ask it to avoid heavy traffic. Whenever you speak to Google Assistant, Siri or Alexa, you are talking to a smart machine. Asking Siri or Alexa to play a song is now standard behaviour for my two sons, aged nine and eleven. They are no longer amazed that a machine can identify the song they want (notwithstanding their less than perfect English pronunciation) and play it for them in a matter of seconds, time after time. For them (and many others), it has become the most normal thing in the world.

Smart computers and algorithms are also playing an increasing role in customer service. More and more call centres are using computers to analyse the emotions in customers' voices, so that the contact centre operative can respond more appropriately. The quicker the operative can identify the customer's emotion, the bigger the chance that the conversation will be a success. Many contact centres now also use computers to draft written answers to the customers who submit their queries by e-mail, although human operatives can still adjust the drafts slightly, if necessary, before sending them on to their intended recipients. As a result of this automation, the operatives work faster and in a more personalised manner, leading to great customer satisfaction.
For the customer, this use of artificial intelligence is completely invisible. The computer predicts what should happen without the customer knowing. Some people are appalled by this idea, without being aware that they have probably already fallen 'victim' to it!

The predictive power of AI is already having a massive impact on the total customer experience. The examples of Starbucks, JD and Meituan Dianping mentioned in the previous chapter all resulted in faster service and greater customer satisfaction. But this was only made possible by the ability of their algorithms to predict customer behaviour.

If Starbucks wants to deliver your favourite coffee to you within five minutes, it can only do so if it knows in advance what you intend to order, even before you have ordered it. DiDi, the ride sharing service in China, also has this same ability to predict when and where the vast majority of its customers will need a lift.

Every consumer has habits and patterns of behaviour. As soon as a certain pattern has been identified, technology can accurately predict that consumer's likely future actions. The better Amazon is able to analyse the totality of an individual's patterns, the more targeted its recommendations for that individual will become. This means that in time Alexa will only recommend a single brand of a particular product, in the near (and some-what frightening) certainty that her recommendation will be spot on.

The future impact of artificial intelligence on customer relations will be centred primarily on this increasing ability to make predictions. As a result, a wide range of processes will become more efficient and more user-friendly than they are today.

At the end of this evolution, the effort that needs to be made by the customer in the purchasing and service processes of many thousands of products will have been reduced to zero. Artificial intelligence will raise customer interfaces to the next level and beyond. It is not so long ago that almost every company had a complex interface. In recent years, they have become simpler and easier to use. Today, they only require the single click of a mouse. Tomorrow, a voice command will be sufficient. The day after tomorrow, the customer will need to do nothing at all. It will all be done for him (or her).

Our lives will be increasingly determined by the calculations of algorithms. Artificial intelligence will not only transform the outward aspects of the customer relationship, but smart machines will also increasingly dominate what takes place behind the scenes. For example, the financial sector is using AI to better estimate its risks, so that bankers and insurers can take more substantiated decisions when assessing whether or not to grant a loan or underwrite an insurance policy. Similarly, the financial markets are already massively reliant on algorithms. 80 per cent of all the transactions on the world's stock markets are no longer performed by people.[27]

A digital companion

In the years ahead, this situation will evolve still further and artificial intelligence will come to play an increasingly important role in all aspects of our lives. At the start of 2020, Samsung unveiled its mysterious Neon project. This is intended to become our digital life partner. The company projects an image of a human being onto a large screen. This man or woman also talks and behaves like a human being, but in reality is a very sophisticated computer simulation.

The first expected application of these simulations will probably be in the commercial field. For example, reception staff at the front desk can easily be replaced by this kind of

realistic avatar. In some museums, the technology could be used to create a virtual guide. In time, a doctor version of the avatar is also likely to be developed. In countries where medical personnel is scarce, AI has the potential to carry out a first medical screening, in a manner that will be much more 'human' than the chatbots currently used.

In the long term, this technology can evolve to become a true 'digital companion'. More and more people are living alone and loneliness is set to become one of the 21st century's major social problems. Imagine the role that a digital companion could play for people who are isolated in hospital with no-one to visit them or for families waiting anxiously at home for news of loved ones during the corona crisis.

The start of the AI curve

Companies are beginning to realise the strategic importance of artificial intelligence, but we are still only at the very start of the adoption curve. A research report published by MIT[28] revealed that 62 per cent of companies are planning to increase their investment in AI. That may seem a lot, but, on the other side of the coin, 20 per cent of companies are currently planning no AI investment whatsoever. Only 5 per cent are thinking about possible AI applications within their own company. And in nearly every case the investments are being used to develop relatively small pilot projects. Notwithstanding the huge hype surrounding AI's potential, its practical implementation in the business world is still very much in its infancy.

If you look back at the examples of AI I have already mentioned, like Meituan, Google Assistant, Waze, Siri, Alexa, Facebook and Netflix, you can soon see that they have something in common: they have all (and particularly the tech-giants) committed themselves 'full force' to the possibilities of AI. As a result, the competition is already light years behind.

Peter Guerra, the chief data scientist at Accenture North America, sees a huge challenge ahead for many company leaders: 'AI is not just the latest cool piece of technology. AI has the potential to totally transform every sector. Business leaders would be smart to think carefully about how their company can evolve structurally as a result of the advent of AI.'

The biggest challenge relating to the implementation of AI is talent. Lack of people with AI talent will lead to a lack of vision and poor execution. The tech-giants succeed in attracting most of this talent, so that other companies are facing the prospect of a serious scarcity of qualified people. The only real alternative is the retraining of their own personnel. The small group of companies that have so far succeeded in implementing AI at a company-wide level were also the companies that invested most heavily in retraining. It is a trend that looks set to continue.

All the research points in the same direction: artificial intelligence is already making clear to the world how the new technology can potentially transform the business environment, with the tech-giants leading the way and almost everyone else hanging on to their coat tails. We are still only at the very beginning of the adoption curve.

Quantum computing

The most powerful computer in your possession is your smartphone. Nowadays, we regard these clever devices as normal, but it is astounding to think that these phones have more computing power than the computers that put a man on the moon in 1969.

That being said, the computers of today still make use of exactly the same principles as those of the 1960s. The core of the computer was and still is the transistor.

Of course, the transistor itself has undergone a gigantic evolution. In recent times, we have seen how Moore's Law has doubled transistor capacity every 18 months. This exponential growth has brought us to where we are today, although the data makes clear that since 2018 this rate of growth is slowing.

Yet notwithstanding this massive increase in computing power, basic computer technology is no different from what it was ten or twenty years ago: computers are powerful calculating machines, making use of a series of ones and zeros to arrive at an answer. This is the binary system. It is either '1' or '0'.

Nowadays, however, scientists are in the process of developing a completely different kind of computer. This new generation of quantum computers will no longer work with bits but with qubits. A qubit is non-binary: it can deal with '0' and '1' at the same moment. As a result, a qubit can store and process much more information. Journalist Mercedes

Cardona helps us to understand this in a visual manner:[29] 'Think of a qubit as a spinning coin and a binary bit as a coin toss: While the toss can either be heads or tails, the quantum principle lets a spinning coin be a measure of both.'

Once quantum computers become operational, we will be able to approach immensely complex problems much more effectively than with existing technology.

It is not intended that quantum computers should replace all our existing computers at home or in the office. These super-powerful machines will be used to solve large and extremely complex problems.

At the present time, companies like Google, Microsoft and IBM are currently racing to try and establish 'quantum supremacy', the moment when a quantum computer achieves for the first time something a traditional computer cannot do. In November 2019, an article appeared in the professional magazine *Nature*, in which Google claimed that it has already achieved quantum supremacy.[30] Their Sycamore computer had solved in a mere 200 seconds a computing problem that it would take the most powerful 'ordinary' computer at least 10 000 years to solve.

Rival IBM was irritated by this claim and immediately disputed the results. According to IBM, the most powerful standard computer could have made the calculation in just two days, not ten millennia! Yet even if IBM are right, the performance of Sycamore still represents a structural improvement. *Time Magazine* certainly regards the Google results as a turning point in computing history.[31]

Once quantum computers become operational, we will be able to approach immensely complex problems much more effectively than with existing technology. Thanks to live data, companies like FedEx and DHL will be able to constantly optimise the routes of their delivery vehicles in real time, leading to an efficiency increase of up to 600 per cent.[32] Similarly, Delta Air Lines are already talking with IBM about ways to make all their airport processes more efficient, ranging from the display of personalised messages on all screens in airport terminals to the better organisation of baggage handling. Airbus and Boeing also want to make use of the phenomenal computing power of quantum technology to make their planes faster and more efficient.

In addition to these potential efficiency upgrades for companies, scientists are also keen to explore the impact that quantum computing might have on the world's more essential problems. For example, ExxonMobil has carried out tests with quantum computers to optimise the power grid. Energy optimisation is one of the key strategies for combating climate change.

Quantum computing can likewise help to design more efficient batteries with a greater storage capacity, which would increase the range of electric vehicles and make them much more popular and practical than is currently the case. Once again, this technology would not only benefit the automobile industry, but also have a positive effect on the climate.

In fact, it may be possible to improve many aspects of the climate problem with the aid of more accurate computer models. Think, for example, of the optimisation of the use of fertilisers in agriculture or the better organisation of mobility in the world's cities. These are two major concerns that both have a huge impact on the climate, but for which we only have incomplete solutions today.
Quantum technology undoubtedly has the potential to provide the key to many of these structural problems. Once we are able to process ever greater quantities of data and test different models simultaneously, society will gain deeper and faster insight into the huge challenges it will face in the decades ahead.

The rapid development of medicines

It seems likely that the first important changes resulting from quantum computing will be seen in the pharmaceutical industry. The huge computing power of quantum computers will make it possible to accurately examine how molecules interact. These molecular processes are extremely complex and their analysis is beyond the capability of existing computers.
Scientific research in this field focuses on the testing of certain chemical combinations, to see how they react. The search for these new molecules and the mapping of their properties is currently a pain-staking and expensive process. In contrast, quantum computers will be able to suggest and test new combinations in a fraction of the time. In theory, a quantum computer can run simulations for all possible molecular combinations, allowing it to suggest the best possible result in the most efficient manner. This potentially opens the door to the development of new medicines for combating terrible diseases, such as Alzheimer's.
Today, clinical trials are carried out on people, which is extremely time-consuming. Once quantum computers are up and running, testing of this kind will no longer need to involve human guinea pigs. In fact, it will not even be necessary to test new medicines and therapies on cells of any kind. All the required tests to guarantee the safety of the new products will be conducted by computer simulation, providing results within a time frame that medical scientists can only dream of today.
And it is not only the processes for making new medicines per se that will be fundamentally transformed. Types of treatment will also be different. Quantum computing will make it possible to develop medicines tailored to the needs of individual patients. Koen Bertels is a quantum expert at the TU Delft and sees huge possibilities in this direction. In an interview with the Belgian *De Tijd* magazine, he offered us a glimpse into the

future:[33] 'At the moment, you need to send blood, saliva or hair to the laboratory and it can take anything from a day to a week before a super-expensive machine provides you with a DNA analysis. These machines are currently far too expensive for ordinary hospitals. But in the future, all you will need to do is to place the patient's finger in a quantum computer and a read-out of the DNA analysis will be available in seconds, so that the doctor has an immediate picture of the patient's clinical condition. And based on the patient's genetic profile, the computer will then be able to recommend and produce personalised medication.'

For the moment, quantum computing is still a promising theory, which it is hoped will be able to help solve many of society's major problems. The development of this technology is still in its infancy, but the results so far give reason for optimism about the future.

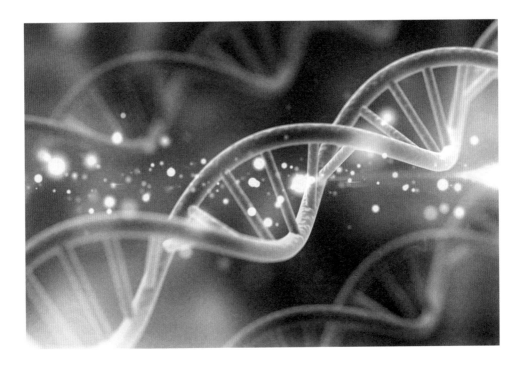

Robotics

On 22 January 1920, more than a century ago, the Czech dramatist Karel Čapek was the first person to coin the word 'robot'. Robot is derived from the Czech word *robota*, which literally means 'work carried out by a serf or slave'. The central theme in Čapek's play was the fear that science might be commercialised in an unethical manner. His robots began to develop more and more human feelings, so that they increasingly seemed to be a more advanced form of human being. By the time the curtain fell, 'classic' humans no longer had a role to play in the world ...

A familiar storyline, don't you think?

Since Čapek's time, scientists and society in general have shown increasing interest in robots. Back in the 1920s, robots were the product of a creative brain; today, factories are full of them and robots are becoming more and more a part of our everyday life. According to the International Federation of Robotics, between 2020 and 2022 some 2 million new industrialised robot units will be installed worldwide.[34] These robots will be characterised by two important trends:

1. **Robots are getting smarter.** The programming and installation of robots is set to become much easier in the years ahead. Improvements in sensors and software will make it possible for almost anyone to train a robot. The most frequently used technique is 'programming by demonstration', in which a human shows the robot a particular movement and the machine then imitates the action. Following this, 'machine learning' will help the robot to perfect the movement.

2. **Robots will collaborate more with people.** Machines will increasingly work together with humans. People and robots will occupy the same working space and will carry out their respective tasks sequentially. The next generation of robots will be able to adjust their behaviour to reflect human actions in real time. This will create a situation that is comparable with two human beings working alongside each other.

In addition to industrial robots, there will likewise be a huge increase in the use of robots in other sectors. There is also a strong likelihood that before too long you will have a robot in your home as well: an automatic lawnmower, a robot vacuum cleaner or perhaps even a programmable Lego toy robot. You may even have all three! One thing is for certain: in the decades ahead, knowledge and expertise in the field of robotics will continue to increase.

Many of the new robot applications will significantly improve both human safety and human efficiency. Think, for example, of crisis situations, where it is dangerous for humans to physically intervene. The robots of Boston Dynamics are especially trained to deal with situations of this kind.

Boston Dynamics was founded in 1992 and is now regarded as one of the most advanced robotics companies in the world. You have probably seen their impressive YouTube films that demonstrate the progress their robots have made over the years. For many people, these machines have a disturbing resemblance to the robots from the *Terminator* films. Even so, every time Boston Dynamics releases a new film, the performance of the robots becomes ever more impressive.

The Boston-based company was bought by Google in 2013. After a difference in vision about future developments, Google sold the company to the Japanese investment fund Softbank in 2017. The Boston Dynamics' robots are now trained primarily for use in the aftermath of natural or nuclear disasters. That being said, it doesn't require much imagination to see their potential military and logistical uses.

These 'health and safety' applications are clearly valuable, but they are far removed from our day-to-day lives. But change is on the way. Cooking robots are a real prospect in the near future and in San Francisco there are already several places where you can make use of a coffee robot. Recently, I also went to eat at Creator, a restaurant where a big robot makes your hamburgers.

The medical world will also increasingly make use of robots. In January 2019, a Chinese surgeon carried out the first 'at distance' operation, assisted by a robot and a 5G connection. The doctor was a full 50 kilometres from the operating theatre and the operation was a test case, involving the (successful) removal of the liver from an animal. The 5G connection meant that there was a delay of just 0.1 of a second between the movement of the doctor and the replicating movement of the robot. Afterwards, the doctor said that it felt as though the robot's hands were his own.

The ultimate fantasy for many people is, of course, the household robot. Which of us hasn't dreamed of owning a multi-functional and super-efficient personal butler? Sadly, this day is still some way off. Most of today's domestic robots have a very specific functionality, such as mowing the grass or vacuuming the carpet. Our invisible robots like Google Assistant, Siri and Alexa come closest to our dream idea, but a lot of work still needs to be done before they can relieve us of all our domestic chores. Although ...

In January 2020 at CES, the largest electronics trade fair in the world, Samsung launched Ballie, which is intended to be a kind of household assistant. Ballie is a ball-shaped robot that makes you think of BB-8 from *Star Wars*. This small robot ball rolls around your home, keeping an eye on anything and everything. Having made its observations, Ballie then acts as a kind of organiser for all your other domestic robots. If Ballie sees crumbs on your carpet, it will order the vacuum robot into action. If the TV is still playing when Ballie notices you are no longer at home, it will arrange for it to be turned off. And if the temperature in your living room is too high, Ballie will ensure that the heating is turned down and/or the curtains drawn.

A robot boom in China

When the Chinese government placed the country in complete lockdown in January 2020, this had a major impact on the world's production capacity. From one day to the next, the world's second largest economy ground to a halt. This was obviously felt in China, but also in Europe and the United States.

By the middle of March, millions of Chinese were once again allowed to work in car, smartphone and other electronics factories. Even so, the greatest technological change brought about by the crisis soon became apparent: a massive increase in the number of robots in Chinese society. Factories had immediately started to investigate ways that they could become less dependent on human input. The quickly discovered that robots not only lower costs and increase productivity, but also (and above all) guarantee continuity of production – even if people in their millions fall sick.

In 2019, China already had more robots than any other country.[35] No less than 39 per cent of all the robots in the world sold that year went to China. And it is expected that this figure will rise to 45 per cent by 2021.[36] At the same time, robotics is one of the technologies in which the Chinese eventually hope to become world leader. This, at least, is the ambition stated in the Beijing government's far-reaching Made in China 2025 master plan. The lockdown had hardly started before it became clear that robots would play an increasingly important role in the future of Chinese society. Within weeks, robots were being deployed in Chinese hospitals for tasks such as disinfection or the transportation of medicines. In this way, the robots served both as a helping hand and as an extra line of defence for the medical personnel. The less the doctors and nurses came into direct contact with the virus, the less likely they were to become infected. Robots were pressed into service wherever they were able to reduce virus exposure levels for their human partners.

But it was not just in hospitals that the robots proved their worth. In the otherwise deserted streets of Wuhan robots soon began to be seen making emergency deliveries of food to people self-isolating at home. The e-commerce giant JD launched a fleet of semi-autonomous vehicles from which people could order food, drink and other supplies in safety. Once the JD initiative became more widely known, the number of orders quickly doubled to 600 000 each day.[37] Robots were also used to disinfect public places and to measure people's temperatures at a distance.

The mature smartphone curve

5G, artificial intelligence, quantum computing and robotics. Four technologies with the potential to radically change society and customer relations within the next ten to fifteen years. But exactly how will this evolution take place? And what will be its consequences? This is something that no-one can accurately predict. But there is one thing that can be said with certainty: all four technologies are only at the very start of their development. The situation is reminiscent of 2007, the year in which the iPhone first came onto the market. This marked the start of the adoption curve for smartphones. During that first year things progressed relatively slowly. After that, there was massive exponential growth and today the smartphone market is mature. In the United States, more than 70 per cent of the population have a smartphone. In most European countries, the figure is between 75 and 80 per cent. Penetration is highest in South Korea, with a remarkable 95 per cent. In the group of rich and well-developed countries, average smartphone owner-ship stands at 76 per cent.[38]

In other words, there is still plenty of room for smartphone growth, certainly in lands where the economy is still in the process of fully developing, although the growth curve is flattening out. At the moment, we are at the top of this S-curve.

Do you remember how Steve Jobs described the iPhone during its very first presenta-tion? He called it 'your life in your pocket'. Today, everyone knows what he meant and we can all recognise our own behaviour in that description. In 2007, we had no idea what he was driving at. 'Your life in your pocket', for a device that allowed you to telephone and send text messages? Okay, in the future there was the prospect that we could use the phone to surf the internet and listen to music, but to immediately describe the phone capabilities as equating to 'your life in your pocket' seemed to most people to be a wild

exaggeration. But they were wrong. In 2020 we can understand the full importance of this visionary comment better than ever before. The smartphone is an extension of our brain and – no matter how often we sometimes curse it – we can no longer imagine our lives without it.

Can you remember how you used your smartphone in the beginning? Most people just made use of the basic services: telephone, texts, photos, music and e-mails. Back then, there were no mobile banking apps, no Spotify or WhatsApp. Uber only arrived much later and Netflix was still renting out DVDs.

In short, we used the smartphone for standard functions and hip mobile gadgets. Do you know what was the most popular app to demonstrate this new type of phone? iBeer was an app that filled a virtual glass of beer on your phone screen. Once the glass was full, you put the phone to your mouth, so that it seemed you were drinking the beer. When the glass was empty, you put the phone down on the table and it gave a loud burp! I can still recall how hundreds of people showed this app to others as a way to convince them of the 'power' of the iPhone. And, in all honesty, I was one of them! I had the app on my phone for ages. Talk about embarrassing! I showed it to my colleagues, friends and family, and I can still remember the look on my mother's face after the phone gave its final belch. You could see her thinking: 'Where did my son go wrong?'

I am only telling you about this example to indicate just how limited people's use of the smartphone was at the beginning of the curve. We used a few basic tools and a number of gadgets, but this did not immediately change the way we lived our lives. That only happened later, as the curve picked up speed. New services and new means of communicating were launched year after year, which allowed the added value of the smartphone to increase dramatically, eventually bringing us to the point where we are today: the smartphone as our digital helper in all possible circumstances.

Alexa, set the timer for eight minutes, please!

If you look at the way today's markets currently use AI applications, you can see that the situation is comparable with the early years of the smartphone. The most tangible of the current markets for these applications is the market for smart voice assistants, like Google Assistant, Siri (Apple) and Alexa (Amazon).

The most mature segment of the market for these products is China, followed by the United States.[39] By mid-2019, some 50 per cent of American households had at least one smartspeaker.[40] This means that the adoption of these devices is progressing faster than was the case with the smartphone.

With a market share of 74 per cent at the start of 2020, Amazon's Alexa is the clear market leader in this new category in the United States. So far, so good.

But if we examine the applications that people are using, the initial smartphone trend repeats itself again. Most of these applications are very basic. 49 per cent of users ask their voice assistant questions about the weather and the news, or else instruct them to carry out mundane tasks, like set the timer in the kitchen. And that's the way it is in the Van Belleghem household as well. 'Alexa, set the timer for eight minutes, please!' is a popular command when the kids feel like a deep-freeze pizza (again). 28 per cent use their assistant to help run the house, which involves controlling the lighting, heating, TV, etc. The current killer application is clearly music. 72 per cent use Alexa and her friends as the most efficient way to play music in the home. But only 14 per cent use them to do the weekly shopping or make other purchases.

All these applications are fun, but they only represent a marginal change in behavioural patterns. Instead of doing all these things on their smartphone, people now ask a smart machine instead. As a result, some of these things happen quicker or in 'hands-free' mode. This certainly has some limited advantages, but not much more than that.

Notwithstanding their popularity, the smartspeakers are still only at the very beginning of their curve. Their adoption is increasing quickly, but their real impact on consumer behaviour has yet to make itself felt. Consumers are currently switching their smartphone habits to voice, but there are no real innovative applications or radical new services. It seems that we will have to wait for the next generation of voice assistants before this phase is reached. We need the smart assistant equivalent of the 'iPhone after BlackBerry' moment. Only then will we see the curve really take off.

The second half of the curve?

5G, artificial intelligence, quantum computing, robotics. Each of these four technologies is in the first phase of its development. We are at the start of the curve. But what will the second half of the curve look like? That is the key question. No-one can predict the future, but every company has the potential to create its own future. So my invitation to companies is this: do not simply wait and see what the second half of the curve will bring, but decide for yourself what you want it to bring. Dare to dream and to fantasise about possible scenarios. Once you have done that, reverse engineer the entire process and start with the implementation.

An interesting exercise to get this process off the ground is to ask yourself 'what if' questions. Decathlon, one of the largest sports retailers in the world, is currently developing its Vision 2030 strategy. As the kick-off for the formulation of this strategy, Charlie Felgate, the vision leader of this project at Decathlon, organised a number of inspiration days. I had the honour to be invited to speak at one of these days. When I had finished giving my talk about my book *Customers the Day After Tomorrow*, the large audience of Decathlon personnel began a 'what if' session. During the subsequent debate, questions were raised such as: 'What if e-sports are more dominant than offline sports by 2030?'; 'What if people delegate the purchasing of their sports equipment to a virtual assistant?'; 'What if physical sports take place in a virtual world?'

Each of these three questions has far-reaching implications. If any of the three 'what if' hypotheses becomes a reality by 2030, the business model of Decathlon will need to be fundamentally adjusted. And by daring to ask these questions, it is possible to already begin the necessary change of the company's mindset. Decathlon will not just 'wait and see'. Instead, they want to shape their own future and that of their customers. They are building the second half of the curve themselves.

The four general purpose technologies will open up many new possibilities in the field of customer experience. The more concretely you can think about these possibilities in advance, the greater the likelihood that you will actually be able to build them the way you want. One of the sectors with huge opportunities as a result of the new technologies is the financial sector. When the internet arrived, banks were the first major industry to make the switch to online. As a result, online banking also became the main reason for many people to start working with the internet at home.

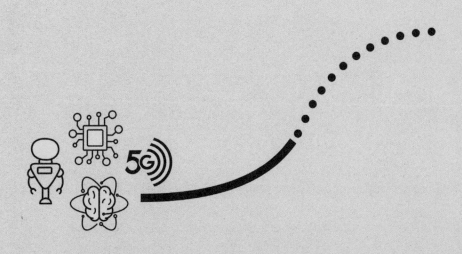

The evolution of mobile applications once again saw the banks at the front of the pack. It began with the introduction of mobile payments but quickly developed, so that nowadays you can have access to almost any financial product through your smartphone.

We are now entering a new phase with even bigger opportunities for banks. For example, the combination of 5G and AI offers new possibilities for payments. From the moment when devices like Alexa and Google Assistant are able to make purchases without the intervention of their human masters, machines will need to find a way to pay each other. Likewise, in the future my car will automatically pay my parking ticket. And my Nespresso machine will know when my supply of capsules is running low and will re-order them independently. In short, there will be countless new payment moments.

FINN is a 100 per cent subsidiary of the ING Bank. Its task is to make payments between machines both possible and safe. Via this spin-in, ING wants to give shape to the second half of the curve. The bank's vision for the future predicts that most product purchases will be replaced by services. What does this mean? Perhaps in years to come we will no longer buy a washing machine, but will rent one instead and pay for each time we use it. In that way, buying a washing machine is superseded by a service.

If a washing machine is fitted with FINN technology, there will be a constant flow of payments between the washing machine and the original manufacturer. Every time the machine is used, it will automatically pay the manufacturer the required fee. This kind of safe machine-to-machine payment opens the door to a completely new business model. What does the second half of the curve look like? To a large extent, you can decide this for yourself.

Technology for good

In the first chapter I talked about the dark side of the digital world. It is sad that new applications are always misused by people with bad intentions. And we should be under no illusions: this will also be the case with the new general purpose technologies. Regrettably, it is inevitable.

But there is also good news. The four general purpose technologies have the potential to improve the world. The technologies of the previous decades – 4G, mobile and social media – have given us greater ease of use for purchasing and communication. These were also improvements, but they were not always visible, even though mobile solutions for real problems have achieved much in the past 20 years.

Some time ago, I had the pleasure of giving a presentation to a team from Vodafone Tanzania. It was there that I first learnt about the M-Pesa mobile payment system. Thanks to M-Pesa, people in different African countries can use their cell phones as a bank account. You don't even need a smartphone. M-Pesa works on a good, old-fashioned Nokia.

In this way, Vodafone, via mobile technology, solved a major problem in lands like Kenya and Tanzania. Many people in Tanzania had no bank account or lived some distance from

their nearest bank branch or simply did not have enough money to warrant it. As a result, people were always obliged to carry ready cash with them – which was a disaster from the perspective of safety and security. Vodafone launched M-Pesa and the problem was eliminated overnight.

In December 2019, almost 300 million mobile transactions were carried out in Tanzania. If you ever have the pleasure of visiting the country, take a good look around each village you pass through. Every one of them, no matter how small, has an M-Pesa location, where people can load money onto their cell phones. It is a great example of how technology can be used for the good of the world and those who live in it.

The combination of 5G, AI, quantum computing and robotics has the potential to implement many (and even more far-reaching) improvements of this kind. Together, they are capable of dealing with challenges in the fields of logistics, energy, health, climate and economic spread. In fact, these four technologies seem likely to herald in the start of the 'golden age' that Carlota Perez has described. In particular, it is these kinds of technology that must help the world to better prepare against the natural disasters and pandemics of the future.

A study by McKinsey[41] in the European Union has shown that there is positive sentiment amongst the population towards innovations like AI. Between 60 and 70 per cent of Europe's citizens see more advantages than disadvantages to these new technologies. In particular, people look forward to the impact on health (the study was conducted before the corona crisis), education and climate.

Even during the early part of the curve fine examples of the benefits of the new technologies are starting to emerge. In one trial project tests with artificial intelligence are being carried out to better map the evolutions of some species of wild animal. Drones constantly monitor the movements of the animals, measure changes in their populations and, in some cases, even catch poachers.

Of course, there will also be benefits for we humans. To feed the world's population in 2050, current food production needs to increase by 70 per cent. There is little or no 'spare' agricultural ground available, so that this increase will have to be achieved by greater efficiency of production. One possible solution is the development of better seeds through a combination of AI and quantum computing. Tomorrow's technology will also be better able to identify crop diseases, following which robots will be dispatched to provide 'personalised care' for each plant type, thereby guaranteeing maximal crop returns, even in difficult years. These and other similar methods must help the world's farmers to continue producing the food we need without the provision of additional natural resources.

The customer wants more – and the technology can provide it!

In the next part of the book, I will discuss each strategic aspect of The Offer You Can't Refuse model in detail. In each chapter, it will become clear that the four general purpose technologies can be a driving force for turning strategy into practice. These nascent technologies have an immeasurably greater potential than the technologies we have seen in recent decades.

As a first step, they will further stretch current levels of user-friendliness. Many more customer interactions will be automated and in chapter 4 I will describe how the transactional convenience of the future is destined to be transformed by more advanced technology. However, it would be a missed opportunity to focus exclusively on the continued evolution of ease of use. The new technologies have the ability to launch our world into a new phase of progress. In particular, they have the potential to satisfy the new expectations of consumers, by helping them to realise their dreams, while simultaneously helping to ameliorate the major problems faced by society.

In chapter 5 I will explain how your company can become a 'partner in life' for your consumers. This obviously implies the need to embrace a new kind of mindset. But if you are capable of doing this, the new technology will allow you to penetrate far further into your customers' lives than ever before. Developing a better understanding of the person

Developing a better understanding of the person behind the customer and responding to that person's aspirations is the key to success.

behind the customer and responding to that person's aspirations is the key to success.

Chapter 6 demonstrates how the four general purpose technologies can make an important contribution towards your 'save the world' strategy by reducing people's negative daily concerns about the future. At the moment, consumers are frequently forced to make a choice between their own interests and the interests of the planet. They also often need to choose between privacy and convenience and/or between privacy and health care. The four general purpose technologies have the potential to ease these dilemmas or, in some cases, even to make them disappear altogether.

The customers of tomorrow and the day after tomorrow expect more than ease of use – and the new technology will be able to provide it!

Being a partner in the daily life of customers

save
time

save
money

facilitate in
life goals

facilitate great
experiences

PART 3

strategies for

the 😀ffer

✌u can't

refuse

In this part I will discuss three of the four strategies for The Offer You Can't Refuse model. As previously mentioned, I will not go any deeper into the basic conditions for making a good offer; namely, a good product, a good price and a good service. I am sure everyone understands that without providing this basic level it is impossible to remain competitive in any market. In contrast, I will devote a full chapter to each of the remaining three strategies, so that their complexities will no longer hold any secret for you.

Ultimate convenience: in the years ahead digital ease of use will become increasingly automated and invisible for the customer. In this chapter, I will explain how you build the interface of the future.

Partner in life: this is all about the person behind the customer. How can you offer services that go further than your core product? In this chapter, I will provide concrete guidelines for developing a 'partner in life' strategy.

Save the world: in future consumers will look increasingly to companies to solve the major problems facing the world. In this chapter, I will discuss in practical terms how you can take your responsibilities in this respect seriously.

ultimate convenience

Tinder wipes its competitors off the screen

In 2007, the classic dating apps like eHarmony, Match.com and OkCupid all underwent the major transformation that saw them change from being a desktop platform to a full mobile dating platform. These apps dominated the market and their biggest asset was their huge database of users. New players failed one after another to break their near monopoly. The network effect and the powerful algorithms of the market leaders seemed to make them impregnable. Until 2012. That is the year in which Tinder appeared on the scene. Within 12 months, this newcomer was the number one app in the dating world.[42]

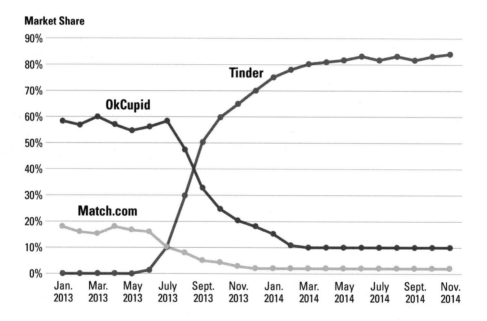

Surprisingly, Tinder did not have what at that time was regarded as the most crucial element for success: an extensive user database. What's more, Tinder chose not to utilise complex matchmaking technology. Classic dating sites encouraged their customers to fill in long lists about their lives. This data was then used to search for a 'perfect match'. The Tinder interface was based on the physical match, although users also sometimes looked for humour in the photo, checked the potential date's favourite song, the biographical information, etc. But the real key was – and still is – the photo. Users are shown a photo and asked to swipe left or right. Swiping left means 'not interested'. Swiping right means 'could be'. If both parties swipe to the right, they are given the opportunity to chat with each other online and, perhaps, make further arrangements to meet.

Young people are more attracted by the idea of online dating than ever before. By the start of 2013, the number of daters aged between 18 and 24 years had grown by 170 per cent. In just two more years (2013-2015), the segment further tripled. The new Tinder interface had turned the market upside down. Ease of use – fast, simple and fun – made all the difference. The classic players had overestimated the value of the perfect match and underestimated the importance of a user-friendly interface.

Personal butlers

Innovation makes it possible for people to spend less time on things they 'must do' and more time on things they 'want to do'. The dishwasher and the washing machine give us more time to play sports, or cook, or watch TV. In other words, more time for the nicer things in life. Even so, you hear some people say things like: 'Since we have a dishwasher, we no longer have those pleasant chats over the washing up.' These comments usually carry the classic undertone of: 'Everything was better in the old days ...' Well, if you so miss those conversations with your partner when you were doing the dishes, nobody is forcing you to use a dishwasher. Wash your dishes the old way, if it means so much to you! Of course, the vast majority of people can no longer imagine living without a dishwasher. When it breaks down, the majority immediately order a new one the next day.

Time is a scarce and precious resource for all of us. The more efficiently we can complete our 'obligatory' daily tasks, the more time there is to do other things. Technology has already saved us huge amounts of time: we can take part in meetings from home, so that we don't get stuck in traffic jams on the way to the office; we can order products online,

so that we don't need to travel to (and hunt for what we want in) physical stores; we can record TV programmes, so that we can 'fast forward' during the commercial breaks …

You can no longer be bothered to search for and buy your own clothes? Then why not make use of a company like Stitch Fix? You fill in a one-off question list about your personal tastes and indicate how frequently you want to receive new clothes. After that, the service starts automatically. In keeping with your instructions, every so often a box with new clothes will be delivered to your front door.

Customers of Stitch Fix allow the company to choose the contents of each box. To make the concept workable, Stitch Fix uses smart algorithms, whose choices are monitored and, if necessary, adjusted by a human stylist. Once the customer receives the clothes, he or she has three days in which to decide whether or not to keep them. New customers pay an initial 'styling fee', but the prices of the clothes they are sent are comparable with the prices in other high street stores.

This kind of company makes it possible for almost anyone to have a personal shopper. Once you have made the initial (and not very demanding) effort, you receive clothing automatically, without any further effort at all. In March 2020, Stitch Fix was valued at 1.3 billion American dollars. Not so long ago, a personal shopper was the privilege of the happy few. Thanks to Stitch Fix, it is now within the reach of the ordinary man or woman in the street.

The automation of your weekly shopping

Every Saturday, I go to a nearby supermarket to do our weekly shopping. Most of my purchases are routine in nature. If you were to analyse what I buy, you would probably find that around 70 per cent of the products are the same every week. A further 10 per cent would be the same every month; washing powder, for example. The remaining 20 per cent varies according to my mood, my tastes, the weekly promotions and how hungry I am when I am in the store.

In other words, most of my purchases follow a clear pattern. In fact, this is true of almost every consumer. And once there is a pattern, it can be programmed and predicted by an algorithm. Wouldn't it be great if the supermarkets could fully automate our routine weekly and monthly purchases? Imagine if a company like Amazon could deliver you a box of groceries each week with everything you need for the next seven days. You could then use the time you save on the things in your life that are really important to you.

McDonald's and Dynamic Yield

New interfaces are appearing all the time, both online and offline. Initially, interfaces were mainly linked with the online world. The Tinder dating app is a pure online interface. To deliver products promptly to your home, Amazon makes use of a mix of online and offline automation. The next step is to integrate these forms of automation more fully into the offline environment.

In recent years, McDonald's has undergone a major transformation. In my previous book, *Customers the Day After Tomorrow*, I described in detail how the company had completely redesigned its classic processes. The roll-out of ordering via digital kiosks with service at tables was implemented with success.

McDonald's now want to take things a step further. In March 2019, the burger giant bought the American company Dynamic Yield for roughly 300 million dollars, McDonald's largest acquisition in the last 20 years.[43] Dynamic Yield is specialised in artificial intelligence and machine learning.

Using this technology, McDonald's now plans (amongst other things) to personalise menus in the Drive Thru. At the moment, every customer is shown exactly the same menu. In the near future, the company wants to adjust its menu to reflect external factors, such as the weather. The ultimate step is the full personalisation of the menu for each individual customer.

For a number of years, McDonald's has been investing heavily in the use of their mobile app. In many countries this app is one of the most popular of all corporate apps, with millions of users. Thanks to this interface, McDonald's has been able to learn a lot about the preferences of its customers. The next phase involves using this information to personalise menus. For example, if, in the future, a vegetarian approaches the Drive Thru, the vegetarian options will automatically be positioned at the top of the menu he or she is shown. The same is true if you are a fan, say, of fish burgers. As a result of this personalisation, customers will not only feel more welcome; there is also a realistic possibility that they will buy more. In other words, a win-win situation: greater satisfaction for the customer and greater commercial value for McDonald's.

Do people really trust all this automation?

I can get very enthusiastic about the possibilities offered by algorithms. There are so many aspects in our lives where smart algorithms can do things better than we humans. Even so, one of the questions I am asked most frequently is: 'Steven, will consumers trust those algorithms? I also like to make my own decisions, without being influenced by a machine.' A lot of people think this way, but in most cases they are deceiving themselves. They are convinced that they critically examine every decision they make and wouldn't dream of listening to algorithms, since this would limit their freedom of choice.

This sounds (and, to a large extent, is) positive. However, research has shown that only a minority of people practice what they preach. Let's take a simple example: Google. If you perform a Google search, you usually get more than a million results. Hundreds of pages with links to the most interesting websites are all placed within your easy reach. In other words, this is a perfect starting point for anyone interested in doing a really in-depth study of a particular product or service. But what does the research show? Almost 95 per cent of people never look further than the first page of results.[44] Why? Because the Google algorithm has being doing its job and doing it well for the past 20 years. In other words, we know that the best results are going to be on the first page. We accept it almost as a fact of life. An independently-minded 5 per cent still refuse to trust the algorithm and plough through further pages of results. While they are doing this, the other 95 per cent are doing something more useful with their time ...

> *Our intuition tells us that we like to make our own decisions, but research demonstrates that this is not the case.*

Put simply, our intuition tells us that we like to make our own decisions, but research demonstrates that this is not the case. A study published by the *Harvard Business Review*[45] has described how people put the results they get from algorithms ahead of the advice they receive from their fellow humans. Their only criterion for making this choice is a consistently high quality of outcome. If an algorithm has proven its reliability over a longish period, people will trust it before they trust the judgement of their family and friends.

When I read this study, it made me think back to the early development of the sat-nav. In the previous chapter, I mentioned how the hit rate of my first navigation system was 50 per cent. This led to some interesting experiences. If I was driving somewhere and the sat-nav said 'Go straight on', but my wife said 'No, I know this neighbourhood, turn left here', then I would usually turn left. At that time, my wife had a hit rate of 85 per cent against the machine's 50 per cent. Today, however, Waze has a hit rate of 99.99 per cent, whereas my wife is still stuck on 85 per cent. So if the computer now says 'Straight on' and my wife says 'No, it's left', I now go straight on – and accept the consequences of the decision …

The conclusion of the Harvard study is clear: as soon as an algorithm keeps its promises, we trust it.

The characteristics of the interface of the future

During the past decade, ease of use has improved dramatically. Today, we can conduct our bank transactions with Face ID. We can confirm our purchases with a fingerprint. We can start up our favourite films by voice command. We can turn on the alarm system in our house from anywhere in the world. If I approach an underground car park, the barrier opens automatically, thanks to a mobile app from my bank. There is no need to mess about with tickets and the payment is made automatically. The app does it all; I don't have to do anything. In some airports, it is now even possible to board a plane without the need to have your boarding pass or passport physically checked. A face scan now decides whether you can get on the plane or not. And as we have just read with McDonald's, in the near future the menus of the fast-food chain will reflect our personal preferences.

If you study the nuts and bolts of all these successful and innovative interfaces, they all have four characteristics in common:

1. **Proactive:** a modern interface anticipates. It needs to discover what the customer wants before the customer knows it himself. A smart interface solves problems before they arise. Think, for example, of the smart fridge, which orders new milk as soon as the last bottle is opened. Or a machine that orders its own new spare parts as soon as the existing ones are showing signs of wear. McDonald's plans for its menus also involve making a proactive choice about what meals best match people's taste profiles. By the time you are ready to order, the menu has already been amended!

2. **Zero effort for the customer:** the international trend in every sector reflects a further decrease in the effort that customers need to make to complete a transaction. If a process is complex and boring, most people leave before completion. To keep people sufficiently interested, interfaces need to be simple and, preferably, fun. McDonald's new Drive Thru concept requires no effort from the customer, not even the pressing of a button. The menu is adjusted automatically as the customer's car approaches.

3. **Invisible:** consumers hardly know that the new generation of interfaces are there. Nowadays, machines can arrange things without any need for human interaction. The McDonald's menu is an example of this. So, too, is the Facebook algorithm. Every

time you log on to Facebook, you are automatically offered a list with updates that reflect the kinds of things you like to see. You don't ask for this list and you don't 'see' that it is being prepared; you just get it. And usually you think: 'Hm, this looks like fun …' In the years ahead, the internet will be literally everywhere, but at the same time it will also be less tangible. If we want to go online today, we first have to click on the Safari, Chrome or Edge app. In the future, the internet will just be there, invisibly built into all the smart devices that surround us or perhaps even in our AR glasses, once these have been perfected.

4. **Personalised:** every customer is different. Segmentation is a concept from a marketing era that has gone forever. Today, the individual needs of the individual customer are paramount. These needs are specific and vary from person to person. The better the ability of your interface to personalise, the bigger your success will be. The McDonald's menus will be tailor-made for every single customer. This is segmentation on a scale of one.

The interface of the future:

automated

invisible

personalized

proactive

Toutiao

Toutiao is one of the most popular news and content platforms in the world. The company was founded in 2012, as part of the ByteDance group (which also owns TikTok). The content of Toutiao is produced by journalists, influencers and bots.

This news app meets all the criteria for an interface of the future. Because it uses bots, the app's publication of new content is super-fast. As soon as, say, a football match is over, the bots provide an almost instant summary (proactive). Toutiao also makes use of artificial intelligence to apply a filter to incoming news for its customers. This filter selects new stories automatically (zero customer effort) and without the need for a filter button (invisible), to provide content that it knows will interest the reader (personalised).

In other words, the AI filter works like the Facebook filter: Toutiao decides which news you get to see and which news is withheld. From a societal perspective, this method of working is open to criticism. Giving people a narrower and more personalised view of the world is not necessarily a good thing at a time when we need to promote greater social harmony and understanding. People are already being pushed more and more into their own bubble by AI, without the need for these kinds of systems to make that bubble even more restricted.

Leaving these societal concerns to one side, the impact of AI on the company's results has been impressive. Toutiao is the most addictive digital platform in the world. A user spends an average of 74 minutes a day on Toutiao.[46] In comparison, the average Facebook user spends 'just' 50 minutes a day on his or her favourite social network. In other words, the Toutiao user is 50 per cent more active on the news app than Facebook users are active on what is the world's second most addictive site.

But this is not even the most stunning Toutiao statistic! The speed with which Toutiao earns money with its app is truly staggering. Unparalleled, in fact. In 2017, a mere five years after its founding, the company generated a turnover of 2.2 billion American dollars. Its business model is based on the sale of targeted advertising and has brought it financial rewards that outclass many of the world's other top tech-giants. In 2003, five years after its founding, Google's turnover was 1.5 billion dollars. The comparable figure for Facebook in 2009 is 0.77 billion dollars. Toutiao is without doubt the digital tool with the fastest rising turnover curve ever seen. And the key to this success is their interface: faster than real time, zero effort, invisible and personalised.

A filter on everything

Toutiao applies a filter to the consumer's news consumption. Facebook applies a filter to posts and messages from your friends, family and colleagues. Netflix applies a filter to the kind of content it suggests. Even McDonald's new Drive Thru menu applies a filter to what you might like to eat.

Looked at from a positive perspective, we call this personalisation. Looked at from a negative perspective, we call this a narrowing of our societal outlook. Although many people are worried by this narrowing, they seem to forget that in many circumstances the human brain also acts as an automatic filter. Even if you and I both take the same daily newspaper, we will probably read, digest and remember different articles. If we both walk through the same town, we will notice different advertisements along the way. That is how our brain works. It filters an excess of information.

What's more, people like filters, even if they don't always realise it. The amount and range of information available to us today is so huge that it is often a welcome relief to have a filter that can cut it down to more manageable proportions. Similarly, lots of consumers still like to visit physical stores where they can receive feedback from sales personnel, who therefore also function as a kind of filter. And if you want to impress your friends with a superior bottle of wine to accompany your latest self-made dinner, you are more likely to pop down to a specialised wine seller than to your local supermarket. Once again, the seller acts as a filter.

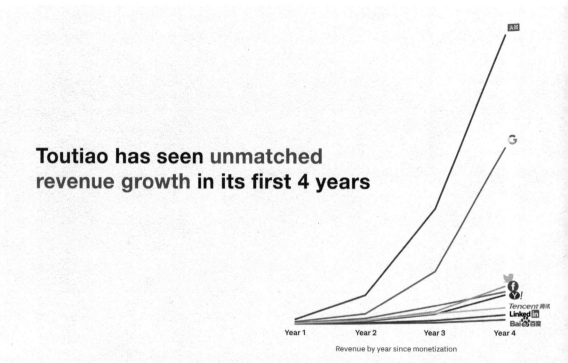

Toutiao has seen unmatched revenue growth in its first 4 years

Year 1   Year 2   Year 3   Year 4

Revenue by year since monetization

The fact that the use of platforms like Facebook and Instagram continues to increase serves to underline just how much we like to work with filters. Often, it is the only way that we can see the wood for the trees.

Given this mass of information and choice, many consumers have developed what is known in the jargon as FEBO: 'Fear for Better Options'. The range of products is so great that people begin to have doubts about what they really want to buy. And because this offer is so huge, particularly on the internet, the value of advice has increased. It is no coincidence that in many countries travel advisers now have more work than ever before. People no longer know what to choose.

In many of the product categories on its website, the Dutch Coolblue company suggests a 'Coolblue's choice', indicating the three products at different price points in each category that represent the 'best buy' for its customers. To make this choice Coolblue analyses mountains of relevant data.

Pieter Zwart, the founder and CEO of Coolblue, told me that nearly 70 per cent of Coolblue's turnover is generated by 'Coolblue choices'. In other words, seven out of every ten customers buy one of the three televisions, computers or washing machines recommended by Coolblue's choice. Again, it proves that consumers just love to be given advice. And the simple truth is that computers are much better able to offer this kind of advice than human beings. Like it or not, digital filters are a part of all our futures.

The next stage in this evolution will occur when the customer gives full autonomy to the filter. In the previous phase, the filter made a number of suggestions and the customer made the final choice. In this next phase, it will be the filter – and the filter alone – that decides what to buy and when. The customer will no longer need to confirm the purchase and will therefore cease to be a part of the transaction process.

Once the consumer has been removed from the purchasing process in this manner, we will have reached the point where machines are effectively doing business with other machines.

So how will this work? Imagine that a consumer decides that his washing machine can automatically buy new supplies of washing powder. There will be a number of agreed guidelines – so much per month, the cheapest brand, etc. – but after that the washing machine does the rest: assessing the level of supply, contacting the supermarket, arranging delivery, and so on. The customer is not involved until the new supply arrives on his front door step.

Once the consumer has been removed from the purchasing process in this manner, we will have reached the point where machines are effectively doing business with other machines. This suggests an alternative interpretation to the title of this book: *The Offer You Can't Refuse*. As a consumer, you can indeed no longer refuse the offered product, because the machine has bought it on your behalf!

Amazon's filter on products and brands

One of Amazon's key objectives for the future is to install the world's biggest product filter in every consumer's home. Once the company's Alexa platform has been refined, it will be the perfect interface to help people make their purchases. When the consumer says: 'Alexa, we need some new cat food,' Alexa will tell you which cat food is best. This will be limited to just one or two suggestions. You might, perhaps, ask for a third alternative, but it is unlikely you will take it much further than that. In other words, you will no longer see the hundred other different types of cat food on offer at the local supermarket, or the dozen or so available via the supermarket website. If Alexa is doing her job properly, your choice will have been reduced to just one brand – the brand that Amazon knows is the best brand for you.

How do they know? By coupling data relating to your previous purchases with the latest price and review data for the cat food category. Amazon builds, as it were, a kind of dating software to link the right consumer to the right product/brand. Is that what consumers want? Yes, on condition that this personalisation works perfectly. Every time you are offered a product that matches well with your preferences, your confidence in the system increases. And if it saves you time as well, there is a good chance that you will accept the system as part of your daily life.

Imagine, however, that you say: 'Yes, but I like a little variety in my purchases and I am being denied this by those damned product filters!' That is a fair point, but it is also one that is easy to solve. In the future, you will be able to programme Alexa so that every so often she suggests a new product that fits your profile. If your purchasing record shows

Amazon invented the product filter

that you like to try new things, Amazon will already be well aware of this. This makes it possible for Alexa to respond to the preferences of each individual consumer, so that her recommendations always feel like a bull's-eye, time after time.

Once enough confidence has been built up in this manner, the purchasing responsibility for entire product categories can be delegated to Alexa and other similar platforms. At first, this will only be for routine products, where the consumer has no clear preference for a particular brand. But in a later phase other types of products will be added to the list.

In the early days of e-commerce, people were convinced that this method of purchasing was only suitable for books, CDs and DVDs: simple products with a low financial risk, so that customers were not too scared that something might go wrong. Today, we buy more or less every product online. The new interfaces of the future will undergo this same evolution.

Assuming that society will continue to make increasing use of product filters and autonomous machine-purchasing, this will have a massive impact on marketing, and in particular on brand strategy.

There are effectively three possible scenarios. The first scenario is where the consumer requests a specific brand:

- **DE-FILTERED**: if a customer specifically asks for Colgate toothpaste, it is clear what the AI filter will do: it will give the customer Colgate toothpaste. In this case, Colgate manages to avoid the filtering process. Its strong branding allows it, as it were, to become de-filtered. This is the ideal scenario for every brand.

What happens if someone gives a brand-free command? 'Alexa, I want some batteries.' What will Alexa give you? Will it be Amazon-branded batteries or will she propose an A-brand? This results in two remaining scenarios for the brand:

- **FILTERED-IN**: if the customer reviews and match-making details of a specific brand are good enough, the Amazon algorithm will know that there is a more than reasonable chance that when the customer asks for a product he will appreciate being offered that particular brand. As a result, the filter will suggest the brand. It is filtered-in.
- **FILTERED-OUT**: if the customer review and the match-making details are less promising, there is a strong likelihood that the specific brand will not be suggested to the customer. In other words, the filter removes the brand from consideration. It is filtered-out. In a world where interfaces of the Alexa type will soon dominate the purchasing process, this means that brands in this position will lose the opportunity to come into contact with consumers. It is almost as if they will become invisible. In today's traditional world, brands can counter this effect with classic-style advertising. But as soon as consumers start to rely more and more heavily on AI filters, the impact of this kind of advertising will decline significantly.

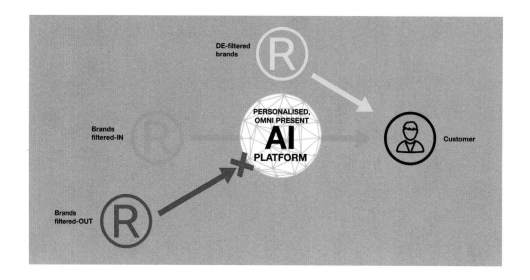

What does all this mean? It means that in future companies will have to invest more heavily in the strength of their brands (allowing them to be DE-FILTERED) or in products and services whose reviews confirm that they are sufficiently high-quality and differentiating to merit noticing by the filters (allowing them to be FILTERED-IN). If your brand is FILTERED-OUT, you will be in big trouble.

Nike pulls the plug

At the end of 2019, Nike decided to end its collaboration with Amazon. The super-brand now wants to focus primarily on direct sales to consumers. In 2019, Nike had a turnover of some 33 billion American dollars, of which 11.7 billion already came from direct sales. These sales were realised through Nike's own stores and online channels. For Nike, it is important that its brand products are offered at a uniform price. Because Amazon works with many small-scale retailers, the range of price variation was too much for Nike's liking. Each of the small retailers offered their own discounts on Nike shoes and clothing, so that the uniformity of the brand was compromised. It was feared that this, in due course, would erode the brand's strength.

Nike understands like few other companies the strategic importance of direct contact with your end customers. For this reason, the organisation plans to invest significantly in its efforts to increase the share of direct sales in its turnover. This is now a crucial part of their brand strategy. In fact, maintaining a direct relationship with the end user must be a priority for every company.

When I discuss Nike's choice with other business leaders, the classic reply is: 'Yes, Steven, but you must remember we are talking about Nike.' Of course, what they are actually saying is: 'Our brand is not strong enough to cut our ties with Amazon. We are too reliant on them.'

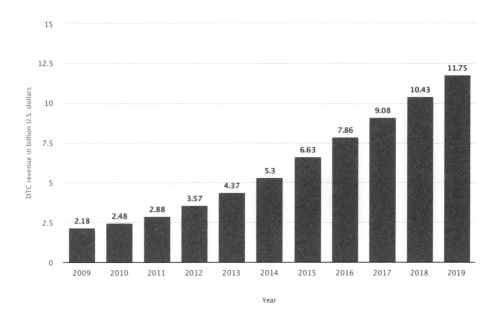

In most cases, both analyses are correct. Nike is indeed a very strong brand, whereas in recent years most other companies have invested insufficiently in their own brand strength. Opting for short-term activations and sales promotions has led to an erosion of their brand value. As a result, their options in the short term are now more limited than for the stronger brands.

In this chapter, I am describing the evolution towards ultimate transactional convenience. The most important consequence of this evolution is the greater urgency to build strong brands. The easier it becomes for consumers to make more and more of their purchases through the big digital platforms, the more important it becomes for consumers to specifically ask for your brand. The moment when consumers only start asking for categories of products is the moment when power will pass exclusively into the hands of the AI filters. When that happens, your only hope is to have a truly top product or service.

Two scenarios

As I see it, there are two possible scenarios for the near future.

The first scenario is the one that the large technology platforms would like to see happen: a market dominated by centralised and automated sales platforms, which manage to interpose themselves between the customer and most brands. And we should be under no illusion that the tech-giants only have this ambition for consumer products.

One of my clients is a world-leader in spare parts for machines. During a strategy meeting he told me how one of his most important customers now made all their basic purchases via Amazon Business. My client can only sell to Amazon, with the end customer then buying everything he needs from the Amazon platform. So why is this customer now acting in this way?

There are essentially three reasons: the Amazon platform is more efficient, Amazon logistics are more reliable and Amazon helps to negotiate the price. As a result, Amazon has wormed its way in between the customer and the manufacturer of the spare parts. The ultimate convenience provided by companies like Amazon works as a magnet on both consumers and companies alike.

In the West, we are rapidly moving towards this scenario; in the East, it has already arrived. In China, the majority of daily transactions now take place via platforms like WeChat and Meituan Dianping. In other Asian markets, the Grab platform (comparable with its two Chinese counterparts but based in Singapore) is increasingly taking on the same role.

two scenarios

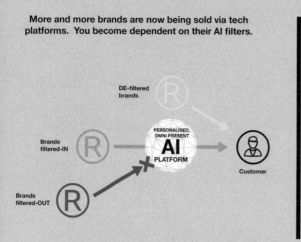

More and more brands are now being sold via tech platforms. You become dependent on their AI filters.

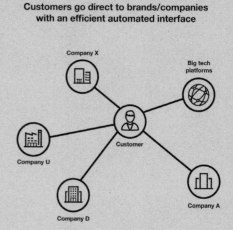

Customers go direct to brands/companies with an efficient automated interface

Scenario one ends in a world where by far the largest share of basic transactions takes place via the technology platforms.

In scenario two a large number of transactions again take place via the technology platforms, but there is still a group of other companies with brands that are sufficiently strong to remain in direct contact with consumers. In this scenario, customers continue to find enough value in maintaining direct interaction with certain 'favoured' providers. Excellent service, warm and personal human contact, an equally performant digital interface, unique products: these are all examples of reasons why customers may prefer to buy directly from you rather than through a fully automated platform. Identifying these differentiating elements in your market and investing in both a strong brand and an outstanding customer experience have never been more important than they are today.

Some companies may opt for a combination of both these scenarios. And they may be right. For many of them, it is indeed interesting to sell their products via the large technology platforms and their turnover from Amazon is now often their most important source of revenue.

Nevertheless, there is a risk in becoming too dependent on the tech-giants. If they decide for whatever reason that they want to change course, they will do so without thinking of you and the significant impact it may have on your results. Or to express it in slightly different terms: even if the tech platforms currently represent a highly important source of income for your company, it is still important to retain a firm grip on your direct relationship with the end consumer.

This can, however, lead to a difficult dilemma: should you work with Amazon or fight against them? The trick, of course, is to keep a foot in both camps. Try to work as successfully as possible with the big platforms, but also work every day at building a strong direct relationship with your customers.

The ultimate convenience: automatic and invisible

The final phase in interface development is approaching. Only a completely invisible and automatic interface will satisfy all the criteria for being successful. This will reduce the customer's time investment to zero. Automation is something that people get used to very quickly. Once you are used to working in an office where the lighting is activated by sensors, you soon regard it as almost medieval that you ever had to search for the right switch! If your central heating decides when its own maintenance is needed, telephoning the plumber for help seems like something from a previous century. As long as they work effectively, trust in these systems develops rapidly.

An invisible and automatic interface certainly helps customers to save time, but also gives rise to a number of questions. As a result, their evolution will trigger a fierce ethical debate in the years ahead. How will consumers know that they are being treated fairly? For example, the use of invisible and automatic interfaces will lead to the disappearance of price transparency.

Imagine that a petrol station is equipped with automatic and invisible interfaces. You drive up to a pump and start filling your car. In the meantime, the petrol station has scanned your number plate. Your number plate reveals your address. An address, in turn, reveals something about your social status. Add to this the type of car you are driving and it is not too difficult to assess whether someone belongs to the top half or the bottom half of the income curve. Based on this information, the petrol station can – theoretically – charge its wealthier customers 5 per cent more than its poorer ones. The customers will not be aware of this, since payment will be made automatically via sensors and the smartphone. In other words, the process requires no effort from the customer (benefit), but some customers pay 5 per cent more than others (drawback). For some people, this might sound like the ultimate form of social redistribution. For others, it will make them furious.

And what if digital tools like Alexa and Google Home learn to better understand the emotions of consumers? Amazon is already working to develop technology that analyses voices. The extra data that this will reveal offers new possibilities for further personalisation.

Consider the following purely hypothetical example. Imagine that Amazon decides to charge a higher price to someone whose voice makes clear that he or she is having a euphoric day. How would we react as a society? Perhaps the data will allow Amazon to conclude that good weather combined with a good mood makes customers willing to pay 5 per cent more than normal. What then? Would Amazon use this information? Would there be a public outcry? Who would decide the rights and wrongs of the situation?

These are just a few examples to underline the importance of making clear agreements and drawing up binding ethical codes in a world where the consumer will no longer need to press a 'confirm order' button. Automation is fantastic, but only if it is honest, fair and ethically applied.

Help! I can see a lion!

How far does your company need to go in pursuit of ultimate ease of use? To a large extent, this depends on the sector in which you are active and the impact that the major technology players have on your company. If you operate in a market where the tech-giants are also active, you will have no choice other than to invest heavily in digital ease of use. Are the digital interfaces of your competitors already state-of-the-art? Once again, there is no alternative: you will have to go all the way.

If, however, your company is active in a sector where the digital revolution is taking place more slowly, your challenge is to be 20 per cent better than your direct competitors. In sectors of this kind it is relatively easy to make the difference with a better interface.

An interesting example of a company in this latter situation is Domino's Pizza. During the past decades, Domino's Pizza shares were among the best performers on the stock market. One of the reasons for this success is that the company invested in performant digital interfaces. The aim of Domino's Pizza was to have the easiest 'pizza ordering tools' in the world. Their motto was: 'It's all-too-easy to order pizzas from Domino's'. And, very soon, it was. In the land of the blind, the one-eyed man is king. Well, in the land of poor digital interfaces Domino's Pizza was the emperor.

To describe the company's philosophy, I like to use a metaphor. Imagine that you are walking across the savannah in Africa with your best friend. It is a beautiful day and the scenery is magnificent. You are taking selfies and enjoying the kind of conversations that only best friends can have. In short, it is one of the best days of your life. And then it happens.

Suddenly, you see a lion.

What is the most important thing at that moment?

If you want to survive, you don't need to be faster than the lion. You just need to be faster than your friend …

This is the philosophy that Domino's used to determine its strategy. Can Domino's be faster and better than Amazon? No, probably not. Can Domino's be faster and better than Pizza Hut? Yes, that is feasible.

You can translate this philosophy to every other sector. Many companies operate in markets where the big tech-players are not active and in which digital interfaces are lagging behind. In these markets, the task is simple: you need to make sure that your interface is 20 per cent better than your rivals' interfaces. If you can achieve this, you will make the difference. In sectors where the Googles and the Amazons of the world are largely absent, being faster and better than your direct competitors is what really counts.

How can I get started?

Offering ultimate convenience to your customers is one of the strategic dimensions of The Offer You Can't Refuse model. So what do you need to do in practical terms?

My advice is to appoint 'friction hunters' in your company. Look for people who are enthusiastic about your customers, but also a little bit frustrated that not enough is done for them. Ask these people to hunt down the frictions in your sales and service process-es. Work through all the steps that your customers need to follow and ask yourself the following questions:
- Where do customers lose time in the process?
- Which steps in the process can be made easier for customers?
- Which aspects are too complex for customers?
- How can the total interaction time be reduced by 10 per cent?

Once you have found the answers to these questions, divide them into two lists. The first list should contain 'quick wins': little things that are annoying for the customer but rel-atively easy for you to fix. The second list will contain bigger projects: important adjust-ments that are necessary to optimise ease of use.
Finally, allocate people and timings to each of the quick wins and projects. After that, you can start with the implementation. Arrange for a meeting of the friction hunters every two weeks, so that they can share updates with each other. Perhaps you can even make a 'wall of ex-frustrations'. Every time a work point is completed and removed from your 'to do' list, make a symbolic medal and hang it on the wall. As the weeks and months pass, the wall will become covered in medals. And once this happens, people will suddenly realise that they are now working in a more customer-friendly organisation.
Using your own people as friction hunters to optimise convenience for your customers is an effective way to get to grips with this strategic dimension of The Offer You Can't Refuse model.

Convenience as the driver of loyalty?

For years, I have been spreading the message that 'convenience is the new loyalty'. In my previous book, *Customers the Day After Tomorrow*, I devoted an entire chapter to the sub-ject. Every analysis carried out during the past decade has revealed that customers were indeed searching increasingly for the interfaces that offered the greatest ease of use. The saving of time, our most precious resource, thanks to the efficiency of good performing interfaces, became an important part of our lives.

In the meantime, good performing interfaces have become the norm. They are no longer a differentiator. Instead, they are the new minimum. Even though there is still room for further improvements in convenience, these gains will never have the same differentiating impact as ten years ago. Yes, the years ahead will see us move ever closer to fully automatic and invisible interfaces, but they will no longer be enough on their own to make the difference.

In future, differentiation will need to be achieved by dealing effectively with all the customer's worries and concerns. Helping customers to realise their dreams and ambitions, while at the same time taking away their fears and making a positive contribution to the challenges faced by society, will be the key to success. In the following two chapters, I will look more closely at two of these differentiating customer strategies.

the ultimate convenience becomes a commodity

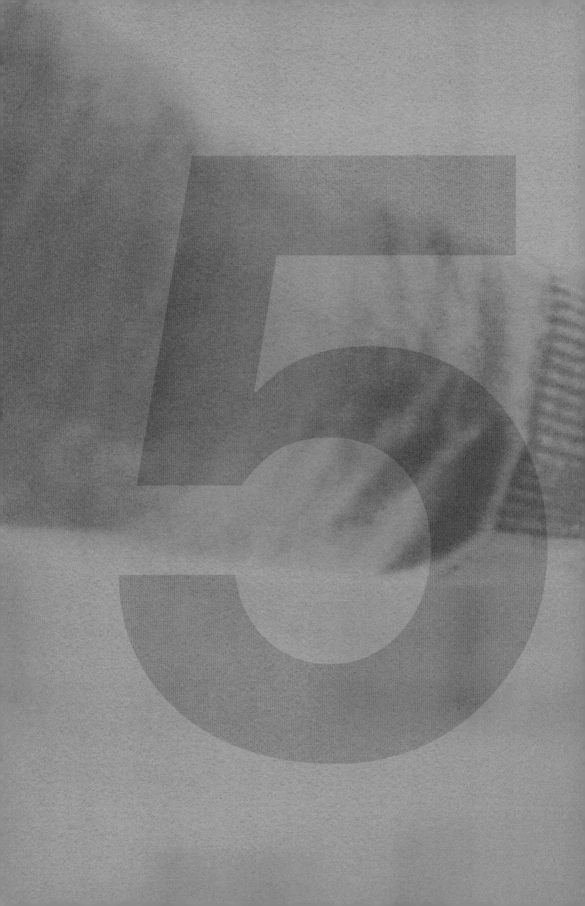

partner in life

Human energy and money are scarce resources

For almost all of us, time is probably our most scarce resource. Because of the limited amount of time we have to do everything we need to do in our daily lives, people attach great importance to ultimate convenience. But after time, our next scarcest resources are money and human energy.

Most of the people I know would love to have more time, money and energy. Very few of us have all three. Many people with lots of money often have no time. And if you have time, you often don't have enough money or energy.

In the film of the consumer's life, money and energy play a major role. This is something you can exploit with your 'partner in life' strategy. I have already mentioned how cheap retailers can be a real financial partner for people struggling to make ends meet or how Ryanair can make it possible for low-income families to enjoy a city trip. Why is the e-commerce site of AliExpress so popular? The answer is simple: because it is 50 to 70 per cent cheaper than the western e-commerce platforms. That helps its customers to save money.

But the biggest opportunities in the 'partner in life' concept relate to the scarcity of human energy. As a company, how can you give people more energy? And have you ever asked yourself that same question? Transactional optimisation saves people time. Emotional optimisation can save people energy or even generate an extra supply of it.

At the start of 2020, Amazon Prime had 112 million customers in the United States.[47] This means it reaches 59 per cent of all American families.[48] So why are so many Americans members of the Amazon club? Once again, the answer is simple: it saves you time, money and energy. For a monthly fee of 10 American dollars, you get free deliveries that are received faster and cost less, as well as benefiting from better recommendations and the free use of a variety of extra services.

> *In fact, it is more remarkable that 40 per cent of Americans have not yet joined Amazon Prime, if you look at all the advantages it brings.*

In fact, it is more remarkable that 40 per cent of Americans have not yet joined Amazon Prime, if you look at all the advantages it brings. After a hard day at work, shopping with Amazon requires little energy and saves you money and time. Not surprisingly, it is a huge success.

The changing mission of Booking.com

More and more companies are moving away from an exaggerated focus on transactional optimisation to adopt a broader, more all-inclusive approach to their customers. In recent years, I have regularly collaborated with Booking.com. I have given a number of talks as a guest speaker and at the end of 2019 I took a group of managers on an inspiration visit to the headquarters of the travel giant. During this visit, it was clear that Booking.com is in the process of changing its mission.

Until recently, this mission read as follows: 'We wish to reserve overnight hotel accommodation throughout the world for every occasion and every budget in the easiest and most customer-friendly manner.' Few would dispute that the company has successfully fulfilled this mission. As a result, it has become a billion dollar concern, and one that is used by many millions of consumers.

But in the years to come Booking.com wants to go even further. Of course, the company still intends to retain its outstanding ease of digital use, but in addition it now also wishes to become a 'partner in travel' for its customers. The new mission therefore reads: 'We want to make it easy and feasible for everyone to discover the world.' In this way, Booking.com hopes to respond to the dreams that many people have of being able to make long and exotic journeys to far-off destinations.

Setting out a new mission on paper is one thing; translating it into practice is something else. This involves a huge transformation for Booking.com. Until recently, their focus has been on hotels, a product that is much easier to sell digitally than a desire to help people discover the world.

Help both B2B and B2C travellers to find an accommodation, for any budget, for any occasion at any location in the world in the easiest way possible

Booking.com

Make it easy **for everyone** to discover the world

As the first step in this transformation, Booking.com has significantly expanded its range. Via its platform you can now also book tourist attractions, as well as the necessary transport and a driver to take your there. Booking these extras via the digital platform remains as quick and as easy as ever, but the dependency on hundreds of thousands of local players means that it not easy to offer the same uniform standard of quality that is generally possible with hotels. To achieve transactional perfection you (only) need to optimise your own channels. But to implement a 'partner in life' philosophy you often need a much wider network of partners.

Google wants to make everything in life easy

Google is undergoing the same evolution as Booking.com. It is engaged in a process that will see its current mission – 'organising the world's information and making it universally available' – transformed into something new. Google's future mission will be: 'To make every part of people's life as easy as possible.' Google wants to invest in saving time (convenience) and saving energy (partner in life). Google Assistant is intended to play a central role in this transformation. Within a matter of years, it is anticipated that users will have delegated a large part of the running of their daily lives to the digital butler. Booking restaurants, making appointments for the hairdresser, arranging a babysitter for the kids: these and many other similar tasks will no longer require any effort by the customer. Just ask Google and it will be done.

To organize the world's information **and**
make it universally accessible and useful

Google

Make every part of people's life as easy as possible

Google is taking a very broad approach to this new mission. For them, the 'partner in life' concept embraces all aspects of an individual's or a family's daily existence. For example, Google wants to be a partner in mobility. As a result, the company is developing a fleet of self-driving taxis with its Waymo division. In addition, Google wishes to be a partner in health care. And in the purchasing of your routine shopping: thanks to its collaboration with major retailers, you can already buy dozens of products via your Google Assistant. But it doesn't stop there. Google also wants to be your partner in living. If your house is equipped with the right Google interfaces, you can literally arrange every aspect of the running of your home via the Google Assistant: turning the lighting on and off, operating the TV, preparing meals via a cooking assistant, etc.

To make this all-inclusive 'partner in life' strategy viable, Google works as far as possible with its own technology, but it also needs the help of an extensive network of partners.

For Google, the 'partner in life' concept embraces all aspects of an individual's or a family's daily existence.

If, for example, Google really wants to become a partner in mobility, it will have no option but to collaborate with as many car manufacturers as possible, since its own vehicle network is far too small to make its ambition achievable.

The three steps to a 'partner in life' approach

To successfully implement a 'partner in life' strategy, you need to generate a continuous process of movement, consisting of three steps:

1. Developing an excellent understanding of the needs and frustrations in the life of your customer.
2. Use this understanding to describe in detail the customer's life journey.
3. Implement 'partner in life' actions.

In other words, you need to acquire insights that will allow you to make a concrete description of your customers' lives, which you then seek to influence positively through concrete actions. If correct, these actions will prompt new behaviour in the customer, leading to new insights, a revised description and a further set of concrete actions. And so the gradual refinement of your 'partner in life' strategy continues. The faster and more effectively you can repeat this circular process, the easier you will find it to differentiate your company from your rivals in your sector.

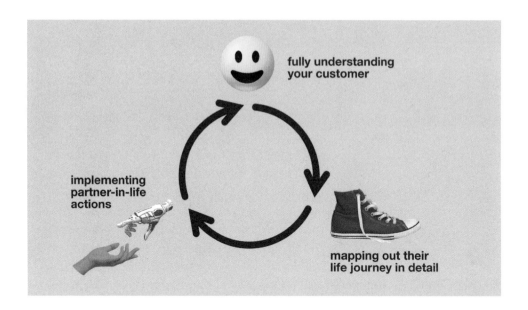

fully understanding
your customer

implementing
partner-in-life
actions

mapping out their
life journey in detail

1. Developing an excellent understanding of the needs and frustrations in the life of your customer

Every customer has dreams, fears and ambitions. As the first step in your 'partner in life' approach, you need to put in place a system that will give you continuous insight into the emotions of your customers. A one-off market research study or a closed questionnaire will not give you the information you need. This can only be obtained by observing consumers in their day-to-day lives.

Many companies still focus their market research almost exclusively on the relationship between the consumer and the company. A bank will look at the extent to which its apps and online tools are suitable to meet the financial needs of its customers. A retailer will look to see if its range and the way it is offered still match customer expectations. A car manufacturer will look at whether its brand is still sufficiently attractive and whether all the functions of its cars are sufficiently well known.

Of course, all these questions are highly relevant but they concentrate on the company's transactional relationship with the customer. To become a partner in life, it is necessary to understand the bigger issues that play a role in the customer's thinking. For example, as a bank it might be interesting to learn about people's dreams and ambitions – a new house, a trip around the world, etc. – so that you can see how the bank can help to achieve their realisation. In much the same way, the customers of retailers might be interested in living a healthier lifestyle, but without exceeding their monthly budget. And the customers of the car manufacturers might have more questions about improved mobility than about the performance of the car itself. Gaining insight into the wishes, dreams and fears of people that relate in some way to your sector is the first step towards becoming a partner in life.

The lessons of President Obama

In September 2018, I had the pleasure of meeting the former American president, Barack Obama. We were both speaking at the same event in Amsterdam. For me, it was an unforgettable moment to be able to shake the hand of this remarkable man. One of the topics about which he spoke was life in the White House. As president, you live in this imposing official residence with your family, but life there is like nothing else in the rest of American society. You are treated in a way that has nothing in common with the day-to-day existence of the average American.

To keep his feet firmly on the ground, President Obama devised a number of specific tactics. One of them was particularly effective and efficient: each evening he asked to see ten letters from ordinary American citizens. During his time in the White House, the president received between 10,000 and 20,000 letters each month. He had a team of more than 100 people to answer all these letters, but at the end of each day he was given a random selection of just ten, which he read as his final task before going to bed. And he did it every day. For a full eight years.

Almost every evening, the president's staff gave him a thick file with briefings that would allow him to prepare for the meetings scheduled for the next day. These briefings might cover subjects as diverse and as important as the war in Afghanistan or measures to deal with the economic crisis. But after he had read and digested all this information, he turned to the ten letters from ordinary people, to find out what was worrying them most. One might be from a couple in Arizona, who didn't have enough money to pay for

health care. Another from a steel worker in Pittsburgh, whose plant was threatened with closure. It was then that the president realised that, even though he had worked very hard that day, he had had no impact on the lives of these ten people, his 'customers', the citizens of the United States.

Gaining insight into other people's everyday concerns takes you outside of your own bubble. The White House is unquestionably one of the largest bubbles on the planet, but we all have smaller bubbles of our own. You can live in the bubble of your company or even in the bubble of your department. I live in my 'crazy Steven' bubble. The trick is to make sure you regularly leave your bubble, so that you can find out what is going on elsewhere in the world and, more especially, in the dreams, fears and ambitions of your customers.

Monzo takes away worries and frustrations

Recent years have seen the emergence of a large number of neo-banks. These new, smaller and generally more innovative banks have taken the market by storm, a success that is usually based on a strong digital and highly user-friendly offering. Monzo is one of the top five fastest growers in this segment.[49] In January 2019, Monzo had roughly one million customers. Twelve months later, that figure had risen to 3.6 million.[50] Other neo-banks, like Revolut and N26, have enjoyed similarly spectacular growth. So what makes this kind of bank so attractive to the market?

A quick glance at the Monzo website makes the secret of their success crystal clear. The team at Monzo first made a summary of all the frustrations, problems and ambitions that people have with regard to their daily finances. After that, the bank formulated a product offer that addresses each and every one of these concerns. In other words, Monzo has not made the difference by simply investing in a good customer journey, but by understanding the financial life journey of its customers.

People who live from pay cheque to pay cheque are often worried about their financial health. Monzo tries to deal with the stress that this can cause. If you agree for your pay to be deposited with the bank, they make sure that the money is in your account 24 hours earlier than usual. In other words, you get 24 hours of free credit.

And if you live from pay cheque to pay cheque, spending too much can also be a major stress factor, often because you haven't got enough money to buy even the necessities of life during the last few days of the month. Once again, Monzo is there to help. They have developed their Salary Sorter. When your pay is deposited into your account, it is divided up into three portfolios. In the first, sufficient money is set to one side to cover all the obligatory monthly costs (rent, electricity, food, etc.). In the (optional) second, money can be set aside for savings. Whatever is left over goes into the third portfolio, which is available for the customer's free use. Of course, the customer retains at all times the right to decide what he spends, but these tools help to give a clearer picture of his or her financial position. As a result, the likelihood that someone will spend too much in any given month

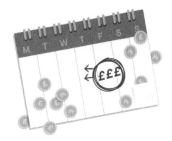

is significantly reduced, allowing them to make it through to the end of the month with much less stress and worry. It is a kind of automated self-protection.

Customers are also provided with a monthly summary of their outgoings. After a number of months, Monzo is usually able to see the emergence of a pattern. If your expenditure at the start of a month exceeds this pattern, the bank will send you a friendly message. This clear and early form of communication hopefully makes it possible for the customer to adjust, so that the end of the month can again be reached without any major problems.

Monzo did not say: 'How can we make our tools as easy to use as possible?' No, Monzo said: 'What emotions and concerns are important in the lives of our customers?' And once Monzo understood what really matters to the people behind those customers, it formulated its product offer accordingly.

2. Describe in detail the life journey of your customer

In recent times, companies have invested huge sums of money to map out the customer journey. This is the path that a consumer follows to finally purchase a particular product or service. The object of this mapping exercise is to allow companies to better optimise their own sales, marketing and service processes. In due course, this leads to transactional perfection. For this reason, the exercise is a valuable one and it forms the basis for the philosophy I described in the previous chapter.

> *This no longer has anything to do with the optimisation of your operational processes. Instead, it aims to reduce the frustrations and help realise the dreams in the life of your customer.*

But to become a partner in life, what you really need to map is the customer's life journey. This no longer has anything to do with the optimisation of your operational processes. Instead, it aims to reduce the frustrations and help realise the dreams in the life of your customer.

The following box highlights the differences between the two journeys.

Customer journey	Life journey
Understanding how the customer buys or uses products.	Understanding the dreams, ambitions and fears in the consumer's day-to-day life.
Removing frictions in the purchasing and service processes.	Removing frictions and providing added value in the customer's day-to-day-life.
Mapping the customer journey.	Mapping life phases and life moments.
Analysing the company's touchpoints.	Analysing the important moments in the course of the customer's day or life.
Transactional optimisation.	Emotional optimisation.

Lumi by Pampers

Perhaps you currently have a baby somewhere in your family? Perhaps it is your baby, and maybe even a first one? If so, congratulations! Many of us will remember the moment when we first took our newborn baby home. We will also remember what our main concerns were at that time.
Most of the concerns of new and inexperienced parents centre on the basic aspects of life. Is our darling eating enough? Is he or she sleeping enough? Is he or she breathing while asleep? Are we changing nappies often enough? Sounds familiar? We even had friends who used an Excel spreadsheet to chart and monitor all these essential elements in their baby's young life.

Lumi, a sub-brand of Pampers, responds to parental worries of this kind in a smart way. It has mapped out these worries and developed a solution to eliminate them. Lumi provides parents with a smart nappy, a sleep tracker, a smart camera and an app, which together provide anxious mums and dads with all the information they need in a clear manner. As a result, the parents know how much their child is sleeping, whether that sleep was peaceful or disturbed, how often the child relieved itself, etc. Pampers could have decided simply to bring smart nappies to market, but a smart nappy only tells parents when the child needs a fresh one. By providing a more broad-based solution to parental concerns, Pampers has become a partner in the life of young parents.
P&G (the mother company of Pampers) also benefits significantly from this approach. The relevant data that P&G collects is very useful for further boosting its own efficiency. For example, it is possible to buy the smart nappies online via the Lumi platform. In this way, the customer no longer needs to go to the supermarket to pick up a new box, while at the same time P&G is able to build up a direct relationship with the end user. As a

The award winning sleep routine system

Paired with an unbelievably good monitor

★ ★ ★ ★ ★

Meet Lumi →

result, Pampers knows exactly how many nappies you use, so that the company can offer you a new supply at exactly the right moment. It is also able to follow how your child is growing, so that it can provide you with the right nappies for each phase of your child's development.

In short, the Lumi concept results in a clear win-win situation. The consumer benefits from greater peace of mind. P&G can benefit from increased direct sales and greater operational efficiency, thanks to the data it collects.

iCarbonX

iCarbonX was founded in 2015 by the Chinese genome expert Jun Wang, the former CEO of the Beijing Genomics Institute, today known as the BGI Group. Right from the very beginning, investors had high expectations of Wang's company. After the first round of investment, to which companies like Tencent subscribed, iCarbonX was immediately worth one billion American dollars.

In 2019, I visited iCarbonX with a group of entrepreneurs and was able to interview co-founder and chief scientist Yingrui Li about his unique company. iCarbonX wants to be a partner in personal health care.

It bases its philosophy on the hypothesis that your quality of life can suddenly and unexpectedly decline as you get older. Your behaviour between your 35th and 55th year largely determines how good this quality of life will be once you are old. If you abuse your body during this 20 year period, through the wrong food, too much smoking and alcohol, not enough sleep, etc., you will pay the price once you pass the age of sixty. The problem is, of course, they you don't feel the negative impact in the short term. You are only confronted with the unpleasant truth much later on, by which time it is already too late.

iCarbonX wants to preserve a high quality of life, even in old age. The company does this by collecting and analysing extensive data about your body. Naturally, this involves the measurement of your basic health statistics and the amount of exercise you take, but it then goes much, much further. For example, you can install an intelligent toilet in your home, which monitors your urine and your bowel movements every time you use it. When I visited iCarbonX, they were even considering the possibility of analysing behavioural data from social media, based on their belief that mental health is every bit as important as physical health. This is a good example of the kind of holistic thinking that is so typical of Chinese companies. iCarbonX attempts to collect as many data points as possible, in order to gain maximum insight into the evolution of your health. This enables the company to give targeted advice that will allow you to maintain your quality of life.

In the long term, this kind of company should be able to predict how long a person is likely to live. For every action that an individual takes, the algorithm can calculate the resulting positive or negative impact on life expectancy. Imagine that you are in the pub drinking a refreshing pint of beer when you suddenly get a message, informing you that you are shortening your life by two days! And that a Big Mac menu might bring the Grim Reaper closer by four days! Most of us are not waiting for this kind of information. Perhaps it would help us all to live longer and more healthily, but it would also take a lot of the pleasure out of life. iCarbonX is not yet going this far, but its philosophy is certainly moving in that direction.

3. Implementing 'partner in life' actions

Once you have a thorough knowledge of the dreams and fears of your customers, you can describe their life journey. Having done that, you then need to move on to the development and implementation of 'partner in life' actions. There are four possible strategies by which you can achieve this. You should not choose just one of these strategies, but must use them in combination. This gives the best results, as the example of the Grab company a few pages further on will show.

Strategy 1: from product to service

The evolution from 'selling products' to 'providing access to services' has already been taking place for quite some time. According to Carlota Perez, this evolution will be one of the main pillars of the next 'golden age' of Smart Green Growth, because it will mean that fewer products will be made and sold, as a result of which we will use less energy to produce less (and less polluting) material.

Thanks to Netflix, we no longer need to buy DVDs, because we have access to an almost limitless library of video content. Thanks to Spotify and other music streaming services, we no longer need to buy CDs, because we have access to their massive digital music archive. Companies like Spotify are now partners for music-lovers.

At the end of 2019, I was able to interview Tien Tzuo (you can listen to the full interview via my podcast). Tien Tzuo is the founder of Zuora, one of the leading software companies in the subscription economy. He is also author of the book *Subscribed*. Tien is convinced that in years to come almost every industry will be able to make the transition to the subscription model. 'This might sound like a big step,' he explains, 'but when Software-as-a-Service (SaaS) and Cloud were first introduced they also sounded like something from another world. But today most companies do not want to return to a model where they are the owners of their own servers and software. As a result, the entire software industry has already made the switch to subscription.'

In the decades ahead, consumers will show less interest in the ownership of goods and more interest in the services connected with those goods. In other words, it will not be about the CD, but about music. People will not want a car, but will want transport. We are already used to no longer buying a daily paper, because we have access to real-time news services online. There will be many more transformations of this kind. Do you want to own a tractor or do you just want to plough your field?

In the near future, it will become possible for entire industries to be converted into service sectors, based on enabling technologies like artificial intelligence and 5G, which will see the evolution of the internet of things speed up dramatically. In theory, this evolution will make it possible to turn every product into a service. Consequently, we will no longer buy a washing machine, but will pay for each individual wash.

In a world where transactional perfection is crucial, the key question is: 'Will my pizza be delivered quickly and correctly?' As soon as services become crucial, the question will be: 'When I am hungry, can I choose what I want to eat from a good range of meals?' With this second question the customer is looking for a partner in life for food. He or she already takes transactional perfection for granted, because it is the new minimum. If companies follow a 'partner in life' strategy, they will also use new ways to secure customer loyalty. The classic approach of discounts and customer cards is no longer relevant in a 'partner in life' scenario. In the old world, companies convinced customers to buy a product and then tried to hold on to those customers using classic marketing techniques. In contrast, the 'partner in life' strategy is based on engagement. The brand must offer a total experience that goes further than the product and the interface. In this respect, data analysis is the best tool to find out if your customers really appreciate your services. Netflix never talks about a loyalty programme. Instead, the company analyses how often you watch a series or film and then adjusts its offer and its interface on the basis of that analysis. Every user is given individual treatment. Netflix also experiments in real time with the thumbnails of its series. In this way, it is possible to measure the level of engagement series by series, which helps to ensure that customers remain more faithful to the platform, not through classic loyalty programmes but by converting data into a personalised offer.

What's more, it is not just high-tech and software companies that are making this transition from product to service. The French national railways, SNCF, recently discovered that many teenagers were no longer using the train for long journeys but instead were making use of the services of the start-up BlaBlaCar. This company arranges for you to ride in the car of someone who is planning to travel to the same long-distance destination as you are. Do you want to go from Paris to Barcelona? On BlaBlaCar you can find potential rides for less than 20 euros.
Young people think this is a fantastic platform. Thanks to BlaBlaCar, they can make long international journeys cheaply and easily. To counter this, SNCF now offers unlimited train travel to 16 to 27-year-olds for just 79 euros per month. This new service was immediately a big hit. More than 100,000 students have paid for one of these 'Happy Cards'. It is encouraging to see how a company that was founded as long ago as 1938 has been able to recapture market share from a trendy new start-up. This new formula has made SNCF a partner in mobility for the young target group.

Strategy 2: from services focused on the core to solutions for the entire problem

During recent times, many companies have focused on top quality for everything related to the own direct service provision. Of course, this is fantastic and logical. But often what the customer really needs is more broad-based help.

A few months ago, we noticed that our home internet was working very slowly. It took ages to upload and download even relatively straightforward files. Clearly there was something wrong with both the internet connection and wifi. We phoned the helpdesk of our telecom provider and were helped in a friendly and efficient manner. An appointment was made and a few days later an equally friendly and professional technician visited our house to assess the problem. His conclusion was the same as ours: the internet was much too slow. He checked the modem in the garage and all the intermediate connections, which allowed him to reach a second conclusion: 'Your modem is working and the connections are all in order. Your problem must have some other cause.' It was hard to argue with this analysis, but we were curious to know what his next step would be. 'I'm afraid that means there is nothing more I can do for you. You will have to call in an IT company to see if they can find out what is wrong. All I can say is that our company is not the cause of the problem ...'

> *Often what the customer really needs is more broad-based help.*

With that, he closed up his toolbox and left. In terms of process, friendliness, speed and professionalism, it was hard to criticise his service and, by extension, that of our telecom provider. Everything was perfect, transactional optimisation at its best. Even so, we, the customer, were still left saddled with our problem. So where to go from here? Honestly, we had no idea. 'Call in an IT company' was his advice. But what company? And what do you tell them? It is at moments like this that a partner in life will investigate the problem until he has discovered the cause and provided a solution. A partner in telecom needs to look beyond his own modem and connections. He needs to keep on looking until the customer has been helped.

If you agree with my contention that human energy is a scarce resource, then helping customers with a 'total package' is a smart strategy. When Centraal Beheer installed smoke detectors in my house, as I described back in chapter 2, my insurance company solved my problem for me fully, so that I didn't need to worry about the quality and safety aspects.

The providers of financial services nearly all segment their customers on the basis of their available capital. The largest group consists of what might be called ordinary customers, followed by a group that can invest a sum of 250,000 euros and a further group that has capital in excess of one million euros (private banking customers).

Private banking customers know what it is to have a financial partner in life. They can call on their bank for all kinds of financial, legal and fiscal advice. The challenge for the banks of the future is to provide this same personalised service on a much larger scale to its ordinary customers, who only have limited capital resources.

Robots are likely to play an important role in this evolution. Powerful algorithms and automated systems will give the banks much greater potential to offer even its largest group of customers personalised advice. The difference in comparison with private banking is that the human dimension will be missing. A private banking client has a personal adviser, which is simply impossible for ordinary customers, given their much greater numbers. Even so, the new technology makes personalised advice for all a realistic possibility, and this can be – or rather must be – supplemented with broader advice about matters other than banking products. In short, the banks will need to help their customers with their wider financial problems.

The Belgian bank KBC has a strategy that it hopes will see it evolve into a partner in payments and daily financial transactions. The KBC app is, of course, a very good banking and payment app, but it also offers a range of other services, such as automatic car park entry and exit, the booking and payment for tickets on public transport, the use of share bikes, etc.

KBC has examined all the services where the payment process costs the customer additional time and effort – queuing up for the ticket machine in a car park, waiting to buy a train or bus ticket, and so on – and has automated these payments via its app. In this way, the bank shows that it is interested in more than selling its own financial products and makes good its claim to be its customers' partner in daily payments.

It is possible for every sector to think about ways to broaden its services and communication beyond a focus on its own core. A retailer must no longer be concerned exclusively with the sale of products, but must seek to help its customers to live healthier and more environmentally aware lives. A car manufacturer must look further than issues like safety and quality, setting a new emphasis on a broader range of mobility services.

Strategy 3: from focus on the core to the blending of industries

During recent decades, the companies in most industries have remained true to their core. Although they may have evolved slightly, car manufacturers have continued to make the same great cars they have always made, just as retailers have continued to sell the same kinds of great products. Media companies that started as pure media companies have, by and large, remained pure media companies.

The past ten years have shown how difficult it can be to transform within that core. The advent of new digital business models has placed many companies in an awkward position. Retailers have found it difficult to make the switch to e-commerce. Media companies clung on to their linear approach for far too long. Car manufacturers took years before deciding to invest in electric vehicles and the sharing economy.

Google is one of the few examples of an organisation that regularly moves away from its core and investigates options in other industries. Google builds balloons to provide the world with internet, manufactures self-driving cars, collaborates with SpaceX to push the boundaries of space travel ... People often look down their noses at Google's innovations, largely because until now they have generated very little revenue. The truth is that they don't need to. In the first instance, Google earns its money (in huge quantities) from online advertising, not from its radical and innovative breakthroughs.

To become a partner in life, it is possible that you will need to leave your core. The example of Centraal Beheer (chapter 2) is a case in point. It may sound strange that an insurance company suddenly starts selling solar panels and offering household help, but it is a logical step in their 'partner in life' process. The projects of Centraal Beheer that go beyond their core are all moving the company in a clear direction.

Centraal Beheer wants to be a partner in living for its customers. Google's ambition goes much further; it wants to be a partner in solving all the world's major problems. Leaving or expanding your core is a necessary component of the 'partner in life' concept, but you need to travel in a particular strategic direction that will result in a broader range of services for your customers.

Toyota has chosen to be a partner for mobility in the lives of its customers. With this aim in mind, the Japanese car manufacturer intends to build an experimental city. Work on the greenfield smart city, known as Woven City, will start in early 2021. To implement this project, Toyota is collaborating with the Japanese telecom player NTT. The total investment of both companies amounts to 1.8 billion American dollars.[51]

This innovative city will be constructed close to Mount Fuji, on the site of an abandoned Toyota plant. It is planned that 2 000 people will live there in the not too distant future. Toyota's city of the future will be an experimental environment, where real-life research will be carried out into countless innovations that will influence our daily lives in the years ahead. The city's energy will be generated by hydrogen fuel cells and all other facilities will reflect a need for greater sustainability. Day-to-day life will be organised by

smart technology. Everything will be connected – people, vehicles, buildings, etc. – and all communication will be via smart sensors.

The purpose of this remarkable initiative is to see how the full potential of a city can be most efficiently utilised, whilst at the same time offering high standard of living to its inhabitants. To travel around the city, the residents use fully autonomous, zero-emission vehicles, while all deliveries of supplies are made by these same self-driving vehicles and robots.

With this project, Toyota wishes to show how the company can become a partner in life and mobility for people. Or as the CEO of Toyota put it during the launch of the Woven City concept at the 2020 CES technology fair in Las Vegas: 'Today, a city is built around the motor car. In the future, we will build cities around people. People must become the focal point of every city.'

The idea of a car manufacturer investigating the potential impact of a city that is no longer built around the 'car is king' model is an inspirational one. By leaving its core in a focused and strategically targeted manner and by taking the future into its own hands, Toyota is paving the way that will allow it to become a partner in mobility for the world of tomorrow.

Strategy 4: **from individual companies to networks of companies**

Offering a wider range of services to customers is only scalable if companies collaborate. At the moment, company A competes with company B. In the future, the competition will be between ecosystem A and ecosystem B.

When Amazon launched its smart voice assistant Alexa, initially it was little more than a fun gadget. Suddenly, we were able to talk with a machine and its answers were logical and interesting. But right from the very start, Amazon was determined that Alexa would evolve from a neat gadget into a full-blown platform. Other companies were allowed to develop applications for Alexa and even to make use of Amazon's speech technology. By the end of 2019, more than 100 000 Alexa skills had been developed by Amazon partners.[52] Google has the same ambition with its Google Assistant. The company wants as many partners as possible to make use of Google technology to offer services to their customers. When I visited the CES trade fair in Las Vegas in January 2020, I was struck by the fact that almost every physical product on display bore a sticker with the words: 'Google and Alexa compatible'.

Of course, it is not only the large technology companies that are now working in partnerships and ecosystems. Since 1 January 2020, BMW and Daimler have integrated their mobility services in a new joint venture: Your Now. Within this new framework, they have already developed a number of interesting projects.

Free Now is the name of their joint taxi and ride-sharing services. This bundles together the previously autonomous brands of the two car manufacturing giants: mytaxi, Beat, Kapten and Hive. The starting capital for the service amounted to two billion euros and Free Now is expected to provide some 300 million journeys each year in eighteen European and South American countries.[53]

Similarly, Share Now is the new name for their car-sharing offer, which was previously marketed as Car2Go (Daimler) and DriveNow (BMW). Via this new combined service people can use cars at moments that are relevant for them.

It is clear that BMW and Daimler have joined forces in an effort to compete with companies like Uber, Lyft, DiDi and Grab. Together they have more impact than alone. As a result, there is now a battle for market share between the ecosystem of two traditional car manufacturers and the ecosystem of the new mobility tech-players.

Who will win? Time will tell. But one thing is certain: a 'partner in life' strategy always demands the expansion of your offer and the development of an ecosystem that helps to realise this objective is an important strategic move in your transformation process.

Grab

Grab was founded in 2012 and has its headquarters in Singapore. Initially, the company was a kind of South Asian version of Uber, with a focus on innovative taxi services. In the intervening years, Grab has evolved into a partner in life for many of its customers. It is a fine example of a company that has combined each of the four above-mentioned strategies to create a strong platform that now forms part of the daily lives of more than 600 million users.[54]

In its early years, Grab focused successfully on mobility. Right from the very start, it specialised in the provision of services. It did not sell cars. It sold movement from A to B. In 2018, Grab's success even forced its main rival, Uber, to leave the South-East Asian market.

It was also in 2018 that Grab decided to broaden its services to include food delivery, travel reservations, financial services and even the purchase of people's daily shopping. As a result, by the end of that year, the company's turnover had risen to one billion American dollars. Thanks to this expansion of its offer, Grab can now meet more or less all the everyday needs of its customers (food, mobility, money). In short, Grab provides people with a total solution. By leaving its core, the company has become a true partner in life.

Grab has been successful in this transformation thanks in part to its ability to create an ecosystem of partner companies. Many thousands of local traders can sell their products or food on Grab. Grab takes care of the promotion and the logistics, while the partners take care of the actual production of what is sold. Moreover, there are many aspects of the Grab platform that Grab did not develop itself. Instead, it opted for smart partnerships with companies like MasterCard, Toyota and Microsoft, seeing this as the best way to expand its offer in a quick and high-quality manner.

Strategy	Grab
From product to service	Mobility services were initially the basis of Grab's offer. Right from the very beginning, the company has offered solutions, not products.
From core service to total solution	Grab has assessed the daily concerns of consumers and responded to them successfully by offering solutions in the fields of mobility, food and money.
From focus on the core to the blending of industries	Grab was founded as an innovative taxi company but is now a logistical company that also provides financial services.
From individual companies to networks of companies	Grab works with a large network of partners. For the development of its services, it has entered into partnerships with companies like MasterCard, Microsoft and Toyota.

How can I start my 'partner in life' strategy?

Nowadays, people expect more than pure transactional perfection. Digital convenience has become the minimum norm. Becoming a partner in life allows you to save your customers' effort and even give them new energy. This is how you will set yourself apart from your competitors.

How can you start to implement this kind of strategy?
First, you need to formulate answers to the following questions:
- What are the frustrations in the daily life of the customer that are broadly linked to your sector?
- What costs your customer energy and what gives them energy?
- What questions does your customer ask you, for which you currently have no answer?
- What services does your customer want from you, for which you currently have no solution?

These questions will help you to gain deeper insight into the life journey of your customers. What are the frustrations and expectations in their lives that currently remain unsatisfied?

Once you have the answers to these questions, it is time to see which of the four above strategies offers the best prospects for implementing effective action.

- Which services can you offer to meet the needs of your customers' life journey?
- What wider service needs do your customers have and how can you adjust your service provision to satisfy those needs?
- Which cross-sector initiatives can you take to adjust your offer to the life journey of your customers?
- With whom can you collaborate or establish partnerships to make this possible?

Your answers to these questions will determine the direction of your strategy.

from customer journey to life journey

save the world

There is a sense of social responsibility in all of us!

During the spring of 2020, more than 3 billion people were confined to their homes as a result of the outbreak of COVID-19.[55] This made it possible to maintain hospital capacity and meant that we, the world population acting in unison, managed to save hundreds of thousands of lives. From time to time, we saw in news reports that not everyone was abiding by the quarantine rules, but the vast majority of people did their best to comply, no matter how difficult it was. This worldwide effort was a gesture of solidarity to protect the weakest members of society, the like of which had never previously been seen. For a few months we were no longer focused on *homo economicus*, but on *homo empathicus*. It was not only citizens who demonstrated this solidarity. Numerous companies also used their strengths in an effort to find solutions for the problems facing society at this difficult time. The luxury company LVMH stopped its production of exclusive perfumes and switched to disinfectant hand gels. Anheuser-Busch InBev quickly followed its example. Coca-Cola cancelled its advertising campaigns in the Philippines and instead invested its money in help for the most needy Philippine communities. Microsoft made its tool for virtual meetings – Teams – available free of charge. When it became clear that the unique snorkel masks of retailer Decathlon could be converted into ventilators, the company donated its entire stock to neighbouring hospitals. Hundreds of companies showed their best side during the corona crisis.

There is a sense of social responsibility in all of us, both companies and individuals. We want to help. It feels good to make a positive contribution towards society. Being part of a positive movement gives people a positive feeling and leads to greater solidarity. Moreover, many companies have felt the positive feedback that has resulted from their humanitarian actions during the lockdown. In the years ahead, having a sense of corporate social responsibility will only increase in importance. Customers will expect it and companies will draw energy from it.

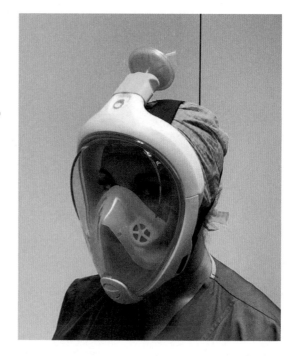

Marks & Spencer has had a sense of social responsibility from its very first day

Of course, the evolution that has led companies to make a positive contribution to society started a long time before COVID-19. Many companies have been doing this for decades – or even centuries! In 1894, Michael Marks and Tom Spencer founded Marks & Spencer. They opened their first small store in Leeds. Back in those days, most people were poor. Poverty was the world norm. For that reason, Marks & Spencer displayed all their products according to price. When

you entered their small shop, all the products in the first section were priced at just one penny. In other words, there was something that everyone could afford.

For its time, this approach was revolutionary and it became a huge success. By offering super-cheap products, Marks & Spencer provided a huge added value for society and, in particular, the less affluent members of the population. During those early years, the company even stopped selling more expensive products, preferring to concentrate its efforts on helping the poor and needy.

The M&S stores came to be known popularly as 'Penny Bazaars'. People were free to look around at their leisure, with no pressure to buy. Nobody had ever seen anything like it.

As time passed, M&S grew significantly. It later bought up a number of its rivals and even became a stock-listed company. During the Second World War, there were serious food shortages in Great Britain. Food had to be imported by sea but the supply lines were constantly disrupted by the actions of German submarines. As a result, rationing was introduced. M&S delivered food to people directly from its lorries. In many cities, it was only the M&S deliveries that kept the shops open. There was also a shortage of material for the making of clothes, so M&S designed a skirt that required less fabric but was still suitable for wearing at work.

> *By offering super-cheap products, Marks & Spencer provided a huge added value for the less affluent members of the population.*

The government adopted this same innovative design and had it mass produced for large sections of the population. Put simply, right from its very first day M&S has applied a philosophy of helping people in need. If there is a social problem in society, M&S wants to use its possibilities and strengths to help ameliorate the situation. During the recent corona crisis, the company supported British medical personnel and care workers. Twice a week, it provided tons of food to people working on the front line in the health sector. It also donated 4 000 pairs of pyjamas to hospitals for patients who no longer had contact with the outside world. More than a century after it was founded, the company is still doing what it can to try and make things better.

How to save the world?

I admit it. It sounds a trifle bombastic. 'How to save the world' is the name I have given to the top level of The Offer You Can't Refuse model. It certainly carries much more weight than 'ultimate convenience' and 'partner in life'. That being said, some people question whether it is properly the role of companies to try and save the world. Isn't that the task of governments? Or perhaps even the task of us all, through a greater sense of global solidarity? But companies?

I thought for a long time before naming this step 'save the world', but I am more convinced than ever that it is the right title. My choice has since been confirmed by the annual 'trust barometer' published by the American PR and marketing advice bureau Edelman. No fewer than 76 per cent of the population hope that CEOs will become the driving force behind positive change in the world. In short, people expect more from companies than from governments.[56]

There is no disputing that companies already have a huge impact on the world and on society. Moreover, that impact is felt in many different fields. Companies not only generate economic value, but also social value and societal happiness. The world is facing so many important challenges that companies are morally obliged to consider how they can make a positive contribution that will improve things for some of us, if not all of us. Has Marks & Spencer saved the world? No, but throughout its existence it has helped to make the lives of many poor families more liveable, thereby contributing towards a better society. Every entrepreneur, manager and company leader has that same responsibility: how can you use the strengths of your company to make the world a little bit safer, warmer, healthier and sunnier?

'Saving the world' will require companies to substantially change a lot of their past thinking. Many of the marketing techniques and hypes of recent decades will need major adjustment if the business world wants to be taken seriously when it talks about social responsibility.

1. **From purpose to problem-solving:** the concept of 'purpose' is very popular in marketing circles. Numerous studies have shown that companies with a strong purpose make bigger profits than others. In other words, the concept has proven its value. In theory. In practice, however, it does not always produce the desired results. A purpose is not always sufficiently differentiating, directing or action-oriented to make the difference. Many companies define a purpose because they 'must', but then proceed not to follow it. Many of their personnel will never even have heard of it. No, there is a need for a more pragmatic and action-focused approach that tackles society's problems in an ambitious and concrete manner.

2. **From authenticity to sense of responsibility:** during the past decade, 'authenticity' has been one of the most frequently heard marketing buzzwords. But it suffers from the same shortcomings as 'purpose'. Many companies want to be authentic because that is what they are supposed to be, but in practice they don't really mean it. The problem with words like 'purpose' and 'authenticity' is that they are so vague as to be almost meaningless. In marketing and leadership circles there is a need to define and implement concepts more clearly. It is not what we say that should make the difference, but what we do. It is time to walk the talk. Today's consumers expect that companies will make the right choices for their customers, their employees and the planet. A company that in future makes these right choices and communicates them transparently will, by definition, be an authentic company, but it will be able to implement those choices more concretely if it takes a sense of social responsibility as its starting point.

3. **From shareholder value to shared value:** 'shared value' was first described by Michael Porter in the *Harvard Business Review* in October 2011. The philosophy behind the concept is simple: to be successful, companies need to undertake projects that create both economic and social value. It is necessary to invent a new form of capitalism, in which companies can still make money and grow, but also have an obligation to generate benefits for society and the world.

4. **From a world with trade-offs to a world without trade-offs:** today, customers often need to make a choice: privacy or convenience, cheap products or ethically correct products, doing good for the planet or protecting our personal freedoms in terms of diet, travel, etc. In the future, companies will need to find solutions that do not require consumers to make choices that often leave them feeling guilty.

Marketing 2010-2020	'Save the world' strategy 2020-2030
Purpose thinking	What problems will you solve?
Authenticity	Sense of responsibility
Shareholder value	Shared value
A world full with trade-offs	A world without trade-offs

The New Year's letter from the CEO of BlackRock

Larry Fink is the CEO of Black-Rock, one of the largest asset management companies on the planet. Each year, at the start of January, he writes a letter addressed to the CEOs of the world, in which he appeals to them to invest the money at their disposal in a responsible manner. Companies like Black-Rock do not invest their own money. Instead, they administer the billions entrusted to them by banks and other investors. They have won the trust of countless companies and private individuals to deal with their money in a correct and socially acceptable way. Their main aim is, of course, to make profitable investments, but they always try to look further than straightforward financial return.

In his New Year's letter for 2020, Fink appealed in particular to his fellow CEOs' sense of social responsibility. In particular, he zoomed in on the risks faced by the climate. 'Climate risk is an investment risk,' he explained. 'As an investor, it is important to opt for companies that in turn invest in a better climate. The climate problem is more actual than ever before and companies that actively attempt to solve the problem will have more chance of financial success in the years ahead.'

Larry Fink also called on all companies, both public and private, to create greater societal added value. 'Society is looking increasingly to companies to solve social and economic problems,' he concludes. As a result, he criticised the short-term thinking of many asset managers, encouraging them instead to invest in companies with a 'purpose': in other words, companies prepared to play a leading role in social change.

The weakness of a purpose

The fact that a powerful CEO like Larry Fink calls on investors to focus on companies with a 'purpose' sends out a strong and positive signal. Having said that (and as we have already mentioned), the purpose movement in the marketing world has its limitations. In recent decades, marketeers have talked and brainstormed for countless hours about their purpose. In your company as well, I bet. Fink's plea underlines the increasing importance that thinking about and acting to create societal value will have in the coming decades. Even so, the situation continues to be a bit hazy

Do you know what the problem is? There is no uniform definition of what the 'purpose' concept is supposed to be. Some company leaders define purpose as creating social added value. Others talk in terms of the problems their company solves for their customers. Yet others see purpose as the company's raison d'être, the reason for which it was founded.

Within the 'purpose' discussion, reference is most frequently made to Simon Sinek and his world-famous book *Start with why*. In this book he describes the 'golden circle' concept. Companies need to ask themselves three key questions.

- What do we do?
- How do we do it?
- Why do we do it?

Most organisations do indeed begin with the 'what'. Many company presentations start with statements like: 'We are a company that sells unique lawnmowers.' Only later will they move on to the 'how'. 'Our lawnmowers are fitted with state-of-the-art AI, allowing them to mow your lawn automatically and with a perfect finish.' But that is where most of the presentations stop. Occasionally, someone will add a 'why'. 'We want to create more free time for families, so that they can enjoy their perfectly mown lawn.' Simon Sinek's theory teaches us that we should always use the 'why' and not the 'what' as the starting point for a company's strategy and communication. It is a very simple but unbelievably powerful model, and one which has conquered the world.

There is, however, a snake in the grass. The most 'start with why' and 'purpose' discussions end with a declaration with which everyone in the company is in agreement, but which has no differentiating effect whatsoever. I have the pleasure of working for many major players in important industries, so that I regularly get to see what goes on behind the scenes. I have lost count of the number of 'start with why' and 'purpose' slides I have been forced to sit through and in one sense this is positive – were it not for the fact that in my eyes the huge majority of them say nothing about what makes the company so special and so different from its competitors.

Here is an example of the purpose of a major bank: 'Empowering people to stay a step ahead in life and in business.' And here is the purpose of another bank in the same market: 'Banking better, for generations to come.' The words are different, so perhaps you could speak of two different purposes, but in essence the core of what they say is exactly the same. Both these banks want to give their customers (companies, individuals, the children of their customers) a better future. This is obviously a valuable and worthwhile intention, but it is hardly differentiating. I sometimes ask myself how many customers could accurately describe the purpose of their bank. Very few, I suspect. Purposes of this kind are too lacking in distinctiveness and direction to generate action that can make the difference. Of course, you can make the same analysis in dozens of other sectors. The purpose of one leading company in the telecom sector declares: 'We want to use technology to make the lives of individuals and companies easier, faster and more pleasant.' What on earth is that supposed to mean?

A purpose can be effective, but only if it allows you to distinguish yourself and gives a clear direction to your strategy, resulting in concrete actions and behaviour. Sadly, in my experience the purpose of most companies fails to meet these criteria.

What societal problems will your company solve?

In many cases, a purpose is too woolly and, as a result, misses real impact. A good alternative is to think in concrete terms about a societal problem that you can (help to) solve. During the corona crisis, we have seen many good examples of this. Companies identified specific needs in society and used their strengths to satisfy those needs, wholly or in part. These were worthwhile actions in the short term that had immediate positive effects. For many companies this also yielded a lot of positive PR, making both staff and customers proud to be associated with the company name.

The actions during the corona crisis were mainly of a temporary nature. The finest examples were those where companies were able to make an important contribution based on their own strengths. At one point, Lego was producing 13 000 face masks per day.[57] The company reconfigurated its machines, so that they were able to help people in the care sector in a concrete way. A nice extra touch was that the masks looked exactly like the plexiglas in the helmets on the miniature Lego figures that children around the world play with every day. And once the Lego masks arrived in hospitals, the medical staff still had to clip them together, providing them with a genuine Lego experience! How cool is that!

The willingness of companies and individuals to help during the corona crisis was heart-warming. The solving of societal problems gave a boost to people's energy and sense of solidarity.

The trick will be to maintain this same altruistic mindset in the years to come, once the crisis has passed. I am convinced that many companies will seize the opportunity offered by this moment to think more deeply about their societal impact, first and foremost because it is the right thing to do, but also because it will help them to differentiate themselves from their competitors. As a company, you don't need to wait for the next world crisis before you start to consider what you can do to improve society. The crucial question is to decide which social problems the strengths of your company are best suited to help solve.

The example of Verstraete IML (chapter 2) is an excellent case in point, in which the plastics manufacturer set out in a very concrete way to address the problems of recycling, reuse and compostability relating to its main product. Its societal objective is to eliminate 'virgin plastic' – plastic that is completely new and used for the first time – from the world.

The strength of tackling concrete problems in a concrete way is that it brings clarity. It is not an everlasting mission; it is a specific challenge. Every employee and every customer will know exactly what problem you are trying to solve, which also makes your communication about objectives clear and transparent. Likewise, measurability will be similarly straightforward. By making the right choices, the world will be able to follow the extent to which you are getting closer and closer to your goal.

Certain aspects of the 'purpose' philosophy can still be very useful when formulating your societal objective. Just like a purpose, a societal objective makes crystal-clear exactly what course you intend to steer and what things in society truly matter to you.

> *The willingness of companies and individuals to help during the corona crisis was heart-warming. The solving of societal problems gave a boost to people's energy and sense of solidarity. The trick will be to maintain this same altruistic mindset in the years to come, once the crisis has passed.*

Purpose	Societal objective
Differences	**Differences**
An everlasting mission, with no fixed end in sight	Tackling a concrete problem, with a clear end point
Low measurability	High measurability
Lack of clarity about the intermediate steps leading towards the purpose	Possibility to communicate about concrete steps on the way to solving the problem
Similarities	**Similarities**
Gives direction to the strategy and the course to be followed	Gives direction to the strategy and to the course to be followed
Goes further than the creation of economic value	Goes further than the creation of economic value
Increases pride and recognisability with both personnel and customers	Increases pride and recognisability with both personnel and customers

From authenticity to a sense of responsibility

As I wrote a few paragraphs ago, 'authenticity' was one of the marketing buzzwords in recent decades. Consumers want genuine brands and not brands that do no more than spread over-enthusiastic messages via glossy adverts and social media. Felicitas Morhart, a Swiss marketing professor, published one of the most extensive research studies on this subject in the *Journal of Consumer Psychology*.[58] She questioned 2 600 American and European consumers to get a deeper insight into the abstract concept of authenticity. The results of the study showed that consumers regard a brand as authentic if it can satisfy the following criteria. (1) Continuity: brands that have been able to withstand the test of time and exude stability. (2) Integrity: a company that remains true to its own core values, even in difficult times. (3) Credibility: a company that always keeps its promises. (4) Symbolism: a brand that serves as a symbol for a life value that is important to many consumers in their own daily lives.

If I study these results, my conclusion is that authenticity revolves primarily around the ability to positively develop both brand and reputation. It is a long-term investment. The hype surrounding authenticity has often led marketing managers to think – incorrectly – that it was enough to talk about the origin and heritage of the brand.

Developing the value of the brand over the long term continues to be of supreme importance. Recent crises have shown that companies that invest heavily in the long-term strengthening of their brand display greater resilience during the recovery process. In other words, the four dimension of Felicitas Morhort's research continue to be important over a period of decades, not just months or years.

In the future, however, the authenticity hype will move more and more in the direction of a sense of responsibility. This will be the new buzzphrase. More than half of all consumers indicate that they only want to buy from companies that make the right choices for customers, employees and society as a whole.[59] And the younger the target group, the more important this social aspect will become.

Twitter versus Facebook

Every company influences the world, but the impact of a company like Facebook is immense. A platform used every day by billions of people, both to communicate and to access information, can have an influence on society that the world has never previously seen.

Mark Zuckerberg and his team have a huge responsibility to deal with this potential influence in a correct manner. With this in mind, Facebook invests millions of dollars to combat fake news, hate messages and digital bullying. Smart algorithms and thousands of human employees study the gigantic amounts of content in an effort to keep the platform as 'pure' as possible. Even so, Facebook has not been able to restore public confidence in its credibility. Only 40 per cent of Americans trust the company. By comparison, 65 per cent trust the government and 72 per cent trust Amazon.[60]

The decline in public confidence in Facebook began when it became known that Cambridge Analytica had misused available Facebook data to influence the results of the American presidential election in 2016. The same company had also played a similarly dubious role in influencing the outcome of the Brexit referendum.

At that moment, offline society was confronted more starkly than ever before with the imperfections of the online digital society. During this period, the dark side of digital was seldom more tangible. And in spite of the huge remedial efforts made by the Facebook group, people still view the platform with suspicion.

One of the main societal worries about Facebook is the perceived (negative) impact on the democratic process. In many countries there are a number of (primarily non-democratic) groups that understand how to make best use of Facebook. Facebook has the ability to deal with this problem, if it wants to. The day the company decides that political messages can only be disseminated organically and not via paying promotions will be the day when it takes its first serious step in the battle against fake news.

But when Facebook's activities were investigated by the American Senate, Mark Zuckerberg refused to promise that he would tackle this problem. He referred constantly to 'the freedom of the individual' and 'the ability of mankind' to decide for itself whether a message was democratic or not. However, in reality it is very difficult to know which messages on Facebook are credible and which ones are fake news. Facebook would be sending out a strong signal if it took a more responsible position on this matter and had the courage to ban politically coloured advertising.

Critics say that Mark Zuckerberg refuses to take this position because of the money. But that is not true. Political advertising only generates 0.5 per cent of Facebook's massive annual turnover, measured in billions.[61] So it is not about the money. It is about the personal conviction of the leader of the most influential communication platform ever.

It could only do the company good were it to show in this matter the sense of responsibility the world expects. Moreover, it is not a question of banning political messages (freedom of speech would remain), but of banning the targeted spreading of such messages on a large scale via extra budget.

Perhaps you are thinking: 'That kind of company will never be prepared to take that kind of step.' But that is precisely the step that has been taken by Facebook's great rival, Twitter. Jack Dorsey, the CEO and founder of Twitter, has decided that the financial promotion of political messages will no longer be allowed on the platform. Politicians and other people will certainly still be allowed to share their opinions about politics; after all, sharing opinions is what people like to do on Twitter. But the pushing of certain messages will henceforth be forbidden. With this bold decision, Twitter is showing its willingness to take responsibility. The company has chosen the approach that is best for the world, even if it costs it money.

I am not naive. I know that fake news will always continue to exist, even if Facebook opts to follow Twitter's example. Fake news plays on people's emotions, and mostly on the emotion of fear. As a result, some messages still spread virally, even though the message has little or no basis in truth.

Fortunately, this is one area where Facebook is taking positive steps. It now employs thousands of people to better assess the credibility of messages: true or fake? But before these efforts can result in a renewed increase in consumer trust, a number of further courageous decisions, each reflecting a greater sense of responsibility, will need to be taken.

How to set your products on fire – safely

None of this means that brands need to be colourless. Brands and companies can and should have an opinion. And it can be an opinion that not everyone agrees with. In fact, disagreement is inherent in the very idea of having an opinion. Consequently, if you have an opinion, you have to accept that not everyone is going to like it or follow it.

In some cases, taking your responsibility means having the courage to express your opinion: in support of others; in support of important social issues; or even to undermine the opinions of others that you believe to be wrong. When you do this as a company, you must be able to mentally reconcile yourself to the knowledge that some people – and therefore some consumers – will not be happy.

Even so, brand activism – standing on the barricades – is a potential strategy to make the difference in today's world. Modern companies make the difference not only with their products, but also with their voice.

In September 2018, Nike, one of the biggest sponsors of the American National Football League, made Colin Kaepernick the face of a major campaign. Colin Kaepernick was a quarterback for the San Francisco 49ers American football team. He was the first American football player to 'take the knee' rather than to remain standing during the American national anthem, as a silent protest against police violence, racism and discrimination. Other footballers followed his example, but Kaepernick paid a heavy price for his pioneering role. After he began his protest action in 2016, no other team was willing to offer him a contract.

It was this that inspired Nike in 2018 to launch a campaign in which Kaepernick and his principled stand were central. The popular brand used a close-up of the footballer's face with the text: 'Believe in something. Even if it means sacrificing everything.' In this way, Nike showed that the company stood 100 per cent behind Kaepernick's silent and respectful demonstration of his opinion. In other words, it showed that it wanted a world without discrimination, racism and hate.

Many thousands of people found this the best Nike message ever. Fans and supporters enthusiastically shared the message with as many people as they could. But not everyone in the United States felt the same way. The day after the campaign launch many people ostentatiously threw their Nike trainers in the dustbin. Social media were overwhelmed with hate messages directed at the company. Some even began the public burning of Nike products.

You can imagine how in these circumstances some marketing managers would have crawled away into a corner to hide. But not at Nike. When people started burning their shoes, they immediately launched a second campaign: 'How to burn our products – safely.' The company even published its own 'burning guide' online.

Nike supporters were delighted with this subtle new form of communication. For them, this amusing, even sarcastic extra message was confirmation that the brand was not having second thoughts about its opinion. It had opted to back the athlete and his mission and it stood by that commitment – and no amount of burnings and no number of hate mails was going to change that. As Phil Knight, the founder of Nike, once said: 'It doesn't matter how many people hate the brand, as long as enough people love it.'

A year after the bitter emotions surrounding this campaign first broke, it became clear that the furore had done Nike no harm at all: the company gained 163 million dollars in earned media, its brand value increased by 8 billion dollars and sales were up by 31 per cent.[62]

When I talk to managers about this case, they often say: 'Yes, but that was Nike. They can get away with that. We can't.' But this is a wrong conclusion. Nike is Nike because the company dares to stick its neck out, time after time. It dares to have an opinion. It takes its responsibility and does what it believes is positive for the world. Helping to eliminate racism is undeniably positive. The only negative about it is the sad conclusion that such a noble purpose can still generate such a hateful reaction from so many people.

Too many organisations are afraid of doing the right thing. Rather than standing centre stage, they prefer the anonymity of a place in the wings. They feel safer in the shadows. This way, things will never change. Improving society starts with having an opinion and having the courage to stand up for it. Even when the going gets tough, even when your products are quite literally going up in smoke. That is the only way to make the world a better place.

The concept of shared value

When Michael Porter published his paper *Creating shared value* in the *Harvard Business Review* in 2011, he said: 'Of all the papers, I have every written, this is the one that I am most enthusiastic about.' In his opinion, his 'shared value' article would herald the start of a new phase of capitalism.

His argument is that (1) the world is facing many challenges and that (2) the companies have the means and the resources to solve these challenges. In this new phase of capitalism, companies, according to Porter, will generate both economic and societal value, by making use of the strengths of their organisations to make a positive difference in the world.

MasterCard is a strong and successful player in the financial world. In 2019, the company had a turnover of 17.2 billion American dollars, a growth of 40 per cent in comparison with 2016.[63]

Via their Centre for Inclusive Growth, MasterCard has been engaged for a number of years in a project to help people who have no access to financial services. The aim was to provide these services to 500 million people worldwide during the period 2016 to 2020. At the start of the project's final year, MasterCard still has 100 million people to reach. In other words, the company has already given 400 million people better and safer financial assistance.

In 2018, MasterCard invested 20 per cent (500 million dollars) of the fiscal benefits it enjoyed as a result of tax reform in Europe and the United States in the fund it had set up for this purpose. That is what shared value means. This project has already created social value for half a billion people and in the long run it will provide MasterCard with a bigger market that will allow the company to create economic value as well. It is an 'and...and' story.

There is one main difference between the idea of shared value and current thinking relating to Corporate Social Responsibility or CSR. CSR, as currently practised by most companies, is a defensive strategy. It often involves the support of worthwhile projects, but these projects tend to remain on the sidelines. As such, CSR is seldom part of the company's core. In fact, it often amounts to little more than donating money to good causes. Don't misunderstand me. There is nothing wrong in supporting good causes. But unless this support is framed within a wider philosophy and a greater whole, it will not contribute to the company's economic value. In fact, if you want to be super-critical, it actually results in a reduction in shareholder value.

Shared value goes further than CSR. Shared value is about a general mindset, which involves the entire company working together to achieve societal value and, at the same time, economic value.

Three strategies for applying the shared value philosophy

How can you identify the problem you want to solve? The best way is to look back through the history of your company. Why was the company founded in the first place? Right from its earliest beginnings, what contribution has it made to society? Once you have found the societal problem you wish to tackle, the challenge is to find the best way to do something positive about it. In his *HBR* article, Michael Porter suggested three strategies for applying the shared value concept.

New products and markets

The first strategy is based on the development of new products and the discovery of new markets. For example, the SodaStream company has helped to reduce the pollution caused by plastic bottles, thanks to its products that make it possible to transform ordinary tap water into delicious sparkling water. A family with SodaStream uses hundreds fewer plastic bottles than a family without SodaStream. In short, SodaStream has exploited a new product and a new market to generate societal added value.

Transformation of the value chain

The second strategy requires the complete transformation of the value chain. A good example of this strategy is Levi's and its Water-Less premium brand. The entire production and life cycle of a standard pair of jeans uses 3 000 litres of water. Some 49 per cent of this water is necessary for the production of the fabric, with a further 6 per cent needed during the production process. The remaining 45 per cent is used by the consumer when washing the jeans. However, Water-Less jeans currently make use of 28 per cent less water, and this figure is likely to increase to 96 per cent by the end of 2020.

This is a good, but the biggest use of water is not a part of Levi's own production process-es to make the jeans. For this reason, the company is now collaborating with the cotton industry to find ways of producing the basic jeans fabric with less water. It is also investi-gating the use of other fabrics that require less washing. In this way, Levi's is attempting to transform its entire value chain.

Redesigning the ecosystem

The third strategy is the most far-reaching: the complete redesign of the ecosystem in which the company operates. If Nestlé wants to start up a new dairy industry in a new country, it needs a good road infrastructure and good milk production. But in many coun-tries the standard of both requirements is too low to guarantee the quality for which Nestlé stands. The easiest solution would simply be to import milk into the new country, but as a matter of policy Nestlé wishes to encourage and make use of local producers.
To make this possible, the company changes the entire ecosystem of the new market. It builds the roads it needs to get the milk faster to its factories, as well as paying farmers a higher price and offering them low-interest loans, so that they can invest in better stables for their livestock. As a result, the children of these families no longer need to help as much on the farm and can go to school more often. Nestlé also organises medical support by working together with local vets.
All these investments ensure a better quality of milk for Nestlé, but at the same time this 'total' approach, initiated by a private company, improves many aspects of life in the host countries: the farmers, the children of the farmers, the logistical infrastructure, food safe-ty, etc. This makes it possible for the company to offer good products – value for Nestlé – and to raise the standard of living for an entire community – value for society.

The end of the trade-off

The world is full of trade-offs. If we opt for an advantage, we usually have to accept that there is a compensatory disadvantage somewhere down the line. Not necessarily for ourselves, but often for others or for society as a whole. Nowadays, we are constantly forced to make choices. For example, we might have to choose between flying to South America for our holidays or doing what is right for the climate. Flying to South America will give us an unforgettable experience, but we know that air travel damages the ozone layer. Instead of going to South America, we could pick a destination closer to home that is reachable by train, but then we would have to miss out on the holiday of a lifetime. Even much smaller, everyday decisions often involve a trade-off. You want to take lots of clothes with you on holiday, but this will make your suitcase heavier. Once again, this is bad for the environment, not to mention the backs of the baggage handlers at the airport.

In the coming decade, we will see an evolution that will reduce the number of trade-offs or perhaps even make some of them disappear altogether. This is a trend you can already see with some of the smaller trade-offs. Delta Air Lines is currently testing exoskeletons for its baggage personnel. An exoskeleton is a robot suit that you wear like a backpack, but one that gives you robot-like strength. Thanks to these suits, the handlers can work with heavier luggage without any negative effects on their health.
When I was at the CES at the start of 2020, I was able to try one of these Delta Air Lines robot suits. They put a case weighing 30 kilograms in front of me. I could hardly lift it until the exoskeleton suit was activated. Then I could lift it effortlessly. It felt as though I was lifting a sheet of paper! Very impressive.

We want our suitcases on the plane

Heavy suitcases are bad for the health of employees

Another example of a trade-off is firework displays. Most people (me included) like to see fireworks, preferably accompanied by some great music. As a Disney fan, finishing off a day in the Magic Kingdom by watching some fantastic pyrotechnics to the accompaniment of some equally fantastic Disney songs is my idea of heaven.

Unfortunately, animals are not such big fans of fireworks. Horses, cows and dogs are all frightened by the succession of loud bangs and can sometimes be aggressive as a result. We humans love the spectacle, but the animals hate it: a classic trade-off.

However, there is a strong likelihood that by 2030 there will be far fewer traditional firework displays. Many of them will be replaced by drone shows. Thousands of light-emitting drones will offer us a new kind of sound and light experience. These small drones come in all shapes and sizes and can be used in combination to create figures that can tell a story, all to the accompaniment of appropriate music. Okay, it is not exactly the same as a firework show, as true fireworks lovers will be quick to point out, but it is an interesting and viable alternative that will save a lot of animal suffering. Drone shows clearly have the potential to eliminate this trade-off. The aim – as is the case for the elimination of all trade-offs – is to allow people to enjoy products and services without feeling guilty.

Like the drones, the four general purpose technologies – AI, 5G, quantum computing and robotics – have the potential to eliminate many of today's trade-offs. For instance, they already allow us to better organise virtual meetings, which in due course will structurally reduce the amount of business travel, with a positive impact on the climate as a result. Another very topical example? People working in the health sector are responsible for caring for sick people. As the corona crisis has shown, this sometimes puts them in danger, resulting in a trade-off between caring for the patient and caring for the carer. In the future, AI-operated robots will be able to carry out many of the tasks currently

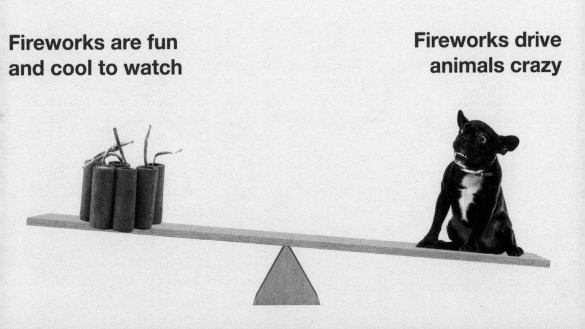

Fireworks are fun and cool to watch

Fireworks drive animals crazy

performed by human doctors and nurses. Similarly, 5G will make it possible for patients to be more effectively examined at distance. In fact, it will even become possible to perform operations at distance, as I described in an earlier chapter. The human surgeon will follow the operation at location A, while the robot carries out his commands at location B. In this way, the new technologies will make it feasible to provide top-quality medical care, while simultaneously decreasing the risk to medical personnel.

Impossible Foods, Beyond Meat, Greenway Foods and many others

One of the most important of the current trade-offs is the balance between what we like to eat and its impact on the planet. I am not a vegetarian. I like to eat vegetarian meals, but I also like to eat meat, even though I know that (too much) meat is bad for my health and for the environment. But I still like to eat it and so occasionally I buy a nice piece of steak from the excellent butcher's shop in our neighbourhood. Is it possible to do something about this trade-off in the future?

Yes, it is. In fact, the first steps are already being taken. Recent years have seen the strong growth of companies like Impossible Foods, Beyond Meat, the Belgian Greenway Foods and the Dutch Vegetarische Slager (Vegetarian Butcher). Vegetarian meat is making its appearance everywhere in the world.

Vegetarian meat does not come from animals, but is made in a laboratory. The products of the companies I have just mentioned are not intended exclusively or even primarily for the vegetarian customer group. They are intended to give meat-eaters a viable alternative that is at least as tasty. They make vegetable-based products that reproduce the flavour, smell, texture and juiciness of animal meat. In the long term, the aim is to make it impossible to tell the difference between vegetarian substitutes and the real thing.

A few years ago, I took a group of entrepreneurs to Silicon Valley for our company nexxworks. When the group asked me on Wednesday: 'Steven, what are we having for lunch today?', I replied with a grin: 'American burgers'. Most of my companions were immediately enthusiastic! When lunchtime came, we tucked into the burger, each of which had a little flag bearing the Impossible Foods logo. At that time, almost no-one had heard of Impossible Foods.

I saw how everyone removed the little flag and took their first big bite of the burger. There were smiles all round. Half way through the meal, I stood up and asked: 'Well, ladies and gentlemen, what do you think of your vegetarian burger?' Everything went quiet in the room. No-one had realised that they were eating a burger that was not made of real meat. Impossible Foods burgers even have juice, which is exactly like the juice that comes out of a medium cooked burger.

When everyone was curious to hear more, I told them the story of Impossible Foods and their ambition to remove animals from the food chain, without depriving meat-eaters of the flavours they love so much. When I had finished, I saw that the majority of those present were pleasantly surprised by the quality of the vegetarian meat. It was only the meat extremists who began to dissect their burger to see what it was made of, but even they could find no difference. And if you don't know that they are vegetable products, you can't taste the difference, either.

When we had a spell of fine weather in Belgium at the end of April this year, one evening I got out the barbecue and grilled some burgers from Greenway Foods. I didn't tell the kids that these were a new kind of vegetable-based burger until after they had gobbled them down and asked for more! Afterwards, they found it 'cool' that they had just eaten their first 'vegan' burger.

During taste tests with culinary experts, the 'meatball' of the Dutch Vegetarische Slager was chosen as the third best meatball in the Netherlands. The jury was not aware in advance that this was a non-meat meatball, and most were surprised when told at the end of the test.

When blind tests were carried out with Dutch consumers by the Albert Heijn supermarket chain, the chicken baps with satay sauce by Vegetarische Slager emerged as the best. As a result, this vegetable-based alternative is now the standard product in the Albert Heijn range. In other words, the quality of this kind of product is already very good and can only get better. We are still at the very beginning of the process. Imagine what they will taste like in 2025 or 2030!

Market penetration is increasing dramatically. Beyond Meat now works with McDonald's and Impossible Foods with Burger King. The entire alternative product range is now available in many supermarkets. Vegetarian meat is many times better for the environment and for our health. If the flavour and the replication of the meat experience continue to evolve in the right direction, there is every reason to suppose that this is one important trade-off that will disappear in the not too distant future.

Three implementation guidelines for your 'save the world' strategy

Deciding which societal problem you wish to tackle and accepting your responsibility are the first steps you need to take to 'save the world'. Of course, no company, not even the biggest and most powerful, is capable of saving the world on its own. No, 'save the world' is all about the philosophy and the intention to help solve a particular societal problem through concrete action. During this journey to 'save the world', there are a number of important elements you need to bear in mind. I have bundled these elements into three broad guidelines, which will help you to roll out your strategy successfully.

Implementation guideline 1: convince your customers – SHIFT them!
As a company, you are no doubt super-enthusiastic about your plan to make the world a better place and your personnel probably share that enthusiasm. But to make a real impact it is your customers that you need to enthuse. Are they on board? Will they be willing to change their pattern of consumption? Information campaigns to make people more aware of the impact of their choices can help, but are not enough on their own. Something more is needed.

In the *Journal of Marketing*, researchers Katherine White, Rishad Habib and David Hardisty published an excellent paper with equally excellent advice about the best way to get your customers on board. Their study focused specifically on the need to convince consumers to make more sustainable choices in their purchasing behaviour and they amalgamated their conclusions in the acronym SHIFT. They argue that it is possible to shift the behaviour of your customers by:

- **Social influence:** others have a huge influence on our behaviour. Communication that emphasises how many people are already displaying a new type of behaviour has a much greater impact than a theoretical awareness campaign. At a certain moment, a group of people will emerge with new behaviour of which they are proud. These people exude self-confidence, which is picked up by others, who then start to imitate the same new behaviour. Make sure that your customers can share their new behaviour with others. Once this behaviour is made visible, its adoption will increase. The 'show-off' factor plays an important role in this.

- **Habit formation:** adopting new behaviour involves more than a one-off action; it is about learning new habits. To deal with the climate problem, for example, many people need to permanently change their behaviour in matters such as diet, transport, energy, shopping, recycling, etc. We need to 'unlearn' bad habits and replace them with new ones. New habits can be encouraged in various ways. Government fines are one possibility, but this is a negative way to change behaviour, which, as a result, often fails to have the desired long-term result. Repression seldom works. People need to be helped to change their behaviour. Most of us are of good will and most of us have positive intentions towards, say, the climate. Many people want to make purchases that are better for the environment and to use public transport more, but it is difficult because these alternatives are often too complex or more time-consuming.

    If you want customers to learn new behaviour, ease of use is one of your most important weapons. Behavioural psychologist Dan Ariely is convinced that the only way to succeed is to make the new behaviour easier for your customers than the old.

    This confirms my conclusion in the second chapter: The Offer You Can't Refuse model can only work if it is implemented in full from the bottom up. If you can make things easy for customers, then – and only then – will they be willing to help you to save the world.

- **Individual self:** people want to have a positive self-image. Changing your own behaviour in ways that have a positive impact on society has a motivating effect. Once it is clear that your previous behaviour had a negative impact, the contrast with your new positive behaviour gives a real boost to your self-esteem.

    But it is not simply our own improved self-image that results in us changing our behaviour. Personal advantage can also be a powerful influence. If new behaviour results in financial gain for consumers, they will be more easily inclined to adopt that behaviour. This dimension was clear, for example, in the action of Tesco that I mentioned earlier, whereby the supermarket chain ensures that healthy products are cheaper than unhealthy ones in every product category.

- **Feelings and cognition:** communication designed to encourage changes of behaviour often makes use of negative emotions, such as fear, guilt and sadness. When you are using emotions of this kind, it is important to ensure that your communication is properly nuanced. If there is not enough fear, people will not be inclined to change; if there is too much fear, they will feel that they have no control over the situation, so that once again they will not be motivated to change.

    Researchers White, Habib and Hardisty concluded that focusing on positive emotions in communication can lead to deeper and more permanent changes of behaviour. For example, it was by emphasising pleasure, pride and the ability to help the world that many people have been convinced to stop consuming water in plastic bottles at home. And just look at the pride on the faces of the increasing number of electric car owners as they drive past you on the street! They are unashamedly proud of the contribution they are making.

During an interview for the nexxworks blog,[64] Costas Markides, a professor of strategy and entrepreneurship at the London Business School, explained about research that had recently been carried out among patients with a serious heart condition. One group were encouraged to change their behaviour with a message that essentially said: 'If you don't want to die, you need to go on a diet and exercise more.' The message for a second group had a different emphasis: 'Do you want to be able to play with your grandkids, go for walks in the woods and enjoy fantastic holidays after your operation? If so, drink less alcohol, eat less fat and do something about your fitness.' The results showed that after six months the majority of the first group had reverted to their old habits. The number of backsliders amongst the second group, which had received a more positive message, was significantly less.

- **Tangibility:** the biggest problem with changes of behaviour that are intended to save the world is that the results of these changes are seldom tangible. This can negatively affect commitment to the new behaviour. Visible results have the opposite effect. During the great corona lockdown, everyone was able to see the benefits of self-isolation in the gradually improving daily statistics for deaths and hospital admissions. As a result, people were more willing to abide by the strict regulations. Helping to achieve an objective with tangible results is a powerful motivator to persist with new behaviour. For this reason, the communication plan for your company's 'save the world' strategy must have clear and objectifiable intermediary objectives. Make your plan concrete and tangible, so that people are encouraged to change their behaviour – permanently.

Implementation guideline 2: perception versus reality

Some companies are expert at formulating brilliant strategic documents. With fine words and pretty pictures they explain to the world how they will contribute towards a better climate for us all. But if you then look at the facts, you will often find a huge gulf between what they say and what they do. At the opposite end of the spectrum, there are companies that are more modest about their contribution, but nevertheless achieve excellent results – although almost nobody knows about it ...

Instinctively, we have more sympathy for the second type of company. A quiet and effective company is better, we think, than a boastful company that fails to keep its promises. Of course, I agree. But from a strategic perspective, neither of these situations is ideal. What we need is a combination of the two.

If you want to 'save the world', you cannot do it alone: it is important to get a movement started. You need the support of your staff, your customers and sometimes even your competitors. And to do that, it is important to let people know what you are doing – and then do it! In other words, it is important to have a credible 'save the world' strategy, but you also need to announce it to the market in a smart way. The PR and marketing relating to your positive contribution are just as important for your long-term success as the positive contribution itself.

It is important to get a movement started. You need the support of your staff, your customers and sometimes even your competitors.

Implementation guideline 3: the curse of perfection

The sports brand Patagonia is well known for its desire to make the world a better place. It does a great deal to try and achieve this ambition and communicates about it brilliantly. One of the company's most striking measures is the self-imposition of an eco-tax of one per cent of its turnover. This money is then invested in projects to improve the environment. In addition, Patagonia has also opted to use brand activism. With a loud voice, it supports various projects in which it believes. For example, this activism helps young people to work against the extraction of oil by fracking in the United States, but the company has also had the courage to sue President Trump personally for what it sees as his failure to sufficiently protect the environment. Patagonia has long been known as a champion for a better climate and a better world.

Even so, the Patagonia website proclaims: 'We are not perfect.' And if you look deeply and super-critically at Patagonia, you will indeed find things that are not 100 per cent good for the environment. So they are not perfect – but they do have an overall positive impact.

Too many companies are frightened by the curse of perfection. Sometimes someone will have a brilliant idea to improve the world, but the company hesitates to implement it, because it is not yet fully in line with its previously announced 'save the world' ambitions. Of course, it is important to strive for perfection as far as is reasonably possible, but if you plan to wait for perfection before starting a movement to improve things, you will be waiting an awfully long time. You will never achieve perfection. No-one ever does. But if your company takes an active role in the solving of problems, there is a good chance that you will be able to stand out from the crowd. This means that you will inevitably come under close scrutiny by both the media and the public, including your customers. And

they will almost certainly find something that is not 100 per cent perfect. You need to be ready for this moment, by preparing arguments which show that, in spite of your imperfections, you are generally moving in the right direction.

In the Netherlands, the Tony's Chocolonely chocolate brand is very popular. Without actively advertising, the brand has captured the biggest share of the Dutch chocolate market. I regard this as a remarkable achievement. The brand was launched in 2005. At that time, it needed to compete with a number of other strong chocolate brands. Even so, in just 15 years it has become the largest player in the Dutch marketplace.

The basis for this success is Tony's Chocolonely's unique positioning. It is the brand's claim that it sells 100 per cent slave-free chocolate. Many of the traditional chocolate brands buy cacao from farms where child labour is still practised. Tony's Chocolonely buys its cacao beans directly from small-scale farmers in Africa, allowing it to make good its claim that its chocolate is completely slave-free. In addition to this unique positioning, the chocolate itself is also innovative (different tastes from the other brands) and its packaging is super-cool. In short, it is a top brand, well marketed. It has a concrete world problem that it wants to tackle and has made its action clear to people in a tangible way. Nevertheless, the company is regularly attacked in the Dutch media. Every so often, people emerge with 'evidence' that the chocolate is not 100 per cent slave-free. Yet even if this is true, it does nothing to detract from the company's many genuine efforts to achieve its goal. Tony's Chocolonely is not perfect, but it focuses attention on a serious problem – child labour – and makes a positive contribution to improve it, which, thankfully, is appreciated by a large section of the market.

Moral? Always strive for perfection but don't be frightened or ashamed if you haven't yet achieved it. Because you never will. Perfection is an illusion. Concentrate instead on the positive impact your company can have.

Tony's Chocolonely buys its cacao beans directly from small-scale farmers in Africa, allowing it to make good its claim that its chocolate is completely slave-free.

PART

4

successful implementation

the 😊 offer ✌️u can't refuse

for employees

One of the greatest myths in the world of customer satisfaction

We have all read the horror stories about the working conditions in the warehouses of Amazon and Zalando. Various undercover reports have revealed that the pressure of work and the productivity targets are so high that some employees doubt whether or not they are actually allowed to go to the toilet. Even so, companies like Amazon and Zalando have millions of satisfied customers. Similarly, working with and for the legendary and visionary Steve Jobs was not always all that pleasant, if we can believe his biography. Yet, once again, the Apple community has many enthusiastic fans.

As a result of these negative anecdotes, some people think that a company always needs to choose between customer orientation on the one hand and what is good for employees on the other hand. But allow me to let you into a little secret: this so-called trade-off between customers and personnel is one of the greatest myths in the world of customer service and satisfaction.

Scientific research[65] has demonstrated that satisfied employees lead to satisfied customers. In contrast, the opposite relationship has not been proven. A company with satisfied customers does not necessarily mean that the employees are also satisfied. But if the employees are happy, this is (nearly always) automatically reflected in happy customers. Sir Richard Branson, the founder of the Virgin group, once said: 'My philosophy is that my team comes first, then my customers, and in third place my shareholders. If you do this right, at the end of the road the shareholders will still be satisfied, the customers will have become fans, and the employees will remain loyal to the company.'

In other words, a company's employees are the driving force behind the satisfaction of its customers. When I was the managing partner of the innovative research company InSites Consulting between 2000 and 2012, at one point I was responsible for our customer satisfaction studies. The conclusions of these studies were different for every company, but there was one thing they all had in common: the super-satisfied customers, the company's ambassadors, were such huge fans because of the people they had met in the company. It was their personal account manager, an operative in the call centre or an assistant in a shop that had made the difference and accounted for the largest part of their satisfaction. The conclusion was the same time after time: it is your personnel who decide whether your customers are satisfied or not.

Today, eight years later, I am an investor in and director of the company Hello Customer, an AI-driven customer feedback platform. And eight years later, my conclusion is still the same. If I look at the data for customer feedback on the Hello Customer platform, that same pattern is continually repeated: customers are made satisfied or dissatisfied by the actions of the people working for the company.

There is no trade-off between customer satisfaction and employee satisfaction. On the contrary, there is a strong correlation between the two. Positive employees radiate a satisfaction that is infectious for their customers, while negatively-minded employees do precisely the opposite.

Whenever I speak at major conferences, many of the questions I receive are about employees, even though the focus of my speech will have been about customers. I speak passionately for an hour about the need for greater customer orientation, and am then rewarded with questions that often deal with the audience's own employees! But that's fine. At the end of the day, they are both closely linked.

Because of these questions and because of the myth about the customer-employee trade-off that still persists in some quarters, I have decided to devote a full chapter of this book to the subject of employees. Employees are the key to achieving customer satisfaction. Consequently, it is important to translate your Offer You Can't Refuse model into practice in a manner to which they can relate.

HR departments in transformation

During the past decade, I have often spoken at HR conferences or during HR training courses at business schools. I was always the odd-one-out: the marketing and customer man in a group of HR experts. Nevertheless, it was always a fine experience. In general, HR people are open and friendly. That being said, I sometimes had the impression that the HR world was less innovative and evolving less quickly than the marketing environment. Fortunately, this is starting to change and the HR deficit is now being rapidly reduced. The current market for HR technology solutions is worth no less than 148 billion American dollars.[66] 74 per cent of HR managers have plans to increase their budget for HR technology during the coming year. What's more, this process has been significantly accelerated by the corona crisis. This crisis meant that for millions working from home became a necessity, leading to immediate extra investment in cloud services and other IT-infrastructure.

When Satya Nadella, the CEO at Microsoft, announced the company's results for the first quarter of 2020 at the end of April, he said: 'The digital transformation in March and April was on a larger scale than the digital transformation we have witnessed during the past two years.'

HR departments around the world are undergoing transformation and are looking for new ways to reinvent themselves. One of the most frequently asked questions in this context is: 'In which technology do we need to invest?' This is an interesting question, but it is also the wrong one. What HR managers should be asking is this: 'What kind of experience and culture do we want to offer our employees?'

The customer experience does not begin with the technology. Neither does the employee experience. What you need to do is start by describing the ideal world for each individual employee and then work backwards. It is only by starting with the employee experience that you will eventually find the right technology. Technology is a means, not an end in itself.

The war for talent

According to a large-scale study conducted by PwC, 58 per cent of HR managers regard the recruitment and retention of human talent as their biggest challenge.[67] A McKinsey report has revealed that companies in Europe and North America are facing an annual shortfall of between 16 and 18 million university graduates to meet their needs.[68] The franchise holders of McDonald's restaurants are also having difficulty to find enough people to work in their kitchens and behind their counters. Fork-lift truck drivers, brick-layers, security guards: they are all in short supply. And the list doesn't end there.[69]

Finding and keeping talent in an era of talent shortage is a real headache for almost every company. The problem is made worse by the fact that in many economies a high percentage of the (potential) workforce does not possess the skills that a modern company needs. The most worrying statistic of all is that 82 per cent of companies say that, even if they can find them, they fail to keep the right people on board.[70]

Finding the right people, training them and holding on to them is one of the biggest challenges in the management of a company in today's environment. This conclusion underlines the urgent need to invest more heavily in the total employee experience. You need to find out what potential employees are looking for and respond appropriately to their wishes and needs. This should now be one of your top priorities.

The Offer You Can't Refuse
for employees

'Customers are just ordinary people,' says my Dutch fellow-speaker and author Jos Burgers. And the same is true of a company's employees: they are just ordinary people. For this reason, it is my conviction that many of the elements that are important for the customer relationship are equally important for the company's relationship with its own staff. As a result of the growing talent scarcity of recent years, the balance of power has shifted from employers to employees. Customers have always had the choice about who they want to buy from, so that companies have already been investigating in the customer relationship for years. They now need to do the same for their personnel.

Notwithstanding the clear need for a better employee experience, companies still give themselves a low score in this domain. Some 80 per cent of company leaders say that the employee experience is very important, but only 22 per cent feel that they are offering a differentiating experience to their own staff.[71]

The challenges for keeping employees satisfied are looking increasingly like the same challenges for keeping customers satisfied. Of course, this requires something more than simply substituting the word 'employee' for the word 'customer' in a presentation or model. It is for this reason that I have adjusted The Offer You Can't Refuse model specifically for employees.

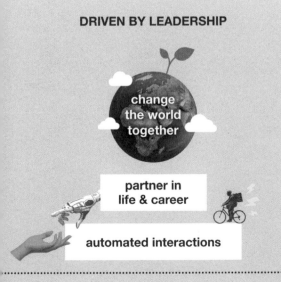

DRIVEN BY LEADERSHIP

change the world together

Adding Value to Society

partner in life & career

Meaningful Work - Continuous Learning
Work/Life - Continuous Feedback

automated interactions

Fast, Easy and Fun place to work

 good product / service & price **$**

Your job function and paycheck

For customers, the bottom level of the model was the need for a good product and good service at a good price. For employees, this lowest level is the need for good job content and a good salary. These are minimum requirements and they are important, but they will not be enough for an employer to differentiate his company.

The second level for customers was ultimate convenience. This also applies for employees. Everyone wants access to smart and easy-to-use tools that save time and energy. As a company, it is important to make the workposts of your employees as user-friendly as possible, equipped with all necessary aids and support mechanisms, so that they can focus their time on the things in their jobs that are truly important. Of course, nowadays it almost goes without saying that these tools also need to work with equal ease in a home environment.

These first two levels form the employee's transactional experience: 'Is the job interesting, am I well paid and is it easy to work here?' The next two levels focus on the employee's emotional experience: 'What is my feeling as an employee of this company, both personally and from a societal perspective?'

The third level relates to the 'partner in life' philosophy. For employees, this not only means a partnership in every aspect of their day-to-day existence, but also a partnership in their professional career. So how can you do this? How can a company be a partner in someone's life and career? Being able to continually offer your employees more and more added value is one of the most important challenges for attracting and retaining talent. What talent wants is to become increasingly interesting for the labour market through collaboration with the employer, whilst at the same time have sufficient time to realise personal dreams and private objectives.

The fourth and highest level of The Offer You Can't Refuse model is, of course, 'save the world'. This level is even more important for your employees than it is for your customers. If you invest all your professional energy in a company, you want that energy to lead to something that goes further than your own or the company's interests. In short, you hope to be able to make a positive contribution to society.

In order to implement this model for employees successfully, leadership is crucial. The manner in which the CEO and senior management communicate and act during the different phases will have a major influence on employee perception.

Ultimate convenience

Simplification of the processes on the workfloor is an important starting point for improving employee experience. A study by Deloitte revealed that 74 per cent of employees regard the processes in their company as being too complex. Only 4 (four!) per cent work in a simple working environment.[72] Moreover, these figures are identical for both large and small companies. Complexity is a general problem in our professional lives.

In my previous book, *Customers the Day After Tomorrow,* I suggested three axes of investment that would allow companies to offer greater convenience to their customers. These same three dimensions can be used for employees.

- **Faster than real time:** if your employees have a problem, try to anticipate it. Making use of data that should be readily available will allow you to gain insight into your employees' levels of (dis)satisfaction and the reasons for them. This insight will help you to identify and proactively respond to particular needs or concerns.
- **Hyperpersonalisation:** we all have our own particular way of working. Investigate how you can personalise your tools and communication in ways that will allow individual employees to make use of their preferred working methods. Nowadays, people want to personalise everything. No two iPhones in the world have the same composition of apps on the home screen. In fact, I would find it pretty creepy if someone else in the world was using exactly the same apps as me! So remember: people like to personalise and do your best to take account of this in all aspects of the employee experience.
- **Convenience:** last but not least, the ease of use of your tools is crucial if you want to spare your employees unnecessary frustration. I have seen time after time how some of my business contacts have stopped communicating with me via their work computer, simply because it is so cumbersome, and have switched instead to their own private computer and gmail address. Many people have better and easier-to-use tools in their private lives than they do in their professional lives. This is seriously detrimental to a good employee experience.

The Evernote dispenser

Some years ago, we were guests of the American company Evernote, creators of the digital note-taking app of the same name. During the tour around their office, we passed a vending machine. From the outside, it looked like any other vending machine, but inside it contained none of the usual unhealthy drinks and snacks. No, it was filled from top to bottom with technological gadgetry: keyboards, mouses, USB sticks, etc. After staring in amazement for a few seconds, we asked exactly what it was for. 'Here our people can come and pick up some IT stuff, whenever they need it. They just punch in the right letter code and out pops whatever they want. A keyboard, for example.' The way our company guide explained it, it all sounded so simple and logical. In fact, you could hear from the tone in his voice that he was surprised we should ask such an obvious question!

Everyone in our group nodded approvingly. Everyone, that is, apart from a senior executive from a large company here in Belgium. He clearly still had his doubts. 'So how do you know when someone really needs a new keyboard?' The Evernote guide now looked even more puzzled, but answered in the same polite and friendly tone: 'We don't. We just let the staff decide for themselves.' Adding as a rejoinder: 'So how do you do it in your company?' In a voice that seemed less confident than just a few seconds previously, the senior executive replied: 'Well, when we need a new keyboard, we submit a request to our IT helpdesk via our internal portal. They send someone down to see if there is a real problem. Sometimes they ask the permission of a more senior IT official to make a final decision. After that, they go and get a new keyboard and bring it back to the person concerned.' Following this lengthy explanation, there was a short but uneasy silence. 'Well, I guess we just trust our people a bit more,' smiled the Evernote guide.

But the executive had no intention of giving up the fight just yet. He thought for a few seconds and then launched his final question, which he assumed would pinpoint the shortcomings of the Evernote system. 'And what if people take USB sticks or mouses for their own private use? What if they steal?' He emphasised the last word 'steal', as though he had just given the coup de grace.

'Now, that's a good point. We know that some of our people sometimes steal, or take things for private use, as we prefer to put it, but we don't have a problem with that. If things get really out of hand, then obviously we will speak to the employees concerned.

But we are convinced that even if 5 per cent of the workforce occasionally takes something home, our system is still quicker and more efficient than the way you do things in your company. We ask our people to give the best of themselves for the company every single day. We sure as hell ain't going to bother them with long and complex processes for routine daily decisions ...' Game, set and match to Evernote.

The 95%-5% rule

This discussion at Evernote highlights how most rules and procedures in companies are made. The vast majority are developed simply to prevent misuse. If you have a crazy rule in your company, it is probably because someone once abused a situation to his or her advantage. And to avoid a repetition in the future, a new rule was introduced. In many companies, internal processes for employees are made much more difficult, simply to stop them from doing something that the vast majority were never planning to do in the first place.

This is the illusion of control. People who want to abuse their positions of trust are often far more 'creative' than people think. In other words, the bad employees still find a way to misbehave; the good employees get saddled with a mass of complex procedures. In reality, the good and trustworthy members of staff, who usually represent 95 per cent of the team, are punished for the undesirable behaviour of a small minority (no more than 5 per cent of the team).

Every company has its own 5 per cent, people who cut corners and bend (or break) the rules. A 100 per cent perfect recruitment policy is impossible. Besides, the actions of this small group might be influenced by mitigating exterior factors: financial problems, a sick child, a broken relationship ...

Of course, this also means that every company has its 95 per cent of good and reliable employees, who are honest and correct. So ask yourself this question: are your processes and procedures made for the 95 per cent or for the 5 per cent? Perhaps it is just human nature to focus on the minority who have bad intentions. Research has shown that our brains attach much more emotional weight to negative matters than to positive matters.

You want proof? Let's say that you get 100 e-mails in a day. Imagine that 95 are neutral in tone, four give you very positive feedback about your work but the last one is scathingly negative. As you drive home that same evening, which of these emails will you be thinking about? Exactly! It will be that single negative email that you keep turning over and over in your mind. Perhaps it will even keep you awake at night. If we were robots, we would react differently. Then we would say: 'Today was a top day! 99 per cent of messages were neutral or very positive, with just one per cent negative!' But we are not robots, and so we look on the gloomy side rather than on the bright side.

If you want to create ultimate convenience for your employees, this is the kind of thinking you have to break. Build your processes and procedures for the 95 per cent, not the 5 per cent. Make things as easy as possible for your good people. Don't slow them down with long-winded and irritating rules and regulations for matters that should be as easy as pie. Instead, give them ultimate convenience. Because this, in turn, will give them more time and energy to make a real difference for your customers and your company.

So, as a manager or company leader, try to focus each day on the positive employees and the positive events in your organisation. It will help to make the life of your workforce – and your own life – a whole lot easier.

Working from home versus working in the office

During the COVID-19 lockdown, many organisations received a boost in confidence in their employees. Millions had no option but to work at home and it all went much better than many people had thought. The manager of a large contact centre told me during this period: 'Steven, before the crisis we had one large contact centre with 500 employees. We now have 500 small contact centres. Everyone is working from home. At first, I was against this. But I have been forced to change my mind. Our customers are still receiving excellent help, even though we have far more incoming requests than normal. It seems that our people are doing their work efficiently, even at home. In fact, we can see that they are more relaxed and more satisfied. Their work-life balance is more to their liking. In short, I was a major opponent of working from home, but know I realise that it can be very effective.'

Before the corona lockdown, this manager was against home working because he was worried about the 5 per cent who would use the situation to avoid doing their work properly. Now he is aware of the positive impact that the 95 per cent can make.

Frank Plehiers is the manager of the ING contact centre. When the lockdown started, his centre was also obliged to shift in just a few days to 100 per cent remote work. Now that the lockdown is over, the centre has not reverted to its pre-corona methods of organisation. The staff have been allowed to continue working at home for an average of two days each week. They are also allowed to choose which days best suit their personal family agenda. On the remaining days, they come into the office, so that interaction with their colleagues and the group feeling are maintained. It is pleasing to see how the crisis has increased ING's trust in its own people. Like many companies, they now realise that it is the actions of the 95 per cent that really count.

GE: a culture of simplicity

General Electric (GE) was founded in 1892. The company has already undergone many transformations in its long existence. Today, it trades in technology, electronics and professional services. According to the Forbes Global 2000, GE is in the list of the 100 largest companies in the world. It today employs some 280 000 people. Its headquarters is in Fairfield, in the American state of Connecticut.[73]

In recent years, GE has worked hard to simplify its internal processes. The company makes complex and innovative products, but both its customers and staff experienced that working with and for GE was getting slower and more difficult. With this in mind, Jeff Immelt, the then CEO, made 'simplicity' a part of the company's strategy in 2014.

In a first step, the CEO asked the management team to remove as many layers in the hierarchy as possible. The internal lines of command needed to be shortened. Next, a critical analysis was made of the number of approvals that were necessary for particular kinds of decision. If decision trajectories overlapped or contained too many levels, the necessary pruning was carried out. At the same time, major investments were made in new digital workforce tools, with the aim of increasing speed and collaboration in the workplace.

A second step to make the lives of the employees more 'convenient' was the 'Fast Works' project. In the first instance, this aimed to increase GE's attention for the needs of customers. By better understanding those needs, it would be easier to set priorities, leading to a 'culture of simplification and greater focus'. This, in turn, would also benefit the employees. In the past, it was often said that companies should: 'Do more with less'. Today, the motto has become: 'Do fewer things better'.

If a company wants to simplify the lives of its employees, technological tools can be used as one of the means, but they are not a solution. This can only be found in a change of mindset, in which the employees are shown greater trust and the leadership team makes clear that it is okay to work on fewer projects simultaneously.

Partner in life and career

A 'partner in life' strategy understands the concerns, dreams, fears and ambitions that people have for their own lives. This strategy is not about the company, but about the person behind each individual employee. Empathy for his or her hopes and worries is a basic requirement for taking the right steps to develop the necessary partnership.

Of course, this partnership is about more than simply being a partner in life. The company also needs to be a partner in the career of its employees. Based on research by PwC and Deloitte, I have identified four elements that are important if you want to establish this dual partnership: a partner in life *and career*.

Meaningful work

One of the best anecdotes about meaningful work dates back to the 'space race' of the 1960s between the United States and Russia. When President John F. Kennedy was visiting NASA, he passed a man cleaning one of the corridors. The president stopped and asked him: 'And what is your job here at NASA?' With a note of pride in his voice, the man replied: 'Mister President, it is my job to help put a man on the moon.' It doesn't get any better than that, does it?

Recently, I have had the pleasure of making a couple of visits to the SpaceX factory in Los Angeles. All the staff wear 'Colonize Mars' T-shirts. Everyone, from the most humble cleaner to the most senior engineer, has the feeling that they are working as part of a unique project. They are convinced that in the foreseeable future people will be walking on Mars. Each time that a SpaceX rocket is launched, thousands of SpaceX employees watch the event on a giant screen in the middle of the production hall. This usually results in a sense of euphoria and loud applause. If, however, the launch goes wrong (which happens only very rarely), you can hear a pin drop in the icy silence that follows.

Of course, these two examples both relate to projects and objectives that are truly unique, but the same philosophy can be applied in any company. Retailer Decathlon wants to make sport accessible and feasible for everyone. That, too, is a noble

Mister President, it is my job to help put a man on the moon.

aim, and one that every Decathlon employee, from the salesperson in the store to the manager in company headquarters, feels able to put their shoulder behind, particularly when you can sense that the company's commitment is genuine.

In 2011, Daniel Pink wrote his bestseller *Drive*, in which he argued convincingly that if you can offer people autonomy, mastery and purpose, they will be happy in their work. His research is now more than ten years old, but the basic principles remain the same.

Continuous learning

Telenor is one of the largest telecom players in the world. Its headquarters is in Norway and the company is active in Scandinavia, East Europe and South-East Asia. Their HR team invited me to give a speech for their top 400 employees.

One of the greatest difficulties facing the company is recruiting and keeping the right talent to tackle the challenges that the telecom industry will face in the years ahead. More than ever, the sector needs people with a technological profile: strong in AI, data analysis and programming. Telenor has been struggling to find these people.

As a result, a few years ago the company decided to launch a large-scale retraining programme for its own people, working together with the online training institutes Udacity and Coursera. Employees with an administrative background were encouraged to follow courses in, say, data science. This kind of talent is often hard to find on the external labour market, so by retraining its own internal candidates Telenor was able to generate a double benefit: the talent was immediately available and the employees concerned were enthusiastic about their change of career direction.

Many people see their job as part of a life-long career trajectory. By continuing to learn and develop throughout that career, they hope to keep their profile interesting for the labour market. Research indicates that employees under the age of 35 years regard opportunities for continuous learning as one of the most important drivers for choosing who to work for.[74]

Companies that invest in the training of their personnel often reap the rewards of their effort. Organisations with a strong learning culture have 92 per cent more chance of bringing innovative products and services to market; are 52 per cent more productive than others; have 56 per cent more chance of being first to market with products and services; and are 17 per cent more profitable than their competitors.[75]

Well-being

Ann De Bisschop wrote an excellent book on this subject entitled *Wellbeing = winst* (Well-being = profit).[76] She contends that companies that invest in the well-being of their workforce book better results across the board. To support this argument, she uses the definition of Karen Danna and Ricky Griffin, the first authors to put literature and research relating to well-being in the workplace firmly on the map: 'Well-being at work is the result of satisfaction in and about the work in question, in combination with good physical and mental health.' A study by LinkedIn has shown that 49 per cent of employees have a preference for benefits linked to health and well-being above all other benefits.[77]

In the United States, the presence of a good quality company health care package is an essential aspect when people are choosing their next employer. The supermarket chain Walmart is the largest of these employers in the United States, with a total workforce in the US alone of more than 1.6 million people.

Walmart does not rely on care insurance, but prefers to work directly with health centres, seeing this as the best way to provide its employees with the best health care. Walmart has even set up a centre of excellence specifically for this purpose. The company focuses on treatments for employees with serious medical conditions, such as heart complaints, obesity, cancer and those in need of organ replacement. In most cases, Walmart pays 100 per cent of the medical costs.

An example of how their system works? One of their employees was anxious to find the cause of the chronic neck pain he was experiencing.[78] The pain kept on getting worse and a local surgeon suggested a back operation to solve the problem. Walmart recommended the employee consult another doctor in a different American state. Thanks to the Walmart care plan, the man was able to fly with his wife to visit a top specialist on the other side of the country. This consultation revealed the real cause of the pain. The man had Parkinson's disease. This diagnosis made it possible for him to receive the right treatment and avoid a pointless and potentially dangerous back operation. Walmart paid for the medical visit, but ultimately saved 30 000 dollars, because the man was able to resume work much more quickly. What's more, this is by no means an exceptional scenario at Walmart. And because only 6 per cent of American companies work directly with medical experts in this way, the Walmart approach is a powerful differentiating factor for its employees.[79]

According to an article in the *Harvard Business Review*,[80] patients covered by the Walmart plan spend 14 per cent less time in hospital and return to work 20 per cent faster than employees who are not covered by an equivalent employer plan.

Walmart is good but Apple has taken things even further in its concern for the health of its employees. Since 2019, Apple offers these employees the chance to have their DNA checked for the presence of certain hereditary diseases.[81] The results of these tests are then used for the development of a personalised treatment approach, designed to keep the health of the employee stable for as long as possible.

Continuous feedback

Researcher Josh Bersin has shown that 70 per cent of multinationals no longer organise annual evaluation meetings with their employees, but have switched to a system of continuous conversations as the best means to discuss performance and plan future career developments.[82]

The classic evaluation procedure focuses on the assessment of past behaviour and then rewards or punishes people via financial incentives. But if you want to be a partner in the life and career of your people, you need to look to the long-term future and plan it together through a process of constant dialogue.

Since 2015, Dean Carter has been the director of HR at Patagonia. When he first joined the California-based company, he was surprised. Patagonia had (and still has) a fantastic and forward-thinking image in society, but its method of giving feedback to its employees was antiquated. The company still used an annual appraisal system with carrot-and-stick rewards. This was something Dean wanted to change as quickly as possible.

In the short term, the annual appraisal was replaced by a technologically supported system of continuous evaluation. Every employee was encouraged to ask for feedback as often as possible from colleagues and managers. At the start, everyone gave everyone else super-positive reports: 'You're doing brilliantly!' After a time, this became: 'You're doing pretty well.' A few months later it was: 'You're good at A, but there is still plenty of room for improvement in B.' People needed time to develop sufficient trust in each other to give honest feedback, both upwards and downwards within the organisation.

The fact that people are able to regularly ask for feedback is one of the success factors of the system. 'When you ask for feedback from someone, a relationship of trust is gradually built up,' explains Dean Carter. 'Once a number of people start to do this, others soon catch on and the demand for feedback explodes exponentially. It is much more powerful to ask for feedback yourself than to be given it without asking.'[83]

Saving the world, together with your employees

More and more people are opting to work for employers with positive, ethical and sustainable values. I increasingly read and hear how young people use their own values as the basis for finding the right employer for them. Some 64 per cent of these young people would no longer accept a job with a company that does not have socially beneficial and sustainable objectives.[84]

For companies, it is becoming ever more important to take account of the opinions of this group. By 2025, 75 per cent of the working population will consist of millennials.[85] This means that in the future war for talent the 'save the world' level of your Offer You Can't Refuse model will become a crucial criterion for making the difference.

When I discussed the model as it applies to customers in the opening chapters of this book, my advice was to benchmark your company against the standard in your sector, so that you could assess just how far you need to go with the model's different phases, whilst at the same time preparing for the evolution that will see your customers demanding more and more as time goes by.

But as far as your employees are concerned, you don't have this same choice. The 'save the world' idea is much more important for this internal target group. And not just for the youngsters. It is a fallacy that it is only the millennials who attach importance to positive values when choosing an employer. Young people may attach more importance, but the 'save the world' philosophy also appeals to a large section of more seasoned employees. 70 per cent of the total working population wants to work for an employer with a strong and positive climate policy. 50 per cent of people are even prepared to work for slightly lower pay, if this gives them the opportunity to find an employer with positive societal objectives and values. For one in three young people the absence of a societal sense of responsibility is a deal-breaker, a view also shared by 17 per cent of older employees.[86]

So why are more and more people opting for companies that have a 'save the world' plan? In my opinion, there are three key motives. In the first instance, a 'save the world' strategy creates a sense of pride in employees. But this pride only emerges when their company exceeds the societal norm. During the lockdown, Panera Bread continued making its delicious salads and sandwiches. Lots of them were sold to customers via home deliveries and street pick-ups, but the company also donated thousands of its meals to poor children. Many American children from poorer families rely on free school meals, so that when COVID-19 forced the closure of schools many families found themselves urgently in need of another source of free food. Panera Bread gave away tens of thousands of sandwiches, far more than any other foodstuffs company, to children who would otherwise have gone hungry during the corona crisis. This is the kind of action that makes employees proud, because it goes beyond the norm of what society expects. And the more the employees can be actively involved in these inspiring actions, the greater their impact will be.

The second motive is a derivative conclusion drawn from the very existence of a 'save the world' strategy. Future employees assume that a company that wants to take care of society will also do a pretty good job of taking care of its own people.

Lastly, projects with a societal added value often strike a chord with the employee's own values. A good fit between personal values and the company's values is one of the most important drivers for intrinsic motivation.

At PPG everyone is a painter

In January 2020, I became acquainted for the first time with PPG, one of the largest producers of paint in the world. The company is more than a century old but continues to grow in size and stature. PPG is not only one of the biggest producers in its market, but is also regarded as one of that market's most innovative players.

For example, PPG has developed scratch-resistant paint exclusively for Mercedes. The company is also working to develop intelligent paint, which is intended for use in industrial applications, such as the painting of oil pipelines, where the paint obviously plays a protective role, rather than a decorative one. The idea is that intelligent paint will know when it needs to be re-coated, thanks to the presence of minute sensors that will be inserted into it during the production process. As a result, the paint serves as an additional safety feature to safeguard the pipeline's structural integrity, thereby helping to protect the environment.

When I was invited to speak at the annual leadership congress of the PPG in Miami, I was hugely impressed by the sense of drive and innovation in everything the company does. My speech was planned for around four o'clock in the afternoon, but I was invited to lunch, so that I could get to know a number of the people who would be present. One of the nice things about talking at a leadership event is that I know I am always going to meet lots of interesting men and women – and that I am going to hear lots of interesting stories about innovation.

The content of every leadership event is different, but there is one aspect they all have in common: the dress code of the male members of the audience. At 99.9 per cent of these events, the men are all dressed in dark blue trousers, blue or white shirts and dark jackets. It is almost as though this 'uniform' is one of the business world's unwritten laws.

Imagine my amazement, then, when I walked out on to the terrace where lunch was being held to see hundreds of people dressed in gaily coloured T-shirts. At first glance, I thought that this made a refreshing change. However, a second closer glance revealed that all these T-shirts bore the logo of the PPG community. So what was going on? This group had not attended the morning's lectures, but had been painting schools in some of the poorer districts of the city. PPG provides the paint and PPG employees provide the muscle power. Neat, don't you think? Moreover, this action in Miami was not just a one-off team building exercise, but part of the company's wider PPG community philosophy.

Via the PPG community, the paint manufacturer and its 47 000 employees want to bring more colour into society. In each of the 70 countries where the company is active, it seeks out buildings that have an important social function, but which lack the funding for proper maintenance. And let's be honest: a freshly painted building has a very different appeal to a building where the paint is peeling off the walls. Wherever its help is needed, PPG donates the paint and sends around some of its employees to do the actual painting. Between 2015 and 2020, the company completed 302 projects of this kind in 41 countries. As a result, 6.5 million people now have a more pleasant setting for their meetings and social activities. Some of them are students and teachers. Others are doctors, nurses and patients. In total, PPG employees have spent more than 100 000 hours to make these buildings once again look fresh, colourful and loved.

This is a perfect example of a 'save the world' project within a company. It solves a clear societal problem, using the company's own strengths and possibilities. Moreover, the added value for society can be linked directly to the company's core. Last but not least, by involving PPG employees, their pride in and commitment to the 'save the world' philosophy of the company is increased.

Adobe makes its employees 'an offer they can't refuse'

A good way to find interesting new employees is via Glassdoor. This is a website on which the current and former employees can anonymously assess a company. Adobe, known for its software like Photoshop, as well as being the inventor of pdf files, has been voted for nine years in a row as one of the top companies to work for in the United States. Since its foundation in 1982, Abode has always had a strong focus on its employees. 'Our best asset goes home every night,' said John Warnock and Charles Geschke, the company's two founders. And it is a culture that still persists today.

Adobe is convinced that it is the enthusiasm and drive of its personnel that is decisive for the satisfaction and loyalty of its customers. Moreover, the company also sees parallels between the wishes of customers and the wishes of its own employees. Okay, there are important differences; but there are also many similarities.

For this reason, Adobe has decided to set up a new department that manages both customer and employee experience. In 99.9 per cent of companies there are two separate departments to deal with these matters and they each follow their own course. At Adobe, they are together in a single team. According to the software giant, every company that is heavily dependent on customer-facing employees should do the same. One of the big advantages of a joint customer-employee experience department is that employees immediately have access to very user-friendly digital tools that were initially developed for customers.

In companies where the customer and employee teams are split, it often happens that the different departments use different interfaces. As a result, innovation happens at two different speeds. It is also often the case that investments in customers take precedence over investment in employees, when it comes to compiling budgets and priority lists.

At Adobe, they want to create the same friction-free environment for both customers and employees. Their CIO, Cynthia Stoddard, fully supports this philosophy:[87] 'From our strength in IT, we want to be an enabler for business, not a roadblock. We need to put the technology in the hands of our employees, so that they can decide for themselves how they can make the biggest impact with these tools.'

One of the jobs they have created to make this possible is the 'employee experience technology partner'. It is a job that is much in demand at Abode! People with this function profile strive to help their fellow employees and to give them the best possible experience when using technology in their professional lives. In other words, these 'partners' must eliminate technological frictions and ensure ultimate convenience on the workfloor.

In addition to ultimate convenience, Adobe is also devoting considerable time and resources to the 'partner in life and career' philosophy. The company has made numerous investments in the physical and mental health of its employees. It pays membership subscriptions for fitness clubs and even arranges massages and dietary advice. But within the 'partner in life' focus, Adobe concentrates above all on the continuous learning and development of its people.

In particular, Adobe attaches great importance to diversity and to giving equal opportunities to everyone in society. One of the strongest elements in this aspect of the model is the Adobe Digital Academy. This is a re-skilling programme that allows people of all kinds to take a new direction in their professional life, but the academy has a specific focus on attracting people from a non-traditional background and offering them the prospect of a fine career.

When Archy Posada started his last year at high school, he had already seen more than a dozen of his friends killed in the gang wars that plagued his neighbourhood. To make matters worse, he was made homeless when he was just 18 years old. However, the young man had a talent for music and, thanks to his effort and persistence, he eventually became a professional opera singer.

Then fate took a cruel turn. During a visit to Los Angeles, he was shot on the street and seriously wounded. Because of his limited financial means, there was a risk that he might be made homeless again. Today, however, Archy is a product manager at Adobe. He learnt about the Adobe Digital Academy, joined up, retrained – and changed his life.

In other words, Adobe invests in the development of its employees before they have even joined the company. And Abode now wants to make its re-skilling programme completely open source, so that other organisations can make use of its methodology.

This brings us to the last level of The Offer You Can't Refuse strategy: save the world. Adobe invests in countless climate, health, youth and poverty initiatives. The decisions over which projects to support are not made by senior management. Each year, the employees are allowed to put forward projects from their own local communities and it is then

the entire Abode community that votes on which ones to approve. In 2019, the company invested 3 840 000 American dollars in projects of this kind.

In short: at each level of The Offer You Can't Refuse model, Adobe works with a clear strategy. Little wonder that it is chosen as one of America's best companies to work for year after year. And its decision to merge customer and employee experience is without doubt one of the key drivers behind its success.

Employee experience goes further than HR

Is employee experience the responsibility of HR?

Yes and no.

It is certainly the ultimate responsibility of HR, but not of HR alone. In customer service there is a saying: 'Customer service is not a department; it a mindset of the entire company.' Unfortunately, the same cannot yet be said – or at least not sufficiently – for employee experience. It is important that the happiness and satisfaction of the employees should not become just another task to be added to the HR pile. It must be a responsibility of the company as a whole. Employee experience needs to be part of the core strategy of every business organisation.

It is surprising how frequently you see the same mistakes being made with employees that many marketing departments make with their customers: short-term actions are all too often preferred to long-term impact. Companies and brands that only focus on the short term may occasionally have success, but they will never grow into the companies and brands that people really love.

The same reasoning applies to employees. In an article in the *Harvard Business Review*,[88] Jacob Morgan concludes that millions of dollars are spent on employee projects that achieve almost no meaningful results. So what goes wrong? This is the way it usually happens. The board sees that the figures for employee satisfaction are falling. The board asks HR to do something about it. The HR team comes up with a number of fun ideas, but nearly all of them are of a temporary, one-off nature. Some of the ideas are chosen and implemented. Employee satisfaction rises marginally, but then tails off and starts falling again. And so the cycle is repeated.

Long-term effects can only be achieved with a long-term vision, which makes clear to every member of staff that employee experience is part of the company's core strategy. It is no problem to make HR responsible for this strategy, but unless the team of senior managers supports it 200 per cent, it will never have the desired impact.

Every company says that its employees are important, but one in every three employees does not believe them – or at least sees no evidence of it.[89] When it comes to employee experience, employees are only interested in actions, not fine words. How does the company react when times are difficult? How does the company behave towards different groups in society? How much time does the presentation at the annual general meeting devote to 'save the world' issues? It is not promises but concrete action that will determine the judgement of your employees.

Employee experience ensures a guaranteed return

In his *Harvard Business Review* article, Jacob Morgan studied the financial return of investments in employees.[90] For his research he interviewed companies where he knew heavy investments had been made in all aspects of employee experience. He called this group the 'experiential' group.

How Investing in Employee Experience Affects Stock Price
Numbers are higher for the 15 experiential organizations—the top 6% analyzed—that invest most heavily in employees' cultural, technological, and physical work environments.

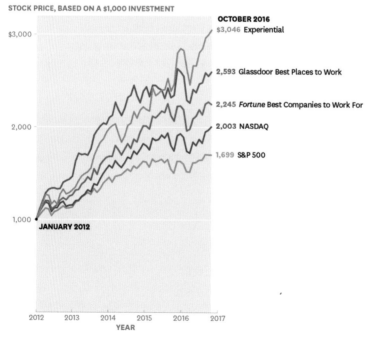

STOCK PRICE, BASED ON A $1,000 INVESTMENT

OCTOBER 2016
$3,046 Experiential

2,593 Glassdoor Best Places to Work

2,245 *Fortune* Best Companies to Work For

2,003 NASDAQ

1,699 S&P 500

JANUARY 2012

YEAR

SOURCE *THE EMPLOYEE EXPERIENCE ADVANTAGE*, BY JACOB MORGAN (WILEY, 2017)   © HBR.ORG

To objectively assess whether or not the companies in this group had performed better than others, he based his findings on the evolution of their share price during the previous five years. He compared his own research group against the financial performance of companies in Glassdoor's Best Places To Work, the Fortune Best Companies To Work For, the Nasdaq and the S&P 500.

The results speak for themselves. The more a company has a long-term vision that embraces employee experience and continues to invest in that vision, the better its financial performance in the stock market.

How can I start to build an offer that my employees can't refuse?

Are you offering your employees an offer they can't refuse? On which dimensions of the model are you scoring well and where do you still need to improve? Perhaps you already have a fantastic 'save the world' project in your company, but are still aware of frustrations within your workforce? If so, this will probably have something to do with the lower levels of the model. Maybe it simply isn't 'convenient' enough to work in your company. There are a growing number of people who choose an employer based on a 'save the world' mindset, but if their daily experience of working in the company is disappointing the strategy will lack impact. As far as customers are concerned, there is slightly more room for manoeuvre regarding which aspects of the model you apply and how, but with your employees you do not have this luxury. You have to score well with every element of the model. You have no choice. Every step in your Offer You Can't Refuse strategy is crucial for determining the satisfaction, pride and loyalty of (and your attraction for) both your present and future employees.

So how do you begin to evaluate and improve your employee experience?
Here are some questions that can help you to identify the actions you need to take.

Ultimate convenience

- Where are the 'roadblocks' that prevent the taking of simple decisions or hinder the efficient performance of processes? How can these roadblocks be removed?
- What are the digital frustrations in the internal operation of your company? How can you ensure that your technology continues to keep pace with the tools that people use every day in their private lives?
- Can you use the same tactic in this area as you use for your customers? Can you appoint friction hunters to search for the irritating frictions in your day-to-day activities, so that they can be eliminated one by one?

- Have you made rules based on the actions of the 5 per cent of less trustworthy employees, so that you are making things unnecessarily difficult for the 95 per cent of good employees?

Partner in life and career

- To what extent does your company make it possible for employees to give shape and form to their own career? Can your people map out their own career pathway, perhaps in consultation with a coach?
- Is there a continuous training trajectory that can help employees to develop the career they want?
- To what extent does your company invest in the well-being of your employees? Is there a strategy to improve their physical and mental health?
- How does your company give feedback? Do you have a low-threshold system that makes it possible for employees to ask for feedback continuously?
- Is your employee experience strategy part of your company's core strategy?

Save the world

- To what extent does your company make use of its strengths to contribute to a better society?
- Do these projects have real added value or are they more concerned with marketing and image-building? It is important to be honest with yourself on these matters. Like customers, employees will be able to see immediately if your commitment is not genuine.
- Are they projects that are consistent with the core and the talents of your company? This is important, if you wish to guarantee the continuity and credibility of these projects.
- Are your employees involved in the creation of your company's societal added value?

DRIVEN BY LEADERSHIP

adding value to society

meaningful work

continuous learning

 work / life

continuous feedback

fast, easy and fun place to work

your job function and paycheck

the h⧗urglass model

a practical innovation model

For this next chapter, I would like to introduce you to a guest author. I have asked my good friend and co-founder of our company nexxworks, Peter Hinssen, to write a chapter for my book. Peter and I have worked together fantastically for more than eight years. Our knowledge and interests complement each other. Peter looks at the world from the perspective of a technologist and a visionary strategist; I see the world from the standpoint of a marketeer and a customer. We see the same things but not in the same way, but together we arrive from different directions at complementary ideas and insights for companies.

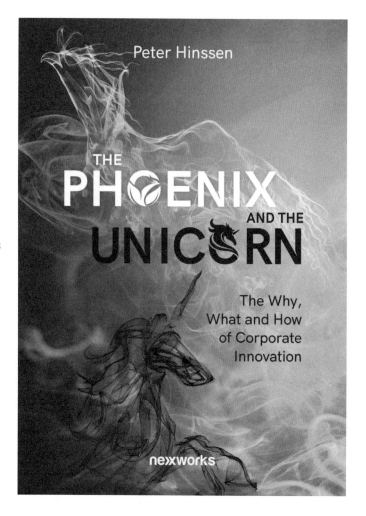

In March 2020, Peter published a new book, *The Phoenix and the Unicorn*. The book describes how companies, which have existed for decades, continue to reinvent themselves time after time, adjusting to new market conditions as and when they arise (the Phoenix). It is an outstanding book, to which I also had the pleasure of contributing a chapter.

The implementation of The Offer You Can't Refuse model will require companies to show a greater innovative spirit than ever before. They will need to introduce new ideas and technologies that make the world more user-friendly, thereby allowing them to remove their customers' worries and improve society as a whole. In this chapter, Peter will share with us a highly practical model that will allow you to deal with innovation in your company in a smarter and more impactful manner.

The Hourglass model – a practical guide for The Day After Tomorrow

By Peter Hinssen, founder of nexxworks, serial entrepreneur, keynote speaker and author

> *If we think long term, we can accomplish things that we could not otherwise accomplish. Time horizons are important.*
> **JEFF BEZOS**

The origin of The Day After Tomorrow

Steven and I have known each other and been inspiring each other for years. The origins of the concept behind the book *The Day After Tomorrow* dates back to a masterclass that Steven had organised in Barcelona. On the final evening, I wanted to use a simple metaphor, so that the group would return home with a clear final message and future mission. Suddenly, I remembered an old schedule I had once seen during my very first job as a young engineer at Alcatel, a company which at that time was the world's most important producer of telecom equipment. I was part of a team that was developing a 'video on demand' system, which would make it possible to view films at home whenever it best suited people's agendas. It was a kind of rough prototype of Netflix. Our biggest challenge was that all the films consisted of a number of compressed video files, stored on a massive hard drive. Back then, this made it very difficult to give a large number of potential viewers access to the same files at the same time.

This meant that if a film was mega-popular – for example, the most recent Star Wars movie – only a limited number of users could watch the compressed files simultaneously, which was hardly satisfactory from a commercial point of view. Faced with this situation, an engineer has one of two choices. You can apply the 'classic' engineer's approach, which essentially consists of opening your engineer's box of tricks and using every piece of technological wizardry at your disposal to ensure that the hard drive can deal with more streams, so that more users can request the same files. Or you can apply an alternative and more practical approach: you simply copy all the most popular film files. This would give you multiple copies of *Star Wars*, making it possible to satisfy multiple viewers at the same time.

A model based on films

As you might have guessed, we chose the second option. This meant that we, as engineers, needed to know which films were super-popular, so that we would make sure we had enough copies. In the end, we divided all films into one of three categories: 'blockbusters', the films everyone wanted to see, so that we would need lots of copies; 'normal' films, which had an average popularity; and 'cult' films, which were only infrequently requested by real film buffs and therefore formed the 'long tail' (as it were) of our video library.

The schedule that we used looked more or less like this:

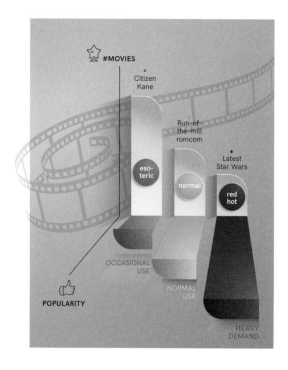

I liked the simplicity of this model, because it was so easy to explain. And when it suddenly flashed into my mind that evening in Barcelona, I realised that we could also use it to categorise our strategic horizons. I sat down in my hotel room and immediately began to develop the idea. In the next morning's workshop, I introduced *The Day After Tomorrow* for the very first time, and it instantly caught on.

Three horizons

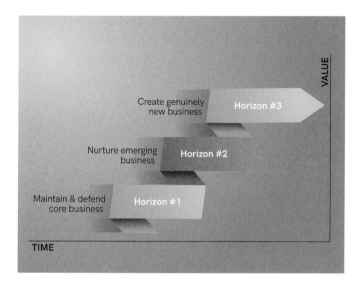

Some time later, someone said to me that The Day After Tomorrow model reminded him of McKinsey's Three Horizons framework. During an enforced sabbatical year between my first and second start-ups, I had worked for McKinsey as an entrepreneur in residence. So it is perfectly possible that I came across their model when I was there, but my real inspiration, as I have just described above, was those three film categories.

The Three Horizons framework by McKinsey is a system to assess the development of your strategic plan, in which you weigh value against time. This results in three distinct horizons. The first horizon is the strategic framework that the company uses to perpetuate and protect its core activity: in other words, 'business as usual'.

The second horizon helps you to focus on the stimulation of newly emerging activities and opportunities, which are often in line with or closely related to your present activities. The third and final horizon involves the development of activities that are completely new for your company. The concept is therefore the same as my Day After Tomorrow.

The Three Horizons model appeared for the first time in the book *The Alchemy of Growth*, published in 1999 and written by Stephen Coley, together with Mehrdad Baghai and David White. Stephen is now emeritus director of the McKinsey office in Chicago. In that book he demonstrated that many companies follow a dangerous path: they concentrate too much on the near future. This tendency is logical, since it is Horizon 1 that provides the largest profits and the biggest cash flow. However, in times of change and uncertainty it is important that companies should not fixate on the 'playing safe' mentality of Horizon 1: they need to look forward to the future. The McKinsey framework makes it possible for company leaders to find a balance between attention for and investment in the good performing activities of the present and the growth possibilities of the future. In essence, therefore, this model has the same content as my Day After Tomorrow model: how much time, effort, budget and resources are you prepared to commit to your 'today' (Horizon 1), your 'tomorrow' (Horizon 2) and your 'day after tomorrow' (Horizon 3)?

For my final version of The Day After Tomorrow model, I amended the old model for popular films and put time on the x-axis, to more clearly define the boundaries between today, tomorrow and The Day After Tomorrow. The most important benefit of these three categories is that they help you to see the impact that each of them can have on value creation for your company. Investing in today is very important for achieving your current targets and objectives. This generates 'current value'. Investing in tomorrow is important for realising 'future value'. But investing in The Day After Tomorrow is essential to secure the huge 'long-term value' that new technologies, concepts or business models can provide.

Most companies are very short-sighted when it comes to looking at the future. Often, they do little more than tinker with their success recipes of today, in the hope that the situation tomorrow will be more or less the same. That is why I find the budget period in companies a delightfully perverse time of year. This sadistic annual ritual forces dozens of managers to pour fake news into flashy-looking spreadsheets, from which they hope to distil a fabricated 'budget' that almost never matches the reality of the coming 12 months.

However, in recent times I have come across an increasing number of companies that no long participate in this budgetary circus. They realise that compiling budgets consumes huge resources and energy, without providing very much in return. They have been clever enough to see that in a rapidly evolving world, in which technology ensures that changes follow each other faster than ever before, the concept of the annual budget exercise is becoming ever more pointless with each passing year.

When I started to use The Day After Tomorrow model, it seemed to encourage people to think for the first time about how they look at the (distant) future and how (if at all) they take account of value creation in their strategic planning. Steven used this same philosophy in his book *Customers the Day After Tomorrow*.

What does YOUR Day After Tomorrow look like?

The most important question is this: 'What is the balance in your company between today, tomorrow and The Day After Tomorrow?' Ideally, the division of time, money, effort and resources should be 70 per cent today, 20 per cent tomorrow and 10 per cent The Day After Tomorrow. If companies are honest, most of them will admit that they commit a disproportionate amount of attention to today. So what about you? If tomorrow and The Day After Tomorrow have no clearly defined place in your company's strategy, what are you going to do about it? I would ask you to sit down (or stand or run or cycle – whatever works best for you) and think about it seriously.

In my opinion, Steven's Offer You Can't Refuse model can also be extrapolated to The Day After Tomorrow model. His first step – quality products and good service at a competitive price – is self-evident. Every company knows and understands this. And the remaining three steps? As I see it, the steps 'transactional convenience', 'partner in life' and 'save the world' can easily be equated with 'today', 'tomorrow' and the 'day after tomorrow'.

Anyone who 'today' is not yet thinking about digital ease of use can forget about the future – because they won't have one. That is crystal clear. Even though it has become a commodity, as Steven explains, transactional convenience is an absolute necessity. Becoming a partner in life for your customers and helping them to fulfil their dreams and ambitions takes us significantly higher on the value curve: this has a much higher 'tomorrow' content. And the 'save the world' concept has a good deal in common with 'the day after tomorrow' approach. Just like The Day After Tomorrow model, the value for companies and their customers increases with each successive step of Steven's The Offer They Can't Refuse model. Which of us would not agree that helping poverty out of the world is higher on the value scale than shopping without the need to pass through a checkout?

For traditional companies – of course, I am not talking about companies like Tony's Chocolonely, where the balance is completely different – that are still largely focused today on the creation of excellent products and services but are also starting (hopefully) to devote more attention to digital convenience, the time spread of The Day After Tomorrow model can perhaps even be a useful indicator. Spend 70 per cent of your time, talent and budget on the streamlining of your products and services, especially by focusing on transactional perfection. Devote 20 per cent of your resources to emotional convenience, so that you can become a partner in the life of your customers. And last but not least, never forget that you need to devote 10 per cent of your resources to the creation of societal value, both for and with your customers; added value that in the long term can give enormous returns not only for those customers themselves, but also for your income, your employees and society as a whole.

In my opinion, The Day After Tomorrow model is so popular because it is so simple. Even so, many people still have doubts and concerns. After I have given my keynote, they often come up to me later on and ask questions like: 'How should I see the difference between today, tomorrow and The Day After Tomorrow? How should I organise those different futures? I understand the WHAT, but HOW exactly do I plan my trajectory towards The Day After Tomorrow?'

As you can see, at the very least The Day After Tomorrow model made people aware of the problem and forced them to think about the future. They finally realised that they had to do something, and for me that was great! But looking back now, I have to admit that I did not say enough about precisely HOW they should approach the challenge. And that began to worry me. As a result, I have now developed the Hourglass model, which forms the core of my latest book: *The Phoenix and the Unicorn: why and how companies must innovate.*

The hourglass model

> *I seem to be able to recognise pieces of the future that arrive just a little too early.*
>
> **WILLIAM GIBSON**

One of the fantastic things about this model is that I owe it all to one of our nexxworks customers! Emile Piters is vice-director IT for EMEA at Medtronic, the world's largest producers of medical equipment. It is the company's proud boast that every second it improves the lives of two patients worldwide. You have probably heard their name, even if only in passing, and they are now the largest med-tech company on the planet. Founded in Minneapolis in 1949, Medtronic initially became famous as the developer of the first battery-operated pacemaker. Before this technology was created, heart patients were already being treated with electronic stimulation, but only by being constantly connected to the electricity net. During a massive power failure in 1957, large parts of Minnesota and Wisconsin found themselves without electricity, as a result of which several heart patients died. It was this tragedy that prompted Earl Bakken, the founder of Medtronic, to develop a portable, battery-powered and transistor-operated device that wasn't dependent on the net – and so the first pacemaker was born. Over the years, the company has grown massively and is constantly looking ahead to find the right Day After Tomorrow strategy. In the rapidly changing world of health care – where big data, sensors and smartphones are creating seismic shock waves – the company cannot afford to limit its horizon to just 'tomorrow'. It needs to look even further. The best example of how Medtronic is capable of transforming its market is Micra, the smallest pacemaker ever. This has knocked traditional pacemaker technology for six, since Micra no longer uses guide wires.

After the publication of *Digital is the New Normal*, Emile and I became friends. Since then, we have regularly exchanged ideas about the newest evolutions in health care. When he began to apply The Day After Tomorrow concept in his own company, his first major challenge was to divide the total resources for IT over the three categories of the model. A large part of Emile's team spent its time on legacy systems (dated but still useable IT) and the implementation of large-scale IT systems like SAP to keep the company running. Of course, an organisation like Medtronic, with an annual turnover of 30 billion American dollars, needs to ensure that its systems work with the precision of a Swiss watch. As a result, the largest part of the budget and human resources were devoted to 'today', and a lot of time was lost dealing with SOY (Shit of Yesterday). When people did finally get around to thinking about the future, they usually did not much more than adjust and expand the existing strategies.

Fortunately, Emile understood that the health sector stood on the eve of some very disruptive changes, which would see it evolve towards a highly personalised form of medical care. The market for pacemakers would change from a sector governed by electronics to a sector in which data and digital platforms would become increasingly dominant. Step by step, he gradually ensured a better alignment between the two elements of his strategic structure (existing activities and emerging activities). He began to devote more attention, money and resources to The Day After Tomorrow.

The metaphor that slowly but surely emerged from this process was that of an hourglass. I don't know how long it is since you last used one, but we all know what they look like. An hourglass has two halves, separated by a narrow middle. The TOP HALF of the hourglass is the half from which the grains of sand trickle out and pass through the middle into the BOTTOM HALF, which gradually fills. If we apply this model to the strategic thought process, the TOP HALF consists of SENSE and TRY.

Sense

In the Hourglass model, SENSE is our radar for everything that is new and interesting: new ideas, technologies, models, concepts, developments and anything else that seems innovative. In other words, it is a way to 'recognise pieces of the future that arrive just a little too early', to use the words of William Gibson.

We live in a Never Normal age: an age in which nothing remains the same or 'normal' for very long, but changes faster and faster than ever before. This pace of change is accelerated by the non-linear dynamic of the network and a series of innovations that constantly strengthen each other. To keep track of all these changes, we need a much better radar than in the past, a radar with a wider field of vision and a detection system that looks deeper and senses more. We need to be more alert, so that we can pick up signals more quickly, no matter how weak they are, and our antennae need to be further refined and sensitised, so that they can identify what the next trendsetting innovations will be. In *Star Trek*, the *U.S.S. Enterprise* was equipped with a 'long-range sensor scan', so that it could detect alien spaceships before they were visible on the crews' monitors. This is the technique that companies now need to learn and develop. If you want to remain fully up-to-date, you will need to do more than attend the annual conference for your sector or professional discipline. You need to go in search of evolutions off the beaten track, following developments in other sectors and being open-minded in response to unexpected opportunities and serendipity. Only then will you be able to truly understand your environment. It is no coincidence that Steven talks in his section on the 'partner in life' strategy about the importance of shifting the focus from the core to the blending of industries and the amalgamation of individual companies into networks.

Try

The second component of the upper half of the hourglass is EXPERIMENTATION. Once your SENSE component has allowed you to establish the ingredients that can lead to change, you need to start investigating what you can actually do with those ingredients. Create an environment where you can test ideas quickly and safely. That is the natural way of working in start-ups: they are great at developing 'lean' methods of experimentation. They make Minimum Viable Products and test them on users.

The lean method was first elaborated by Eric Ries, a young engineer from Silicon Valley, who discovered at first hand that the limited budgets of start-ups necessitate a particular way of working. In start-ups, development processes are naturally lean: they test different versions of a product on users to get concrete feedback from an early stage. They learn from this, improve the products and repeat the tests as quickly as possible. Do you want to know why start-ups work in this helter-skelter way? It is because they have no choice. They are engaged in a constant race against time. Their big fear is that their money will run out before they have a marketable product that can generate a sustainable turnover.

Unfortunately, large and established companies do not have this problem. Why do I say 'unfortunately'? Because their slower approach means that by the time they have actually developed something, it is already too late. Or else they get things completely wrong. When Ries decided to go and work in the venture capital sector, he gave advice to hundreds of start-ups. He later wrote his conclusions in a book, which was published as *The Lean Startup*. The book was a best seller and his ideas began to be adopted in many companies, not just by start-ups but also by traditional organisations. The most important element in Ries' philosophy is how you can speed up the feedback loop.
When start-ups develop a product, they first make an MVP: Minimum Viable Product. The difference between a 'normal' product and an MVP is that an MVP is just 'good enough' to be tested on the public.

The aim, of course, it ultimately to produce a Viable Product, one that will earn you enough to survive. There are probably companies with a lot more money than you already trying to do the same thing. So time is of the essence. A Minimum Product is a poorly performing – perhaps even a badly performing – version of the concept you want to test. In fact, it is so bad that nobody would want to use it. But if you combine a Viable Product and a Minimum Product, you end up with a Minimum Viable Product, the best possible version that you can make at this stage to have it tested by early adapters. These tests provide valuable input for the following iteration.

According to Ries, this is a fairly simple cycle: make, test, learn and start again. If you have your MVP, you launch it and immediately start collecting as much feedback from the users as you can. You analyse their findings and learn what they have to tell you. This makes it possible to develop a second version of the product in a relatively short space of time.

It is only after you have repeated this lean process a number of times that you can actually start to develop a real product or service that can be viable. Since Ries first described the process, his approach has been adopted on a wide scale, both by start-ups and established names. The Ries method is often combined with Design Thinking, because this helps customers to better understand and use the product, which in turn helps to clarify the requirements that the subsequent MVP must satisfy.

This TRY compartment of the hourglass results in the creation of a remarkably efficient system for conducting lean experimentation. By borrowing the techniques used by start-ups, companies of all sizes and ages can organise test departments to search for what works and what does not, so that the necessary adjustments can be made that will lead on to the next stages of development.

Scale and Run

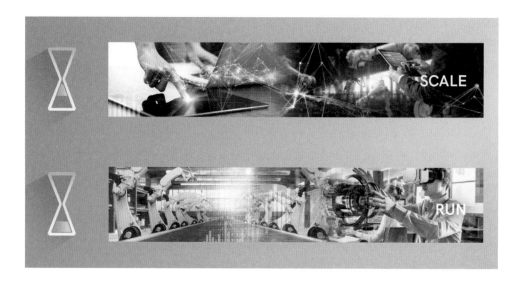

This brings us to the bottom half of the hourglass, which is the place where you need to SCALE and RUN. It is not difficult to understand why these elements are best developed in successful traditional companies. This is the point at which concepts, ideas and projects have now passed through the narrow middle of the hourglass. As such, the bottom half becomes the place where companies decide which of their test products or services really cut the mustard, so that they are worthy of further significant investment. When a concept, idea or project has managed to squeeze through the narrow middle and has convinced you that it is likely to become a success, you need to upscale it as quickly as possible throughout the entire company. Having done this, it is crucial that you next IMPLEMENT everything rapidly, efficiently and reliably.

As Emile Piters has shown, it is possible to apply the Hourglass model exclusively to your IT department, although an increasing number of companies prefer to apply it to their entire strategy.

Leaders become losers

When Google decided to give itself a new name – Alphabet – in 2015, it seemed a strange move for a company that had conquered the search engine market with such amazing speed. What's more, Google was by no means the first player in that market. It is reasonably easy to conquer a market, if that market is new and you are the first on the scene. As far as search engines are concerned, Yahoo and Altavista had already been active for quite some time before anyone had ever even heard of Google. Nevertheless, the newcomer walked all over them in double-quick time.
But that was in the past. Google knew that it had to be vigilant to avoid going the same way as Kodak or Xerox, and perhaps even General Motors or General Electric. These companies were all leaders which grew to become the symbols of their market, but which fell into decline and eventual decay because of their inability to reinvent themselves. As Google burgeoned in size, it became clear that it would not be easy to continue innovating in its core activities. It was afraid that it would suffer the same fate as its former competitors: become obsolete.

Alphabet turned out to be much more than a cosmetic change of name. It was a carefully considered exercise in strategic planning. The parts of the company that were growing fast and making huge profits (including the search engine, YouTube and Android) were incorporated into the core of Alphabet: these are the pillars that need to provide the bulk of the income, cash flow and profit. An example: in 2017, Alphabet generated 86 per cent of its revenue from advertising income via its search engine.

But in addition to this powerful core, Alphabet has also been branching out into more experimental fields. There is Nest, specialising in the automation of houses; Verily, which focuses on technology and research for health care; and Waymo, which is involved in the development of self-driving cars.

But perhaps the most significant (and most well-known) venture of all is Google X-lab, Alphabet's factory for 'moonshot' projects. If you look at this from the perspective of the Hourglass model, you can see that within the context of 'try', Alphabet is already engaged in a number of daring experiments, such as connected contact lenses and internet balloons. Alphabet knows that these experiments could never survive if they were tested in its core activities.

From zero to one and from one to N

In his brilliant book *Zero to One*, the American entrepreneur Peter Thiel gives what is unquestionably one of the most fascinating descriptions of the world of start-ups. Amongst other things, he founded PayPal with Elon Musk and he is one of the most influential investors in Silicon Valley. He also shares his experience of running and investing in start-ups during his lessons at Stanford. It was this lesson material that he eventually worked up into book form for the publication of *Zero to One*. In his book, he contends that making something out of nothing – from zero to one – is the core of a start-up.

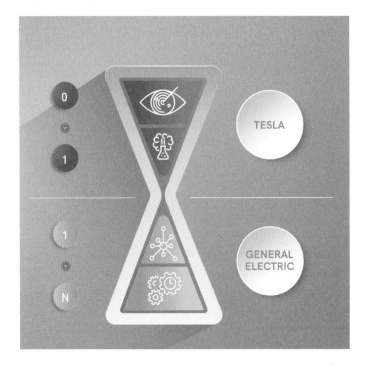

In my opinion, this same dynamic is also the core of the TOP HALF of the hourglass. In both cases, you look with a broad view and an open mind for disruptions and opportunities; you set priorities; you select; and then, finally, you start to experiment and test. It is exactly the same process, repeated until you find the nugget of gold you are searching for. This then needs to be transferred to the BOTTOM HALF of the hourglass. The purpose of this second half of the process is to make the step 'from one to N'. Whatever the product, service or activity is, you need to upscale it and let it grow as quickly and as efficiently as possible, so that you can go from one to a hundred and one, a thousand and one, a million and one ...

Very often, the necessary UPSCALING is embedded in a project and a dozen or so nervous project managers attempt to roll out brand new concepts in the company. IMPLEMENTING is the operational heart of the company: that is where you can feel its pulse beating, where traditional management techniques and Key Performance Indicators are used to successfully achieve concrete results.

One of my favourite quotes is by Nelson Mandela: 'I never lose. I either win or learn.' For me, this is the essence of learning from your mistakes. Likewise, everyone will have heard of the expression 'Fail fast, fail often', which has become a mantra for the world's start ups. Of course, this does not mean you must fail. If you get it right first time, so much the better. But if you do fail, make sure you learn something from it.

A LAT relationship

In the top half of the hourglass – the Day After Tomorrow part – you need to be open to new things. You must also be willing to fail fast and learn from your failures, so that you get greater clarity about the ideas on which you should focus for further development. Once you have identified and refined these ideas, the bottom half is about upscaling and efficient implementation. This half forms the basis of your activities and represents what you will do today and tomorrow.

I have seen how Emile Piters has pushed his company, step by step but with great purpose, in the direction of the Hourglass model. He first ensured that a large share of the total IT budget was shifted to the TOP HALF. Initially, this was limited to just 5 per cent, with the remaining 95 per cent all going to the bottom half. At the time of writing, this split is now 30/70. However, Emile realised that it was not enough simply to redistribute the financial cake in this manner. He saw that the two halves of the hourglass require different skills, a different mentality, and a different culture and leadership. They also need to be organised, managed and controlled in different ways.

But the most important thing of all? They need to be properly connected. In fact, Emile needed to create a perfect LAT (Living Apart Together) relationship. To make this possible, he installed a new mentality throughout the organisation, as a result of which the TOP HALF of the hourglass understood that it could not realise its full potential without the support of the bottom half, which provided the necessary resources, cash flow and upscaling. At the same, the BOTTOM HALF now knew that it had to put its full weight behind the top half, since its creativity was of crucial importance in the battle to remain relevant in The Day After Tomorrow. Both halves need each other, if the company is to have a long-term future.

I have seen many companies where the bottom half of the hourglass is brilliant, but they fail to organise the top half in a way that would allow them to look forward to the future with optimism. I have also seen many companies where the top half is functioning well, but they are unable to create the necessary alignment with the bottom half, so that the formulation of common objectives remains difficult. It is only if you can get both halves working together in perfect harmony – zero to one and one to N – that you will have a solid basis for dealing with the challenges of your Day After Tomorrow.

To me, that sounds like the ideal recipe for a phoenix: a mechanism that allows you to keep an open mind, gives you insights into new possibilities and provides opportunities for developing innovations, from the initial idea to the large scale production of an end product, and this is a continual process.

Apple is the ultimate phoenix. Some of you will know that I am a fanatical collector of Apple memorabilia. And if I say fanatical, I mean really fanatical: I have computers, software, advertising material and almost every book that has ever been written about the company. I have even set up a little museum where I can display all the things I have collected over the years. But I digress. Let's get back to business: Apple had a 'near-death' experience (in fact, many people thought that the company was well and truly dead), but it bounced back, stronger than ever before, and ultimately grew to become one of the most valuable commercial organisations on the planet.

But even before that *annus horribilis* and the subsequent resurrection of Apple, its charismatic founder, Steve Jobs, had already predicted what would happen. In one of the few interviews he gave, which appeared in *Playboy* in 1985 (yes, there are some people who do actually read the articles as well), just a few months before he was sacked from his own company, he made it very plain that Apple needed to reinvent itself, if it wanted to survive.

During that interview, Jobs said: 'Companies, as they grow to become multibillion-dollar entities, somehow lose their vision. They insert lots of layers of middle management between the people running the company and the people doing the work. They no longer have an inherent feel or a passion about the products. The creative people, who are the ones who care passionately, have to persuade five layers of management to do what they know is the right thing to do.'[91]

Jobs was 100 per cent correct, and that is what later happened. The different layers of middle management changed Apple from a sparkling and lively trendsetter into a bureaucratic monster, producing dull and uninspiring products that nobody wanted to buy. Jobs probably had no idea that he was about to be kicked out of Apple just weeks later, because this is how he finished the interview: 'What happens in most companies is that you don't keep great people under working environments where individual accomplishment is discouraged rather than encouraged. The great people leave and you end up with mediocrity. I know, because that's how Apple was built. Apple is an Ellis Island company. Apple is built on refugees from other companies. These are the extremely bright individual contributors who were troublemakers at other companies.'

The rest of the story is well known. An angry Jobs left Apple and invested his entire fortune in NeXT computers. NeXT was a commercial flop and Jobs lost millions. But when Apple bought NeXT and Jobs returned to the company, he used the innovation and creative power of NeXT to give his own career and the fortunes of Apple a real boost. In this way, the company rose from its ashes and was soon making history. For our generation, Apple is the clearest and most visible example of a phoenix.

Use your Offer You Can't Refuse strategy as fuel for the zero to one element of your hourglass

In December 2017, Beth Comstock celebrated 30 years at General Electric, first as chief marketing officer and later as vice-chair innovation. With memorable phrases like 'marketing is about innovation', she proved time and again that she knows just how inseparable these two elements of strategy really are.

And she is right, of course. Marketing and customer experience need to reinvent themselves continuously, if they wish to keep up with the constantly changing behaviour of customers. Together, this tandem has been responsible for some of the most successful innovations in recent years. Think, for example, of the McDonald's kiosks, or the frictionless KBC app for effortless entry and exit from car parks, or the odd jobs service of Centraal Beheer, all of which Steven mentioned earlier in the book.

For this reason, you should regard part 3 of Steven's book with strategies for The Offer You Can't Refuse as a handy guide for the top part of the hourglass of your company. The guidelines that he gives should inspire you to ask a number of highly relevant and intelligent questions, which can feed first the Sense element and later the Try element of your business model.

1. Does your company provide ultimate transactional convenience?

As Steven indicated, the interface of the future will be proactive. It will require no effort on the part of the customer and will be both invisible and personalised. Is that the case with your company? Compare your own situation regarding your interaction with customers with the following examples:

- Is your interaction as proactive as the smart fridge, which orders you a new supply of milk before the old one runs out?
- Do your customers need to make as little effort as the customers who can walk into and out of an Amazon Go without the need to queue and pay at a checkout?
- Is your interface as invisible as the Facebook algorithm that gives you automatic updates?
- Do you provide the same level of personalisation as McDonald's, which adjusts it menus customer by customer?

No? Then the bad news is that you need to do much better. The good news is that this is a perfect trigger for the Sense element of the Hourglass model. Perhaps it is time for you to appoint some friction hunters, as Steven so appropriately calls them. Let them check, for example, where customers lose time in your processes, where things are too complicated and need to be simplified, how the total interaction can be cut by 10 per cent. Customer frustrations are the perfect breeding ground for innovation.

2. Are you doing your best to become a partner in the life of your customers?

Does your company devote sufficient attention to the life journey of your customers, or do you still focus exclusively on the customer journey? Customers now expect more than that. As Steven writes, you need to try and understand the dreams, ambitions and anxieties that play a role in their day-to-day existence. Find ways to make yourself indispensible to them by responding effectively to their hopes and fears.

Once again, Steven gives plenty of practical advice for the Sense element of the Hourglass model. How can you evolve your products into services? How can you transform your core offer, so that it completely solves the problem(s) your customers are experiencing? How can you shift from your current focus on your core to participation in a blend of industries, based not on individual companies but on networks?

The example of Ping An from my book *The Phoenix and the Unicorn* is a good example of most of these necessary changes. Ping An was a classic Chinese insurance company that suddenly decided to transform itself into the world's largest platform for health care. In the following quote, Ma Mingzhe, chairman and CEO of Ping An, almost literally describes Steven's 'partner in life' approach: 'We must not only be the insurance expert of all our customers, but also their best financial consultant and an assistant in every aspect of their lives.'

It bears repeating: a life partner in every aspect of their lives, in which health (certainly in the post-corona era) is naturally a crucial part. The Ping An transition was a great success: by the end of 2018, more than 265 million customers were registered on Ping An Good Doctor, a platform that links doctors and patients, so that they can make appointments for consultations, as well as offering first advice with regard to diagnosis and treatment. In no time at all, 3 000 hospitals and 15 000 pharmacies had joined the platform, which in the meantime has also become an ordering service for medicines (delivered within an hour) in almost 100 Chinese cities.

Ping An has made the shift from product (insurance) to service (health care); from core (insurance) to full problem (health); from core sector (insurance) to new industry (health); and from solo player to a network of companies (hospitals and pharmacies).

So how is your company planning to deal with all this? The time has come to develop an appropriate strategy, don't you think?

3. What is your company doing to save the world?

As Steven wrote about Michael Porter: 'The world is confronted with many challenges and companies have the resources to do something about those challenges.' Every form of innovation solves a problem. Sometimes we don't even know that the problem is there, because force of habit has made us blind to its existence. But these problems are real and our planet and our society are currently facing plenty of them: global warming, migration, poverty, violence, the ageing of the population, obesity and, last but not least, a future wave of pandemics, of which COVID-19 was merely a precursor. Instead of just waiting for the next disaster to happen, think about how your company can help to resolve one or more of these huge issues, whilst at the same time strengthening your long-term commercial position. This is a perfect angle of approach for generating ideas through shared value for the Sense element of the hourglass.

As Steven explained, Porter's three strategies for the application of the shared value philosophy can provide numerous creative ideas and insights. Are you – like Soda stream is doing with its efforts to reduce the plastic problem – looking at how you can develop new products and explore new markets that will create societal added value? Or are you investigating how you can transform your entire value chain, like Levi's did with its Water-Less premium brand? Perhaps you are even planning to remodel your entire ecosystem, like Nestlé has done? If you look around, there are sufficient inspirational examples to allow you to make a concrete start on the Sense and Try elements of your strategy for making the world a better place.

By now it should be clear, I hope, that customer experience is the perfect source of inspiration for the top half of the Hourglass model. It is a fantastic ideas machine, where you can carry out dozens of tests (Try), before subsequently feeding them into the Scale and Run machine. Don't allow yourself to be paralysed by the 'curse of perfection', as Steven puts it. If you have too many ideas, select a few of the best ones and trial them on a small scale. If they work? Great! Make any necessary improvements and re-launch them on a bigger scale. And if they don't catch on? Too bad! Just move on and test another idea. It can be that simple. The secret of successful innovation is to keep on going. If at first you don't succeed, try, try again! So what are you waiting for? The time has come to apply the Hourglass model and build up your very own Offer You Can't Refuse. Good luck!

The Hourglass Model

SENSE — **YOUR RADAR SCREEN** for all things new & exciting: new ideas, technologies, models, concepts, ...

TRY — **EXPERIMENT** with ingredients for change: create a suitable environment to test ideas fast and safely.

SCALE — Which concepts, ideas and projects are really worth **SCALING OUT** throughout the organization?

RUN — **RUN THE OPERATIONS** as smoothly, efficiently and reliably as possible

do it better

This is the final chapter of my book. By now, you will be more than familiar with the principles and philosophy of The Offer You Can't Refuse model. Thanks to Peter's input in the previous chapter, you now also know how to better manage the innovation projects that will allow you to implement that philosophy in practice. What I want to do in this final chapter is to set out a number of criteria that will help you to travel in the right direction. If you hope to bring The Offer You Can't Refuse concept to successful fruition, you need to test your strategy and each of your decisions against these key criteria. I have bundled them together in the acronym: 'BETTER'. Do it 'BETTER'.

- **B**lend of industries: you won't always find the solution in your own industry. If you want to become a partner in the life of your customer and help to improve society, sometimes you will need to have the courage to cross over the boundaries of your own specialisation.
- **E**thical choices: there will always be a temptation not to make these choices. New technologies and burning ambition make it all too easy to put the interests of your shareholders ahead of the interests of other stakeholders. You must resist.
- **T**ransparency: build up trust with your stakeholders by striving for complete openness and honesty in everything you do. In the long term, that is the only way to develop a 'partner in life' relationship with your customers and your employees.
- **T**ailwind market: these are the markets you need to find. Even if you have the best idea and the friendliest personnel in the world, you can still fail. If your market is a market that has been going backwards for years, so that you have to fight tooth and nail for a minimal market share, there is no strategy in the world that can help you. Search instead for markets that have the wind in their sails and where your strengths will allow you to surf on the crest of the market's waves.
- **E**nd customer: the be-all and end-all of everything. Always. In the final analysis, there is only one customer and that is the end customer. Even if you work for a company with various intermediaries in the sales chain, you must be constantly aware of the need to develop your feeling for and relationship with the end customer.
- **R**esponsible decisions: the world has need of good and brave choices. Your company must dare to make these choices, so that it can contribute towards a stronger society.

Luigi's cafe starts an online game show

When the great COVID-19 lockdown of March 2020 obliged cafes, pubs and restaurants around the world to close their doors, it soon became clear which ones were enterprising and which ones were not. Some businesses disappeared from sight; others came bubbling to the surface. For many restaurants, it seemed a logical step to start a take-away service: this matched well with their core and they were usually in a position to offer something to customers quite quickly. But for pubs and cafes this was more difficult.

Luigi's Café is a small bar in the Dutch village of Voorhout. The owner of the bar is a warm and pleasant host, who delights customers each day with a fresh pint, delicious coffee and a tasty selection of snacks. Like every other bar in the Netherlands, Luigi's was forced to close in mid-March. But unlike most others, it soon opened up a new line of business. Luigi's Café became active in the world of online entertainment, which was something completely new for its owner. Every Saturday evening, the bar organised an online bingo session. Within a matter of days, Luigi's had built a new website, on which customers could buy bingo cards for 12.50 euros per card. Depending on the number of players, the bar staff bought a number of prizes at local shops, thereby doing their bit to support the local commercial community. On Saturday, the bingo cards were delivered to the players' homes. To call out the numbers, a livestream was organised for later on Saturday evening. Within weeks, six or seven hundred people were taking part in this new form of online entertainment. For me, this is a fantastic example of an entrepreneur who was compelled to stop his normal core activity, but immediately sought an alternative in a completely different industry. Luigi had no experience with this new activity, but

'Voorhout's online bingo. Play and directly support a Voorhout entrepreneur!'

by daring to move beyond the boundaries of his own specialisation he was able to open up a new channel of business. This was win-win-win: for the bar, a new source of income in difficult times; for his regular customers, a change to strengthen their relationship in an amusing and entertaining way; and for the other residents of Voorhout, a chance to discover the charm of Luigi's Café. But it would never have happened unless the owner had the courage to step out of his own comfort zone. It is a strategy that can often be highly beneficial.

Blends of industries

In the 'partner in life' chapter, the strategy was presented as a way to better respond to the needs of customers. Here, I would like to reiterate this point, not only because of the role it plays in the 'partner in life' philosophy, but also because of its impact on the total innovative power of your company. By cleverly exploiting your strengths, it is possible to develop new services that can create extra value for both the customer and the company. In particular, by carefully following evolutions in the market and monitoring the changing behaviour of consumers, you will often be able to discover new opportunities beyond the boundaries of your own industry.

In recent years, Elon Musk has been able to surprise the world on more than one occasion with his spectacular innovations. From SpaceX to Tesla, from his Boring Company to the Hyperloop: these are all brilliant new ideas that have the potential to change the world. In September 2019, Tesla launched yet another innovation, but one that this time failed to make the news headlines, even though it has the same global potential as many of the others. Admittedly, the subject – car insurance[92] – is not as sexy as space rockets, but the new Tesla product could revolutionise an entire industry. During the first months, this new product is only being offered to a number of customers in selected US states. Tesla sees this as a test case, before it commits itself to the market lock, stock and barrel. For the time being, this means that Tesla insurance can only be taken out by the owners of Tesla cars. The price for this insurance is 20 to 30 per cent lower than the current market average. How is this possible? Tesla has at its disposal real-time data for the driving behaviour of all its drivers, which makes it feasible to accurately estimate the likely cost per driver and therefore set its tariffs accordingly. Herein lays one of the possible weaknesses for upscaling the concept: without the same data for the drivers of other brands of car, it will not be possible to offer the same low tariffs to people who do not drive Teslas. In contrast, before too long companies like Google probably will have access to that data, now that more and more car manufacturers are making use of Google Assistant in their vehicles. In the years to come, insurance products will inevitably be driven by data, collected and processed in this manner by AI. As a result, customers will increasingly be given individual product offers.

To combat this prospect, the classic insurance companies now need to convince their current customers to install a sensor in their car, so that their driving behaviour can be analysed. This model has two main disadvantages. Firstly, convincing the drivers will not be easy. These sensors are highly visible for the customer, so that they need to take a conscious decision to have them installed or not, which is more difficult than working with an integrated data collection method. Secondly, you only begin to collect data from the moment of installation. This makes it impossible for the insurer to calculate an initial tariff based on past driving behaviour. For this reason, many companies now work with reimbursement models. If your collected data later demonstrates that you are a good driver, part of your premium is repaid to you at the end of the first year. Not a bad idea, but not as good as starting with a low premium in the first place. Tesla can already do it for the drivers of its own cars; Google will soon be able to do it for the entire market. In other words, whoever possesses the data of the end user is capable of making a new product offer that crosses the normal industrial boundaries.

There are different possibilities for building up value outside your own industry. For instance, the Tesla example is based on the company's own strengths: Tesla is using these strengths to gatecrash the market of another industry. Another option is to collaborate with or acquire companies from complementary sectors. By buying Nest, Google was able to break into the market for the internet of things and physical products much more effectively. Almost overnight, the company was in a position to start marketing smart thermostats and smart cameras. And the same principle applies to Woven City, which we looked at in chapter 5. Toyota is building this city of the future in collaboration with other companies from other sectors.

Ethical choices: machines that lie?

New technology could become a kind of *Temptation Island* for marketing people. Most marketeers are decent and well behaved, but what happens if someone puts you on an island where you are surrounded by temptations. What will you do when it is possible to personalise prices in a manner that is anything but transparent? Imagine that you can assess your customer's mood in real time and so discover whether they are willing to pay more or less for a particular product? How will you deal with that information?

Do you think that we humans will ever be able to build machines that can lie?

We already know the answer to that question. Of course we will be able to build machines that lie. In fact, we are already doing it. Do you remember the Dieselgate crisis that swamped the Volkswagen group a few years ago? That is a perfect example of a lying machine. If the mechanic did the emission test with the bonnet open, the software manipulated the figures to produce a more 'ecological' result. If you programme a machine to lie, you can rest assured that it will do precisely that. The Volkswagen case is widely known, but I am certain that there are many other comparable cases the world has never heard of. In my previous book, *Customers the Day After Tomorrow*, I called for the setting up of an ethical committee to draw up an agreement for the use of advanced technology and to monitor the algorithms that companies use. Algorithms are nearly always a black box for the customer. The more algorithms play a role in our purchasing decisions, the greater the need for a supervisory body will become. It will be the only way to make sure that consumers are being treated fairly. During the past three years, there has been much talk about the need to create such a body, but a generally agreed system is still a long way off. If there are no ethical rules and no ethical monitoring, the responsibility for acting correctly rests entirely with the company. Every company is free to draw up its own ethical code of behaviour for the use of the advanced technology it links to its customers and employees. Organising this debate proactively is an important first step. In this respect, Microsoft has been setting its own ethical standards for years. Satya Nadella, the CEO of the software giant, is a strong advocate of 'technology for good'. He regards ethically correct behaviour as a minimum condition. According to Nadella, the most important ethical responsibility of the business community is to employ technology to build a better society. Only then will we be wholly ethically correct.

Ethical choices: do you ever want to let go?

In addition to the business context, there is also need for a serious societal debate about the use of technology. How far are we willing to let technological evolution develop? One fine day in February 2020, the South Korean Jang Ji-Sung put on a pair of virtual reality glasses. Seconds later, she burst into tears. In the virtual world, she had been reunited with her seven-year-old daughter, who had died three years earlier. They 'met' each other in the girl's favourite playground. When the child asked in her own voice: 'Mama, do you still think of me?', it was all too much for the courageous Ji-Sung. 'Always. Every day,' she stammered.[93]
At the end of it all, Jang Ji-Sung was happy with the experience. She was pleased to see her daughter and to hear her voice again. However, not everyone is enthusiastic about technological possibilities of this kind. Some people, no matter how much they miss their lost loved ones, prefer more human memories. Some of them even fear that with this kind of technological wizardry they might never be able to truly let go of people who were dear to them.
So just how far do we wish to push the boundaries of technological advancement? This is a very important question. Today, virtual reality is still in its infancy. In comparison with the kind of VR we will be experiencing in 2035, today's technology will seem positively

medieval, like comparing a Commodore 64 with the present generation of iPhones. Thanks to data analyses, realistic image forming and powerful artificial intelligence, it will be perfectly feasible to make a virtual version of a man or woman. The technology will make it possible to have real conversations (based on past data) with someone who has died. And it will all seem so real. But is that what we really want? Do we all want to become virtually immortal? Would we like to be able to ask our dead parents for advice? Or let the kids meet their great-great grandparents? And would we, like Jang Ji-Sung, have the courage to virtually meet our lost child? To be honest, I really have no idea. There are positive and negative points on both sides of the argument. Loneliness in older people is a serious social problem. If one of the partners dies after a marriage of more than 50 years, life can be terribly empty for the partner who is left behind. Perhaps a virtual version of the decreased can help to ease the pain? Or would it make the sense of loss for the real person that much worse? We simply don't know.

What we do know is that in the decades ahead technology will become much more powerful than it is today. The possibility to transcend the distinction between the human and the divine is getting closer every year. Opening a societal debate about the proper boundaries of technological power, conducted by governments, companies and various groups of experts (philosophers, behavioural scientists, sociologists, etc.), would be an important first step in the right direction.

Eternal

Writing about ethics in a management book is always something theoretical. For that reason, I have decided to write a three-part fiction series. The first book in this trilogy will be published in November 2020 and its title is *Eternal*.

It is about a company, X-COM, which brings a new and groundbreaking technology to market: *Eternal*. This technology means that human beings no longer need to die. Thanks to a combination of nanobots and brain interfaces, people no longer get sick. At the same time, the technology also makes it possible to proactively eradicate criminality from society. When the technology is first presented, the whole world reacts enthusiastically. Everyone is overjoyed at the prospect of living forever. Full of nerves, Romy Bell, the project leader of *Eternal,* is watching the presentation, when she learns that one of her colleagues has just been killed in an accident with a self-driving car, while the presentation was taking place. She has the feeling that something is not right: self-driving cars have made accidents a thing of the past. She digs deeper to try and find the cause of the accident. When she suddenly receives a message from her dead colleague, she realises that someone is seeking to abuse the possibilities of technology in the most terrifying way. A race against the clock begins.

I have always wanted to write a fiction book and am delighted that this dream will very soon come true. But the book is also more than that. I hope that it will trigger a debate about the limits of technology. *Eternal* is a realistic science-fiction thriller, in which both sides of that debate are clearly defined in a manner that makes the theme more chillingly immediate than ever.

Transparency in everything you do

If people trust a company, this will have a positive effect on that company's results. One of the factors with the biggest impact on trust is transparency in all aspects of the business process. Consumer research has shown that 94 per cent of consumers intend to remain faithful to companies that offer complete transparency. 73 per cent are even prepared to pay more to shop with a transparent company.[94] Transparency goes further than the sharing of superficial information and attractive photos. A study published in the *Journal of Business Ethics* has revealed that companies that are transparent about their production process and working conditions enjoy a higher degree of trust from consumers, which in turn leads to better financial results and a positive word-of-mouth.[95]

Trust has become a scarce commodity. People no longer always know who or what to trust. The world is awash in fake news and coloured communication. Finding the truth is no longer easy. The only way for a company to build up a relationship of trust is to be consistently transparent in the long term about matters such as the company results, internal processes, purchasing philosophy, pricing, values, employee relations, etc. Even when things go wrong, transparent companies will not attempt to hide the truth. On the contrary, they will be the first to communicate it.

Don't misunderstand me: being transparent does not mean sharing everything about your company with the entire world. There is a huge difference between transparency and publicising your most sensitive commercial secrets! As a Disney fan, I am curious about how Disney treats its employees and what things are really like behind the scenes, but I don't want to know who is actually inside the Mickey suit! That is no longer transparency; that is taking away the magic.

Case: Veja

Veja was founded in 2004 by Sébastien Kopp and François-Ghislain Morillion. The headquarters of this sneakers manufacturer is in Paris, France. In 2018, the brand sold 550 000 pairs of shoes, yielding a turnover of 21 million euros.[96] Veja is regarded as one of the most ethical and transparent brands in the fashion industry.

In 2003, the company's two founders visited a Chinese factory, as part of an audit for another French fashion brand. At first glance, the working conditions in the factory seemed to be okay, but when they saw the conditions in which the workers lived, they were appalled. At that moment, they decided to develop a fashion brand that could be both successful and have a socially responsible method of production.

They opted for sneakers. As a result of their market knowledge, they knew that 70 per cent of the cost price for well-known brand sneakers goes on advertising and communication. The materials and the production cost just 30 per cent. With their business model, they planned to turn this distribution on its head: by minimising advertising and

investing much more in production, they hoped to be able to sell their shoes at the same price as the famous brands.

When they signed their first cotton contract in 2004, they paid double the market price. The local producers couldn't understand what was going on. Kopp and Morillion soon became known as '*Los Frenceses Locos*', the crazy Frenchmen.[97] All their contracts are concluded in accordance with fair-trade principles: paid in advance for a previously agreed price. In this way, the farmer knows exactly how much money he will receive at the moment when he is sowing his seeds. As a result, he is protected from unexpected price fluctuations in the market and has a greater degree of financial flexibility. And in order to ensure complete transparency, Veja publishes all its contracts on its website, right down to the smallest detail. Everyone – competitors and consumers – can see exactly how the deal was done.

As this suggests, Veja transparency policy is far-reaching. It not only publishes its supplier contracts, but also issues a certificate for all the products it uses. In this way, customers know where the materials come from and can be confident of their quality. Veja also wants to produce as sustainably as possible. Via the information on the website, customers can follow the progress they are making towards the realisation of this goal.

In this same spirit of openness, the company is not afraid to highlight its own imperfections (do you remember the 'curse of perfection', which we discussed in chapter 6?). One of Veja's objectives is not to work with companies that are registered in a tax paradise. In this context, Veja makes use of the list of companies and their financial constructions published each year by La Nef. However, on its site the company also makes clear that its e-commerce activities in many countries mean that today it has little option in some situations other than to co-operate with partners who do make use of tax havens. In other words, at the present time Veja is not in a position to make good on all its promises, but it is doing what it can to move in the right direction.[98] This kind of transparency results in huge customer trust and appreciation for the company.

Tailwind markets

What sector do you work in?
Is it a sector with the wind in its sails? One that is constantly seeking new horizons? Where double-digit growth is still possible?
Or is it a sector that is struggling? One where there is constant pressure on prices and margins? Where new types of competitors are making things difficult in a way that almost seems unfair?
The sector in which you work makes a huge difference.

Some of you will have the wind behind you; others will be sailing into a headwind. Having the wind in your sails gives you energy; battling against the wind often means making little or no progress, in spite of all your hard work.
Wouldn't it be great if every company could have the wind in its sails? Of course it would – but I know that such a thing is not possible. However, there is nothing to stop you from searching for your own tailwind market.
At one point, e-commerce was certainly a market that had the wind in its sails. The growth of the digital companies was spectacular. Those who missed the boat were full of criticism for the new model: it wasn't profitable, people would never want to buy everything online, etc. The critics emphasised the disadvantages of e-commerce and in doing so overlooked the opportunities that the new market offered for getting some wind back in their own sails.
Every so often, new possibilities and opportunities emerge in every sector, possibilities and opportunities that can fill your sails with fresh wind. But navigating the right course to find this wind is not always easy. Developing a mindset to be constantly on the lookout for new winds is an important part of any modern business strategy.

How Egmont got the wind in its sails

The Danish Egmont group was founded in 1878 by Egmont Harald Petersen, as a one-man printing business. Egmont quickly became a company specialising in magazines. In 1914, the name was changed to Gutenberghus, in honour of the inventor of the printing press. This name was kept until 1992, when it was changed back to Egmont. Today, Egmont is one of the largest content producers in Europe. It not only prints books and magazines, but also makes films and television series.

In his final will and testament, the founder expressed his wish that the resources of the company should be used for the support of social, cultural and scientific projects. As a result, Egmont evolved into a foundation that seeks to improve the quality of life of children and young adults. Since 1920, the company has invested more than 235 million euros in various projects that were compatible with this mission.

In September 2019, I had the pleasure of being able to talk with the management of this remarkable company. Before I gave my speech, the CEO of the company, Steffen Kragh, addressed his team. He outlined the Egmont vision and strategy for the coming years.

I was very impressed. Steffen said literally: 'I am no longer interested in being part of a failing and highly competitive market. Our magazines, books and TV-formats are holding their own, but the competition is fierce, and will continue to be so. I want to be active in tailwind markets.'

It was during this meeting that I first became properly acquainted with the 'tailwind markets' concept. As far as Egmont was concerned, this meant looking at markets like e-commerce and gaming. These are both industries where strong growth is still possible. However, they are also both markets where it is currently not easy to make the difference, since both are already populated with plenty of powerful players. Even so, Egmont decided to commit itself fully to e-commerce and gaming, but in a manner that was different from these other players.

In the field of e-commerce, the company opted deliberately for categories where players like Amazon were less active. This led them to set a focus on products for parents, outdoor hobbies and kitchen material. Of course, Amazon also sells products in these categories – Amazon sells everything – but by searching for the right niches Egmont hoped it could make the difference. In the meantime, their e-commerce portfolio contains seven

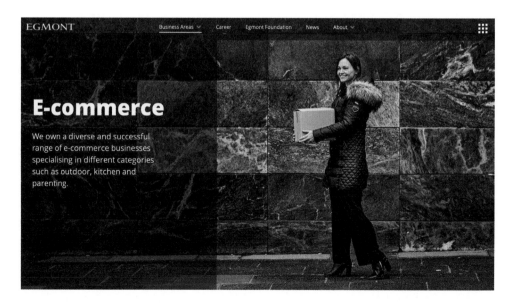

EGMONT

Business Areas | Career | Egmont Foundation | News | About

E-commerce

We own a diverse and successful range of e-commerce businesses specialising in different categories such as outdoor, kitchen and parenting.

strong Scandinavian e-commerce brands, such as Jollyroom, Fjellsport and Outnorth. This portfolio now generates an annual turnover of more than 360 million euros. Likewise, Egmont made the increasingly important gaming market one of its strategic priorities. In 2016, the company began to develop a portfolio of game studios. It deliberately opted not to adopt a blockbuster strategy. Many games are incredibly popular for a short period of time, but thereafter quickly fade away, at which point the search for a new blockbuster begins. Egmont decided to set its sights on other types of games for other target groups. One of their most successful games is called *Hunter: Call of the Wild*, in which people can hunt virtually in beautiful natural settings.

These gamers are older and therefore more loyal than the players of, say, *Fortnite*. And because their loyalty is greater, they are prepared to spend more money on this and other virtual products. You want a virtual hunting lodge in which to hang your virtual trophies? Not a problem if you are prepared to pay – and many are.

The Egmont case clearly demonstrates the benefits of tailwind markets. The company exploited its competencies as story-tellers to go in search of new market segments. Even if these segments already seemed to be well occupied, Egmont found a way to make use of its strengths to fill its sails with fresh wind, so that it could reap the rewards of fast progress, while always remaining true to its wider mission.

The end customer. Always.

Some companies sell directly to end users. Others sell to end users via intermediaries. But whichever of these models your company uses, it is crucial never to lose your focus on the end customer. New trends, changes in demand, variations in behaviour: they all begin with the end customer.

So the message is simple: always base your strategy on this end customer. If you gear your strategy too much to the role of the intermediaries, there is a good chance that you will one day wake up to find the market completely changed. Maintaining contact with and having a good understanding of your end customers will allow you to make necessary adjustments in good time.

For this reason, more and more companies are opting to sell direct to customers, even in sectors where the use of intermediaries has been common until now. For example, the manufacturers of consumption goods traditionally sell their products via retailers. They advertise directly to their customers, but the sale occurs through retail.

In an earlier chapter, we saw how Nike had decided to break this chain and focus fully on direct sales. This was also the case with Lumi (Pampers), where a major consumer goods manufacturer now invests heavily in the development of a direct relationship with its end users.

In the summer of 2020, Unilever looks set to follow this trend with its ice-cream brands Magnum and Ben & Jerry's. In many major cities throughout the world, both brands will use large street freezers to sell directly to customers 'on demand'. And no matter where you are in the city, your ice-cream can be brought to you, thanks to collaboration with Uber Eats or Deliveroo. In this way, the classic retail or 'out-of-home' distribution channel can be (temporarily) bypassed. Unilever now wants to serve its end customers directly.

End customer focus in B2B

More and more B2B companies are starting to determine their strategy based on a closer end customer relationship. Some months ago, we bought a new central heating boiler for our house. It was a 'smart' boiler by Viessmann, which was installed by an excellent local professional.
After the installation, we downloaded the Viessmann app, which linked the boiler to the internet. In this way, the manufacturer can follow in detail everything that happens to its boiler in the home of the end user; in this case, the Van Belleghem family! They can monitor when routine maintenance is necessary and, consequently, contact us proactively to arrange it.

The introduction of sensors into products offers manufacturers ever greater opportunities to collect information about their end customers. In the past, this kind of information was often difficult to obtain in the B2B market. It was the intermediary who knew most about customer feedback and use, which made the manufacturers highly dependent on these intermediaries.
Sensors, data and social media have changed all that. Today, establishing a relationship with the end customer in B2B is much more feasible. Moreover, the knowledge that the manufacturer will receive about his customers will be more objective and will be in real time, in a way that human intermediaries can never hope to match.

Disney+

Disney built up an empire based on cartoon figures. Who doesn't know Mickey, Minnie, Pluto, Donald, Buzz Lightyear, Anna and Elsa? My favourite Walt Disney quote? 'It all started with a mouse!' The films were distributed by cinemas, supported by a large-scale merchandising programme. Later, a number of theme parks were developed, followed by spectacular Broadway shows. In short, the Disney empire is a machine. The company possesses a priceless library of content and related intellectual property rights for all its many iconic characters. The only thing it was lacking until recently was a channel to bring all that content directly to the end users. For distribution, it was still dependent on cinemas, streaming services and television channels. But not anymore.

In August 2017, it became clear that Disney had a new plan. It announced that it was planning to end its collaboration with Netflix: within a matter of months, Netflix would be denied further right of access to Disney content. The market was in no doubt as to what this meant: Disney intended to start its own streaming service.

In March 2019, Disney completed its takeover of 21st Century Fox, for more than 70 billion American dollars. This instantly gave Disney the largest content library in the world.

On 12 November 2019, the inevitable finally happened. Disney+, the company's own independent streaming service, was launched. For a fixed monthly fee, customers gain access to the entire content library of the Disney group. This is more than just Mickey Mouse and friends. It means Disney, Pixar, Star Wars, Marvel and numerous other items of world-famous content.

By February 2020, Disney+ already had 28 million customers. The outbreak of the corona crisis led to further spectacular growth. By the start of April, the number of subscribers had risen to 50 million.[99] I know of very few other product launches that have attracted 50 million customers in just six months time. To call it a huge success is an understatement.

For Disney, Disney+ was the missing link in the chain that led directly to the end consumer of its content. In its theme parks and on its cruise ships, Disney has been able for years to shape the entire customer experience. Now it can do the same in people's homes, thanks to its new direct link with its content customers.

Responsible decisions

There is need for more courage in the business world. The courage to make brave decisions, to swim against the tide, to do what is 'right'. Think back to the example where the CEO of Twitter decided to prohibit paid advertising from politicians, while the CEO of Facebook was unwilling to do the same. Courageous decisions of this kind can be taken at both the strategic and the tactical level.

Tactical decisions often require courage at the customer level. If your company does everything it can to make customers happy, but notices that one particular customer remains dissatisfied, you can legitimately decide to no longer try to help that customer. Sometimes it is simply better to break the customer relationship. A customer relationship that generates negative energy for the company and will never yield positive results, no matter how hard you try, is probably a poor match that cannot be corrected. Even if the customer brings in revenue, it can still be the right decision to cut your ties with him or her.

Of course, it takes even more courage to make brave decisions at the strategic level. The most difficult culture of all for a company to develop is the culture in which everyone will, by nature, 'do the right thing'.

There is a clear distinction between being ethically correct and accepting your responsibility. They often overlap, but are actually two separate dimensions. A company can be ethically correct towards it customers and employees, but still neglect to use its strengths to improve society.

Accepting your responsibility means daring to stick your neck out. It means having an opinion as a company and doing everything possible to transform that opinion into concrete and positive action. This kind of culture does not need to make use of business cases to make certain ethical choices. At the moments when a difficult decision needs to be made, such companies follow their instincts and do what needs to be done, even if that can have a negative impact on financial results in the short term.

If you want to make your customers an 'offer they can't refuse', at some point in the future, especially when difficulties arise, they will want to check that you are being faithful to the mindset you advocated when things were going well. It is during the bad times that you can really see whether or not a company is capable of making responsible choices.

Finally. I can't wait!

You have reached the end of my book. I am delighted you have managed to finish it. I can hardly wait to read, hear and see how you will put my new concepts and theories into practice.

I am curious to find out what new ideas your friction hunters will propose. Their input will undoubtedly help you to take your standards of convenience to the next level. That is the first step in The Offer You Can't Refuse philosophy: ensuring that your transactional processes function as optimally as possible.

Brainstorming sessions about the 'partner in life' aspect of the model are always interesting. These sessions encourage you to think about services that go further than your product and allow you to dream about perfect customer service, which takes account of the person behind the customer. This second step in The Offer You Can't Refuse philosophy offers huge potential for developing a broader and more complete service for your customers.

Last but not least, I hope that many among you will take your responsibility seriously and use your strengths to make a positive impact on society. Do not work with a fluffy purpose, but search for a concrete societal problem for which you can be a part of the solution. This creates huge amounts of positive energy, energy the world sorely needs. This is the third step in The Offer You Can't Refuse philosophy.

What intrigues me most is how you will apply this philosophy to your customers and your employees.

I cannot wait to see what impact you will have, dear readers. I wish you lots of enthusiasm, tons of positive energy and fantastic results during the development and implementation of your very own The Offer You Can't Refuse strategy.

Thank you

For me, writing a book is one of the most exciting aspects of my professional life. *The Offer You Can't Refuse* is my fifth management book, but the nervous tension and the butterflies in the tummy are just the same as they were for the first one. Every time, I hope that I will be able to inspire people and persuade them to look at their customers in a different way.

The process of writing a book has been the same on all five occasions. Roughly 12 months before I start the actual writing, I embark on a research and reflection phase. It is only once this phase has been completed to my satisfaction that I start typing out my thoughts and conclusions. After that, I hand over the manuscript to my publisher, who turns it into a wonderful book.

In each of these phases – research, writing, publishing – I have the pleasure of being able to collaborate with and receive inspiration from a large group of clever, positive and creative people. I would like to expressly thank everyone who has helped me during the past year to make this book what it has finally become.

Right from the very beginning, I was able to work with an outstanding research team, who helped to keep the book's subject matter sharp and relevant. Thank you to Laurence Van Elegem and Cédric Gilissen, for your passion, insight, hard work and help in all aspects relating to content. I greatly appreciate the contribution you have made.

A big thank you also to the people who added their creativity to my content. Karl Demoen has been my designer for the past ten years. He is able like no-one else to translate my ideas in a powerful and distinctive 'Steven style'. Thanks, Karl. As always, it was a pleasure to work with you. My heartfelt thanks likewise go to Piet Goddaer, better known as the artist Ozark Henry, for composing the sound of this book. I am amazingly proud that we were able to do this together, resulting in the first management book with its own soundtrack. I owe you, Piet!

Peter Hinssen, thank you for the powerful chapter you have written for this book. It has been an honour and a delight to work with you for the past eight years: inspiring companies, setting up new ventures, exploring the world.

I would also like to express my gratitude to my good friend, mentor and first employer, Professor Dr. Rudy Moenaert (Tias Business School). He taught me to look critically at the world. What's more, it was Rudy who years ago dropped me in at the deep end by persuading me to give lessons at the Vlerick Business School just two months after I had graduated. It is thanks to him that I learnt quickly how to give good presentations.

Of course, my two publishers also deserve a mention. In recent years, we have collaborated together brilliantly. Thank you to the teams at LannooCampus and Van Duuren Management, and in particular to Niels Janssens, Hilde Van Mechelen and Roderik Teunissen.

The same applies to all my fine colleagues and partners at Snackbytes, nexxworks, the Vlerick Business School and Intracto. Sam Berteloot, Matthias De Clercq, Julie Vens-De Vos, Marion Debruyne and Pieter Janssens: your teams are not only fantastic, but also a joy to work with. My former colleagues at InSites Consulting likewise continue to help me with my story. A special thank you to Kristof De Wulf and Tim Duhamel for their support, friendship and years of fruitful collaboration.

As part of the preparation for this book, I have visited hundreds of companies. I would like to thank each of them for their openness. I have also conducted interviews with a specific group of people, who also merit my deep gratitude: Professor Dr. Filip Caeldries (Tias Business School), Philippe Rogge (CEO Microsoft CEE), Tom Debruyne (CEO Sue Amsterdam), Albert Spijkman, Yvette Stegeman, Peggy Spaapen (Centraal Beheer), Ynzo Van Zanten (Tony's Chocolonely's evangelist), Tien Tzuo (CEO Zuora), Herman Toch (CEO Flrish), Thierry Geerts (CEO Google Belgium), Nico Van de Walle (circular economy manager at Verstraete IML) and Steffen Kragh (CEO Egmont).

It goes without saying that my deepest debt of gratitude is owed to my family. In normal circumstances, it was planned that I would write this book while I was travelling around the world, from Australia to Kuala Lumpur to Panama and back to Europe. In spring 2020, I had a series of planned speaking engagements that would take me to the four corners of the globe. My idea was that I could use all those long hours in airports, on planes and in hotel rooms to do my writing. But then came COVID-19 and all my plans were changed. I ended up writing the book at my home in Knesselare, Belgium.

It was an often fun, sometimes challenging and occasionally stressful experience writing a book in the presence of my wife and our two children, Siebe (eleven) and Mathis (nine).

All my texts first pass through the hands of Evi. There is no-one better than her when it comes to making my texts easy to read, detecting mistakes, identifying illogical thoughts and offering good solutions. It is wonderful to be able to work that way. For the past ten years my faithful second reader has been my father, Pol Van Belleghem. Thanks again for all your help, papa.

Our children are becoming increasingly interested in what I do. Both of them are fascinated by innovation and science. Without knowing it, they are a daily source of inspiration for me. Observing the way they look at things and seeing what they regard as their new normal has given me a new window on the world. I am lucky to have a fantastic family and am truly grateful for it.

Finally, I would like to thank each and every one of you, my readers. Thank you for reading this book. Thank you, perhaps, for also following me on Facebook, YouTube, Instagram, LinkedIn and Twitter or for listening to me at one of my presentations. The boost I get from my public is one of my biggest sources of energy. Many, many thanks to you all.

Steven

End notes

1 https://www.edelman.com/trustbarometer
2 https://sciencebasedtargets.org/2019/09/22/87-major-companies-lead-the-way-towards-a-1-5c-future-at-un-climate-action-summit/
3 https://www.fastcompany.com/90459443/what-will-it-take-for-the-75-of-companies-that-dont-have-climate-commitments-to-step-up
4 https://www.bnnbloomberg.ca/shopify-surges-after-cto-touts-black-friday-level-traffic-1.1423058
5 https://www.microsoft.com/en-us/microsoft-365/blog/2020/04/30/2-years-digital-transformation-2-months/
6 https://www.sciencealert.com/one-third-of-the-worlds-population-are-now-restricted-in-where-they-can-go
7 https://venturebeat.com/2020/04/02/zooms-daily-active-users-jumped-from-10-million-to-over-200-million-in-3-months/
8 https://www.cnbc.com/2018/11/06/starbucks-ceo-were-going-to-apply-to-the-us-what-we-learned-in-china.html
9 https://www.forbes.com/sites/jonbird1/2019/01/15/roasted-how-china-is-showing-the-way-for-starbucks-u-s/#609405a9d443
10 https://www.fastcompany.com/90298866/meituan-grab-most-innovative-companies-2019
11 https://www.nytimes.com/2020/04/30/world/asia/coronavirus-poverty-unemployment.html
12 https://ourworldindata.org/wrong-about-the-world
13 http://www.shaperssurvey2017.org
14 Accenture's Fjord Trends 2020 Report.
15 McKinsey Quarterly, Five ways that ESG creates value, November 2019.
16 https://www.lseg.com/resources/1000-companies-inspire/2018-report-1000-companies-europe/food-drink/max-burgers
17 Carlota Perez, Technological revolutions and financial capital, 2002.
18 https://www.theguardian.com/technology/2019/jan/20/shoshana-zuboff-age-of-surveillance-capitalism-google-facebook
19 https://musically.com/2020/02/05/spotify-ended-2019-with-271m-listeners-and-124m-subscribers/
20 https://www.dailymail.co.uk/sciencetech/article-472032/Illegal-music-downloads-hit-time-high.html
21 https://scitechdaily.com/food-waste-study-reveals-much-fridge-food-goes-there-to-die/
22 https://www.verstraete-iml.com/nl/wat-is-iml
23 https://www.theguardian.com/science/2019/dec/04/china-gene-edited-baby-experiment-may-have-created-unintended-mutations
24 Ericsson Mobility Report, www.ericsson.com/mobility-report
25 https://www.zdnet.com/article/south-korea-secures-4-million-5g-subscribers/
26 Netflix figures.
27 Accenture's Fjord Trends 2020 Report.
28 Report MIT SMR SAS 2020.
29 https://cmo.adobe.com/articles/2019/10/can-quantum-computing-one-day-solve-all-of-our-business-problems.html#gs.0226xp
30 https://www.nature.com/articles/s41586-019-1666-5
31 https://time.com/5708220/google-quantum-supremacy/
32 https://www.tenfold.com/IT/the-vast-and-far-reaching-applications-of-quantum-computing
33 https://www.tijd.be/tech-media/technologie/de-meest-baanbrekende-technologie-ooit/10088681.html
34 https://ifr.org/ifr-press-releases/news/top-trends-robotics-2020
35 https://ifr.org/downloads/press2018/2019-09-18_Press_Release_IFR_World_Robotics_2019_Industrial_Robots_English.pdf
36 https://www.cnbc.com/2020/03/02/the-rush-to-deploy-robots-in-china-amid-the-coronavirus-outbreak.html
37 https://technode.com/2020/02/07/jd-completes-first-unmanned-delivery-for-coronavirus-aid-in-wuhan/
38 https://www.statista.com
39 https://medium.com/voiceui/journey-to-the-global-voice-market-the-us-europe-china-and-russia-8b47a4c3f8e
40 Business Insider Smart Speaker Report, January 2020.
41 McKinsey, Tech For Good research 2019, https://www.mckinsey.com/featured-insights/future-of-work/five-fifty-tech-for-the-greater-good
42 https://sloanreview.mit.edu/article/dating-disruption-how-tinder-gamified-an-industry/
43 https://techcrunch.com/2019/03/25/mcdonalds-acquires-dynamic-yield/
44 https://www.brafton.com/news/95-per-cent-of-web-traffic-goes-to-sites-on-page-1-of-google-serps-study/
45 https://hbr.org/2018/10/do-people-trust-algorithms-more-than-companies-realize
46 https://blog.ycombinator.com/the-hidden-forces-behind-toutiao-chinas-content-king/
47 https://www.statista.com/statistics/546894/number-of-amazon-prime-paying-members/
48 https://finance.yahoo.com/news/amazon-prime-members-59-per-cent-of-us-households-rbc-150743767.html
49 http://www.netimperative.com/2020/01/27/the-top-5-fastest-growing-neobanks-of-2019/
50 https://monzo.com/blog/monzo-in-2020-looking-back
51 https://www.japantimes.co.jp/news/2020/03/24/business/corporate-business/toyota-ntt-smart-city/#.XpbDZC9Y7Vk
52 https://voicebot.ai/2019/10/01/amazon-alexa-has-100k-skills-but-momentum-slows-globally-here-is-the-breakdown-by-country/
53 https://automotive-online.nl/management/laatste-nieuws/internationaal/26668-bmw-en-daimler-clusteren-mobiliteit-in-your-now

54 https://expandedramblings.com/index.php/grab-facts-statistics/
55 https://www.weforum.org/agenda/2020/03/todays-coronavirus-updates/
56 2020 Edelman Trust Barometer.
57 https://www.businessinsider.com/lego-goggles-protective-a-day-for-coronavirus-outbreak-ppe-2020-4?international=true&r=US&IR=T
58 Brand authenticity: An integrative framework and measurement scale, journal of consumer pshychology, april 2015.
59 http://www.millwardbrown.com/mb-global/our-thinking/articles-opinion/articles/brandz/global/2019/people-prefer-brands-they-can-depend-on-to-do-the-right-thing
60 https://www.statista.com/chart/17646/americans-trust-in-facebook/
61 https://techcrunch.com/2019/10/30/zuckerberg-political-ads/
62 https://www.fastcompany.com/90399316/one-year-later-what-did-we-learn-from-nikes-blockbuster-colin-kaepernick-ad
63 https://www.forbes.com/sites/greatspeculations/2020/01/29/will-mastercard-miss-earnings-expectations-for-fy19/#65d5a7d477e9
64 https://nexxworks.com/blog/strategy-structure-and-leadership-are-the-holy-trinity-of-disruptive-innovation-interview
65 The relationship between employee satisfaction and customer satisfaction, Journal of Services Marketing 26, July 2021, Hoseong Jeon and Beomjoon Choi.
66 PWC 2020 HR Technology Survey: https://www.pwc.com/us/en/library/workforce-of-the-future/hr-tech-survey.html
67 PWC 2020 HR Technology Survey: https://www.pwc.com/us/en/library/workforce-of-the-future/hr-tech-survey.html
68 https://www.mckinsey.com/business-functions/organization/our-insights/attracting-and-retaining-theright-talent
69 https://www.vdab.be/sites/web/files/doc/trends/Knelpuntberoepen%202020.pdf
70 McKinsey Global Survey: War For Talent.
71 Deloitte Global Human Capital Trends.
72 Deloitte University Press.
73 https://nl.wikipedia.org/wiki/General_Electric
74 https://www2.deloitte.com/us/en/insights/deloitte-review/issue-16/employee-engagement-strategies.html#endnote-44
75 https://www2.deloitte.com/us/en/insights/deloitte-review/issue-16/employee-engagement-strategies.html#endnote-45
76 Wellbeing = winst, Ann De Bisschop.
77 https://business.linkedin.com/talent-solutions/blog/trends-and-research/2018/linkedin-research-perks-benefits-employees-care-about
78 https://hbr.org/cover-story/2019/03/how-employers-are-fixing-health-care
79 https://www.willistowerswatson.com/en-US/insights/2018/01/high-performance-insights-health-care-delivery
80 https://hbr.org/cover-story/2019/03/how-employers-are-fixing-health-care
81 https://www.businessinsider.com/apple-color-bring-genetic-testing-to-employees-2019-12?international=true&r=US&IR=T
82 https://hbr.org/2016/10/the-performance-management-revolution
83 https://hrexecutive.com/future-of-feedback/
84 https://www.pwc.com/m1/en/services/consulting.html
85 https://www.forbes.com/sites/workday/2016/05/05/workforce-2020-what-you-need-to-know-now/#7da7bb0a2d63
86 https://solarbuildermag.com/news/survey-employees-more-likely-to-work-for-company-with-sustainability-programs/
87 https://www.cmo.com.au/article/641639/how-adobe-cio-turning-her-team-into-customer-employee-experience-orchestrators/
88 https://hbr.org/2017/03/why-the-millions-we-spend-on-employee-engagement-buy-us-so-little
89 https://www.kincentric.com/-/media/kincentric/pdfs/kincentric_2019_trends_global_employee_engagement.pdf
90 https://hbr.org/2017/03/why-the-millions-we-spend-on-employee-engagement-buy-us-so-little
91 Interview met Steve Jobs in Playboy, februari 1985.
92 https://www.tesla.com/blog/introducing-Tesla-insurance
93 https://www.reuters.com/article/us-southkorea-virtualreality-reunion/south-korean-mother-given-tearful-vr-reunion-with-deceased-daughter-idUSKBN2081D6
94 https://www.labelinsight.com/Transparency-ROI-Study
95 Journal of Business Ethics, september 2013.
96 https://en.wikipedia.org/wiki/Veja_Sneakers
97 https://project.veja-store.com/en/story/
98 https://project.veja-store.com/en/single/limits
99 https://www.theverge.com/2020/4/8/21214236/disney-plus-50-million-subscribers-international-europe-india-netflix